ATLANTIC SEAFARING

ATLANTIC SEAFARING

*Ten Centuries of Exploration and Trade
in the North Atlantic*

Roger Morris

First published in the United States in 1992 by
International Marine, a division of McGraw-Hill, Inc.,
in association with David Bateman Ltd., Auckland, New
Zealand.

10 9 8 7 6 5 4 3 2 1

Library of Congress Cataloging-in-Publication Data

Morris, Roger, 1935-
Atlantic seafaring / Roger Morris
p. cm.
Includes bibliographical references and index.
ISBN 0-87742-337-7
1. Atlantic Ocean—Navigation—History.   I. Title.
VK15,M65   1992
623.89'09163—dc20   91-45676
                                           CIP

Typeset in 10/11 Schneidler medium by Typeset
Graphics Ltd, Auckland, New Zealand.
Printed in Hong Kong

Design by Errol McLeary.

CONTENTS

PREFACE

This book sets out to illustrate some of the sailing ships which were engaged in exploration, settlement and trade across the North Atlantic, and relate a few of the events in which they were involved. The subject is so vast that it has been necessary to cull the possible selections ruthlessly so that the reader is not subjected to a battering of abbreviated accounts of voyages. Thus only the initial exploratory and settlement voyages are included, and even here there may be gaps. Some of the transatlantic trades, firstly with the Caribbean and later with the eastern seaboard of North America, are included. Throughout the whole period, the industries of fishing and whaling were based in Atlantic waters. From Europe, annual fleets set out for Newfoundland and the Grand Banks to fish for cod, while whalers scoured the ocean from Spitzbergen and the Greenland Sea to the Davis Straits, the coast of Labrador and gulf of St Lawrence. Later, Americans hunted the sperm whale in the south. Also, ranging the whole 4 centuries of the predominance of the sailing ship in the Atlantic was that grim commerce, the slave trade.

This is an illustrated book and as such presents the author with a daunting task. It is easy, when writing about the physical aspects of a subject, to leave out the bits where either one is not sure, or there is just no information. In an illustration, it is not the practice, nor is it desirable, to leave blank any area where a detail cannot be proved by the rigorous discipline of historical research. With regard to the illustrations of earlier ships there is a great deal of conjecture, and likewise regarding some details of later ships. Complete accuracy is obviously impossible; the paintings are as accurate as the author

can make them, and their purpose is to interest and entertain as well as, perhaps, instruct. Some technical detail is described, firstly to assist readers with little knowledge of the mechanics of sailing vessels. Secondly, anybody with experience in modern sail will undoubtedly look at details of the rigs of some of the old ships and wonder how the whole complex mess was handled in practice. Consequently, there is an emphasis on general layout, rig and sailing practice rather than the detail of ship construction.

To those who may be disappointed that some aspects of the North Atlantic's multifarious explorations, settlements and trades have been ignored, I apologise. Much of the exploration of the Caribbean and South America north of the equator has been skipped. Nothing has been included, except in passing, of the search for a North-west Passage, for to do justice to this topic would require a whole book in itself. Details of the sugar, log-wood, cotton and many other regular trades have had to be either ignored or only incidentally mentioned. The ships hauling these cargoes were not specialised and were run-of-the-mill merchantmen of the period, and the purpose of this book is to study the ships, rather than the trade as such. Naval vessels, other than Spain's 'Silver Galleons', are eliminated except where they occur in the course of a tale. I know that many of the adventures of the sailors of the nations of Europe have been ignored and, as I speak no other language, admit to favouring resources available in English.

The sailors of old were a hard and often-abused class. In the North Atlantic they suffered cold and ice, storm and calm, sweltering heat, exposure, fever, shipwreck, pirates, their own nation's press gangs and predators from other lands. On a diet and in

conditions that would revolt a westerner today, they worked the ships across the ocean and more often than not brought them home safely and profitably. The development and expansion of western civilisation would not have prospered without deep-sea ships and the courage and skills of those who sailed in them.

INTRODUCTION

A thousand years ago Norse seafarers were sailing their small ships directly from Norway to Greenland, and unless indisputable evidence comes to light to show that there were predecessors, it is to those hardy and truculent viking sailors that the accolade must be given for the first transatlantic voyages.

Although the Norse settlements in Greenland survived for perhaps 5 centuries, they passed away leaving only a whisper of a faraway land beyond Greenland, the 'Vinland' of the *Sagas*. The Norse voyages failed to have any lasting impact on the course of European history, and even their cherished and beautiful little ships, limited by the nature of their clencher, or lapstrake, construction, were superseded by larger, more capacious and powerful classes of vessel.

It was the voyages led by the Genoese mariners Columbus and Cabot, spearheading the expansion of an awakening Europe, that turned the North Atlantic from being the edge of the known world into a highway to a New World. Within a very few years of these initial voyages, hundreds of sailing ships, in fleets and alone, were regularly plying the North Atlantic sailing routes. It has been said that during the mid nineteenth century so many ships were voyaging between the United States and Europe that, throughout a passage, it was rare not to have at least one other ship in sight.

The winds and currents of the Atlantic

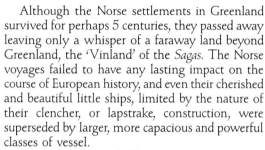

Over all the face of earth
Main ocean flow'd, not idle, but with warm
Prolific humour soft'ning all her globe . . .
– John Milton

The ocean is not just an enormous static body of water. Shaped by the forces of the Earth's rotation, climates, tides and geography, it has within it gigantic rivers, sometimes flowing one above the other, sometimes side by side and elsewhere mixing, bringing together warm tropical flows with Arctic waters and creating the climates of the surrounding continents and the winds which prevail across its surface.

Without the warming influence of the Gulf Stream and the North Atlantic Current, European civilisation may not have grown to the stage where it could look beyond the confines of its home and master the skills to seek other lands beyond the ocean. The sailors of the great age of exploration soon learned to harness the winds and currents of the seas to their advantage, rather than battle with the relentless elements.

The circulation of winds and surface currents of the North Atlantic were quickly understood and their direction and distribution influenced the whole subsequent history of discovery, conquest, settlement and trade. It was the prevailing northerlies, or Portuguese trades, off Portugal and the north-west African coast which encouraged that nation to open up the west coast of Africa. The north-east tradewinds, luckily prevailing well north in that year, bore Columbus across the Atlantic, and the westerlies brought him safely home. Cabot struggled and finally beat these westerlies in the middle latitudes, and later ships bound for the Newfoundland fisheries and the northern continental seaboard found an easier summer passage in the north. By far the most favoured route westward was south to the region of the north-east

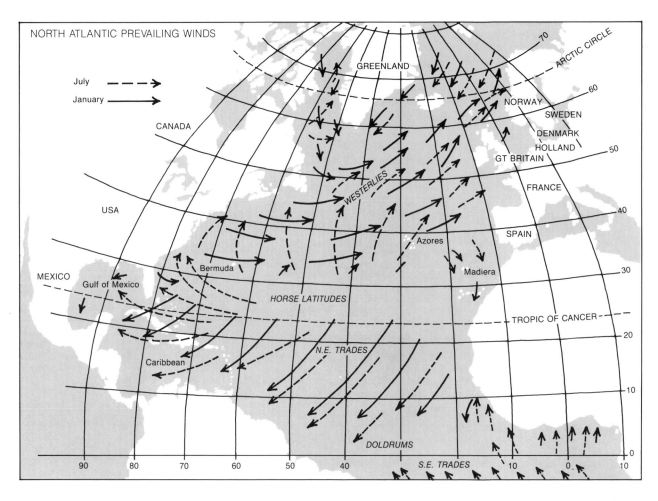

NORTH ATLANTIC PREVAILING WINDS

July ⟶
January ⟶

GREENLAND
CANADA
USA
MEXICO
Gulf of Mexico
Bermuda
Caribbean
WESTERLIES
HORSE LATITUDES
N.E. TRADES
DOLDRUMS
S.E. TRADES
Azores
Madiera
NORWAY
SWEDEN
DENMARK
HOLLAND
GT BRITAIN
FRANCE
SPAIN
ARCTIC CIRCLE
TROPIC OF CANCER

trades for a warm, brisk run across the ocean with the whole eastern seaboard, Gulf of Mexico and Caribbean to leeward. From the Caribbean, the Gulf Stream and the west winds sped the ships home to Europe. It was on these winds that the various triangular trades depended, and without the tradewinds the slave trade would have been hamstrung.

Regions of calm were to be avoided if possible.

The doldrums, between the north-east and south-east trades, were crossed as far to the west as possible by vessels bound to and from the South Atlantic. The region of variable winds between the tradewinds and the westerlies, known as the horse latitudes, can bring calm or light winds, but, apart from rain, the weather there is generally fair, and the region in the North Atlantic is virtually an extension of the north-east trades.

Down from the Arctic regions, cooling the whole north-eastern seaboard of the North American continent, flows the Labrador Current, providing the hazard of iceberg and the blessing of the bountiful fisheries off Newfoundland. Off the eastern borders of the Grand Banks the cold, green Labrador Current flows south-west alongside the deep blue Gulf Stream flowing north-east, creating a phenomenon known as the *cold wall*. To sail from the Gulf Stream

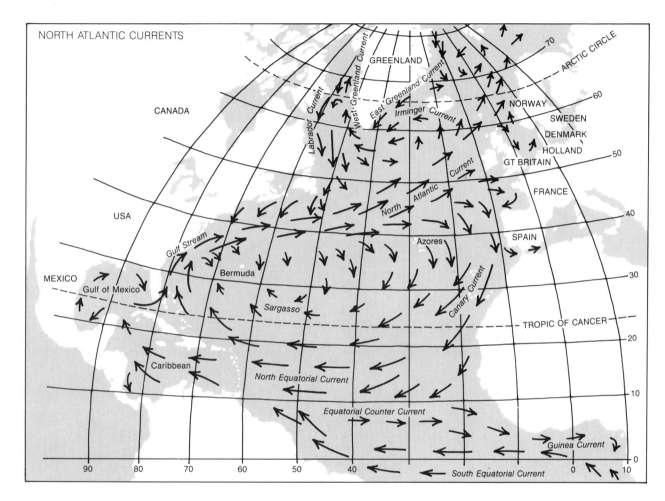

NORTH ATLANTIC CURRENTS

into the Labrador Current is similar to opening the door of a refrigerator. The temperature drops many degrees and the transition from blue to green water is sharp and immediate. In these regions, in all seasons, fog is the navigator's most frequent hazard.

Winter in the forties and fifties of the North Atlantic is predictably vile, and storms can occur in all regions in any season. However, the most fearful storms are the hurricanes which sweep in from the tropical North Atlantic to cause havoc in the Caribbean before they either march clear across Mexico or the southern States, or curve up the eastern seaboard. Winds of between 34 and 40 knots are reckoned a gale. Any wind above 64 knots is blowing with hurricane force and, in the tropics, hurricanes have been known to produce wind speeds of over 175 knots (324 kmph or 201.4 mph). The survival of any sailing ship caught in such winds at sea, or in anything but the most secure harbour, would be doubtful. The following old adage warns the sailor:

July; stand by
August; you must
September; remember
October; all over

DEEPWATER SAILING SHIPS UNTIL 1700

Long, long before Columbus, the Chinese had their tradition of the battened *lugsail* and the Arabs their graceful, triangular *lateen*. Europeans in the Atlantic and, from the fourteenth century, in the Mediterranean, favoured a single simple *squaresail*. Properly cut and set, this is easily handled and reasonably efficient, capable of driving a ship between 65 and 70 degrees of the wind, and for a running sail it cannot be bettered. The Norse *khörr* used just this sail. (*Illus. 1*)

The learning years

After the demise of the khörr in the thirteenth or early fourteenth century, ships continued to use the single squaresail. Then, probably early in the

illus. 1

fourteenth century, a small *bowsprit* was fitted. To this were led the *bowlines*, lines which flatten and hold taut the *luff*, or leading edge of the squaresail when closehauled. Later in the century a *lateen mizzen*

illus. 2

came into use and, probably before the century was out, some Henry Ford of the Mediterranean maritime world stepped a *fore mast* and created the prototype three-masted, square-rigged ship. (*Illus. 2*)

By the time of Columbus the bowsprit boasted a sail of its own, the *spritsail*, which was hoisted out on a parrel and was brought inboard to stow, usually on the port side of the forecastle. The bowsprit was secured on the starboard side of the stem and foremast. *Topmasts* and *topsails* were also an innovation. Sailors, being as they are, would find the large flagstaffs, lashed at the mastheads, irresistible – just asking for a sail to be set on them. The basic three-masted rig proved ideally suited to ocean sailing and, in principal, has remained unchanged since then. A fourth mast, initially only an improvised boat mast and lateen sail, was stepped well aft. This

became known as the *bonaventure* and was common until the early seventeenth century.

The smaller versions of these ships, such as the *Santa Maria* and the *Matthew*, were referred to as *nao* or *navio* in Spain, *navicula* or *bark* in England and *barque* or *nef* in France. In those days rig did not class a vessel; rather, special features of its size, structure and purpose determined its designation. Thus a *patache*, a swift, small *caravel* type of vessel used for carrying dispatches, among other things, was normally lateen-rigged but retained her class when she was square-rigged for ocean sailing. (*Illus. 3*)

illus. 3

The caravel

However suitable the square-rigged nao was as a freighter, it was the *caravel* which led the vanguard of early Atlantic exploration. (*Illus. 4*)

illus. 4

illus. 5

She was the creation of the Portuguese, who used the Arabic lateen sail to drive their hulls, which also may have been inspired by Arabic craft. As a lateener, the caravel was fast and weatherly. She drew little water and was ideal for the exploratory work on the African coast. However, when it came to long ocean passages the Portuguese found it preferable to set squaresails on the foremast as the lateen could be nerve-racking, if not dangerous, when sailing downwind for long periods. The Spanish preferred to give their caravels the standard square rig, and rigged as such, they were known as *caravela redonda*. (*Illus. 5*)

The caravel was in use throughout the sixteenth century, gradually increasing in size and bearing a variety of rigs. (*Illus. 6, 7 and 8*) However, her advantages were eclipsed by the *galleon* with which she seems to have merged, and thereafter she vanished. Her descendants lived on in the little dispatch boats and brigantines used to speed messages between Spain and her colonies.

The nao or carrack

During the early years of the sixteenth century larger and larger naos were built, more or less to the same basic design. Some enormous vessels were built in the Mediterranean, so stacked with superstructure that they could barely sail. In Atlantic waters these ships were more moderate but still extreme, with towering forecastles and aftercastles. These vessels, ranging from 200 to sometimes over 1000 *toneladas*, seem to have been differentiated from the barks and navios and became referred to as *carracks* and naos. This class of ship lasted throughout the sixteenth century and was favoured by the Portuguese in their trade with India, for they were easily defended as well as being enormous load carriers. The open-water passage around the Cape did not stretch their limited manoeuvrability, but the slow rate of

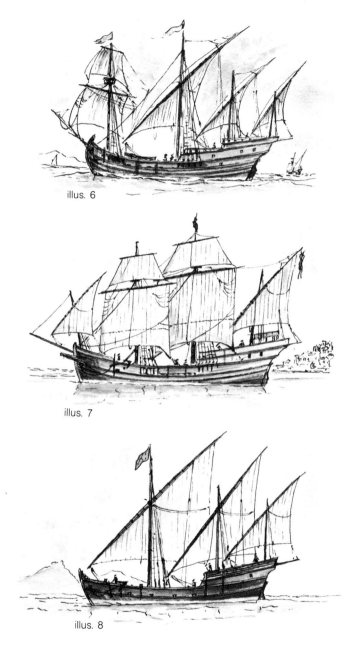

illus. 6

illus. 7

illus. 8

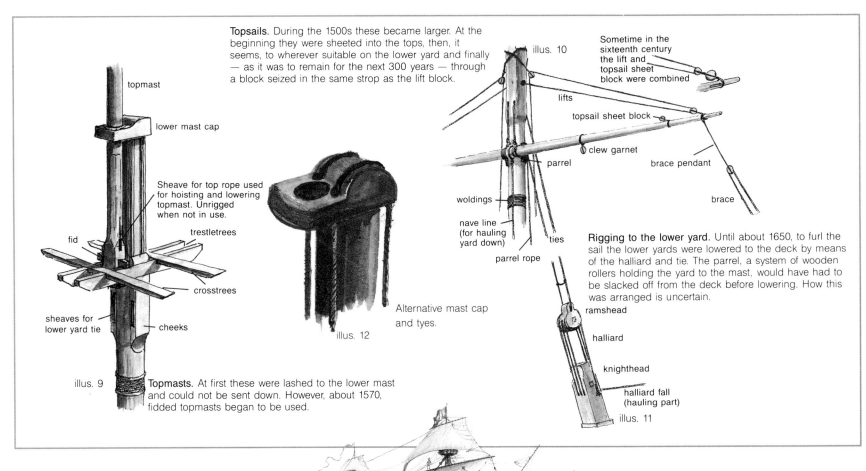

Topsails. During the 1500s these became larger. At the beginning they were sheeted into the tops, then, it seems, to wherever suitable on the lower yard and finally — as it was to remain for the next 300 years — through a block seized in the same strop as the lift block.

topmast

lower mast cap

Sheave for top rope used for hoisting and lowering topmast. Unrigged when not in use.

trestletrees

fid

crosstrees

sheaves for lower yard tie

cheeks

illus. 9

Topmasts. At first these were lashed to the lower mast and could not be sent down. However, about 1570, fidded topmasts began to be used.

Alternative mast cap and tyes.

illus. 12

illus. 10

Sometime in the sixteenth century the lift and topsail sheet block were combined

lifts

topsail sheet block

clew garnet

parrel

brace pendant

brace

woldings

nave line (for hauling yard down)

ties

parrel rope

Rigging to the lower yard. Until about 1650, to furl the sail the lower yards were lowered to the deck by means of the halliard and tie. The parrel, a system of wooden rollers holding the yard to the mast, would have had to be slacked off from the deck before lowering. How this was arranged is uncertain.

ramshead

halliard

knighthead

halliard fall (hauling part)

illus. 11

progress of the stately argosies decimated by starvation and disease those who sailed in them. Queen Elizabeth of England's 700-ton *Jesus of Lubeck*, loaned to and lost by John Hawkins, appears to have been a carrack or nao, and they were also used by the Spanish in the *Carrera de Indias* until they were superseded by the galleon. (*Illus. 13*)

illus. 13

The galleon

During the 1520s and 1530s a new class of vessel appeared in the Atlantic. Referred to as a *galeon* or *galion*, she may have been initially a modified type of galley, fitted with the standard three-masted square rig and as such much faster and more manoeuvrable than the carrack type. During the following decades the galleon, improved and enlarged, became the preferred freighter and warship of the Spanish. Other nations swiftly followed by building galleons of their own until, at the end of the century, the carrack or nao was nearly extinct. In the 1560s, John Hawkins, who had no love for the Spanish, admired their ships and, too closely for his own good, observed the vessels the Spanish were using in the *Carrera de Indias*. It was only after his return from Mexico, where his fleet had been trapped and destroyed by the Spanish, that the English began to produce their superb *race-built* galleons which were to desperately harass the Spanish. Could it be that the royal galleons of the Spanish *flotas*, designed to outfight and outrun predators and safely bring home the gold, silver and jewels of the Americas, inspired the English to build the ships which were to defeat the Armada? One should be careful about believing all the insulting remarks made by Elizabethan Englishmen regarding Spanish naval architecture.

In the terminology of Spanish sixteenth-century documents, there remains a very grey area as to the exact definition of *nao* as apart from *galeon*. Without other evidence, present-day authorities generally accept that a galleon can be differentiated from a carrack by the arrangement of the forecastle and beakhead and by the shape of the stern. The galleon, like the caravel, had a flat tuck, whereas the carrack's stern was rounded up to a transom beam. However, the difference is in reality not all that clear, particularly in regard to the Spanish word *nao*, which virtually means ship, and is sometimes indiscriminately applied. Also, there were ships with galleon sterns and carrack bows and vice versa, and the beakhead seems to have lent itself to all sorts of experimentation. At first it may have served as a ram, but it soon fulfilled the purposes of a platform to handle the spritsail, a solid structure to which the bowsprit was secured with gammon lashings and a handy, self-flushing head for the crowd. (*Illus. 14, 15 and 16*)

From the 1570s the identity of the galleon was clearly established. (*Illus. 17*)

illus. 15

illus. 14

illus. 16

illus. 17

13

About this time the ships began to boast *quarter galleries*, which not only formed secluded promenades for the officers but also a convenient shelf for their jakes. The rigging and sail plan was becoming more efficient, with larger topsails and greater use of topgallant sails on bigger ships. Topmasts were no longer lashed to the lower masthead, but properly supported by cap, cross and trestle trees and fid. (*Illus. 9, 10, 11 and 12*) The lateen mizzen course now had its own bonnet, giving it the configuration of a sail known as a *settee*. (*Illus. 18*)

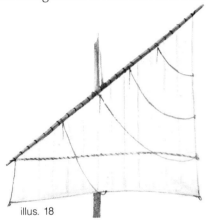

illus. 18

Towards the end of the century, ships were beginning to experiment with mizzen topsails; firstly rather unhandy lateen topsails (*Illus. 19*) and then a square topsail, set above a barren yard, known in English as the *crossjack*. (*Illus. 20*)

Miniscule spritsail topmasts made their appearance, and during the early decades of the seventeenth century gradually increased in size. For the next hundred or more years, nearly all ships of any size sported the precarious spritsail topsail, so it must have earned its keep.

From the time that the three-masted square-rigged ship first sailed, it must have been found absolutely necessary to balance the rig. When closehauled, with no headsails, a ship's tendency to carry severe

illus. 19

illus. 20

illus. 21

weather helm, or fly up into the wind, had to be controlled.

Firstly this was done by raking the foremast well forward, then by means of the spritsail. Ships got by with this for the next hundred years, but no matter how elaborately a spritsail is trimmed to the wind, it does not set when the wind comes forward of the beam, as there is nowhere to get down the tack. Closehauled, without the spritsail, the ship could only be balanced by reducing sail aft, spoiling her windward performance.

When the spritsail topsail came into use, the spritsail yard, significantly, was moved further forward, out beyond the forestay collar where the old parrel, although retained in some cases, no longer could serve its purpose in allowing the yard to be hoisted in and out. The lifts of the spritsail yard served also as sheets for the spritsail topsail; their standing part was just unhitched and bent to the clew of the sail. Now the spritsail yard could be swung so that the weather clew, or tack, of the sprit-topsail was extended and stretched beyond the end of the bowsprit. By this means the spritsail topsail, far out on the lever of the bowsprit, exerted a force out of proportion to its size, not adding much drive to the ship as did the staysails and jibs of the next century, but enabling the seventeenth-century galleons to set and balance a full suit of canvas when sailing to windward.

Although I have had experience in handling an eighteenth-century spritsail, the foregoing manner in which I have suggested the spritsail topsail was used is theory. It has been claimed that, however the yards are braced, the sail would be grossly distorted when set in the manner I have described. However, I have experimented with a model and find it works perfectly provided the tack and sheet are adjusted properly. The set can be further improved by hauling on the weather spritsail topsail lift and hauling the spritsail yard a little further outboard by means of the spritsail halliard. (*Illus. 21*)

To anyone with any understanding of rigging, it is startling to realise how little lateral support bowsprits were given. In the seventeenth century it had become a powerful spar, stepped on the centreline, to which was led all the stays of the foremast. On it was set the spritsail and the spritsail topsail, yet no shrouds or guys were provided to support the spar sideways. Powerful *gammon lashings*, at first single, and then double in large ships, held the spar down, and the heel was massively chocked against the foremast. The bowsprit passed over and was seated down on the stemhead. I cannot see what prevented it from working frightfully if the ship was rolling and no sail was set on it. It was not until 1700 that *bobstays* came into use, to be followed by *bowsprit shrouds*.

By 1620 the sail plan of the standard three-masted sailing ship was set for the next 100 years. Refinements to the hull and rigging followed one upon the other. During the early decades of the century the Dutch rose to the height of their seaborne power and, naturally, their preoccupation with ships inspired some practical and often pleasing developments in marine architecture.

The fluyt

The greatest contribution to the world of merchant shipping was the *fluyt*, already in service before the end of the sixteenth century. Perhaps this vessel was inspired by the herring *buss* or even the ancient *dogger*. What sort of ship the latter was is unknown, except it was Dutch in origin. It was used throughout the Middle Ages for trading and fishing, and made voyages to Iceland and probably Greenland. Whatever her ancestry, the fluyt was an immediate success. (*Illus. 22, 23*) She was capacious, but not a

illus. 22

illus. 23

tub, having a greater length-to-beam ratio than most other contemporary sailing ships. She was a wonderful sea boat, with full rounded bows and stern, and she carried less superstructure than the galleons. Her aftercastle was low and narrow, projecting distinctively over the tiller-port in what was to become known in later years as the *pink stern*. Her rig was simple and could be handled by considerably fewer hands than a comparable galleon.

During the seventeenth century fluyts were built in various sizes and modified for their particular trades, which might include anything from fishing to piracy. In fact, they were particularly well suited to whaling and fishing, working in the seas from Spitzbergen to the Grand Banks of Newfoundland. The *Zeehaen*, one of Abel Tasman's ships, was a fluyt, and well able to keep company with his other ship, the *Heemskirck*, a fast war yacht. Other nations used and adapted the Dutch fluyt. In England she became sometimes a *flyboat*, and later, with some modifications, a *pink* and a *cat*. The latter were employed as colliers in the North Sea, and were used by James Cook and William Bligh in the Pacific. In Spain one often comes across the term *urca* in reference to a purely merchant vessel; some of these

at least were certainly fluyts. Whereas the galleon, as did nearly all early ships, had to fight as well as trade, the fluyt was primarily a merchant ship, although she was often well armed.

Gradually, influenced mainly by the Dutch and Flemings, the outward appearance of ships began to change. Superstructures became lower and the hulls more graceful. Previously, in most cases the *wales*, or projecting thicker planks of the hull above the water, followed the line of the decks. Usually there was a wale at the point of maximum beam, below the gundeck, one level with the gundeck, a wale above the ports, another at upper deck level and one at the top of the bulwark, known as the *gunwale*. Other smaller wales often ran the length of the superstructures which, in northern ships, were often lapstrake for lightness. It was desirable to give the wales a steep sheer, particularly towards the stern, but this was limited if the deck was not to be laid at a very uncomfortable angle, with unpredictable and undesirable effects on gunnery. From the early years of the seventeenth century, more and more ships, particularly Dutch and Flemish ships, began to have their decks laid level, or almost level, fore

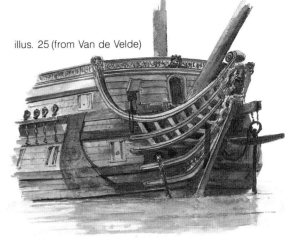

illus. 25 (from Van de Velde)

and aft, and the wales were free to rise gracefully to form the lovely hulls of the mid century. (*Illus. 24*)

The stem and beakhead also underwent a gradual change, first sweeping upward to a greater extent and then becoming shorter. While the often elaborate and highly decorated sterns of seventeenth-century ships draw a wondering attention, the complicated curves of the beakhead head-rails developed into an art form in their own right. (*Illus. 25*) The *knee of the head*, or the knee which supported the beakhead,

illus. 24

illus. 26

became more powerful, filling entirely the curve between the beakhead and the stem. (*Illus. 26*)

Sometime mid century, the sailors' life aloft became a little easier. Although it was often managed aloft, it was common practice for ships to lower their course yards to furl. As the yard came down, the *clew garnets* and *martnets* gathered the sail to the yard. With the yard not far above the rail, the sailors made their way out to pass the *gaskets* or lines used to secure the sail to the yard. To furl the sail at the ends of the yard projecting beyond the ship's side was relatively easy, as it was firmly held to the yard by the martnets. Likewise, shortening sail by removing the drabbler and bonnet was comparatively simple, given the manpower. (*Illus. 27*)

During the first half of the seventeenth century topsails became larger and were found to be much more effective in ocean seas, where the lower courses often lost the wind in the troughs of the waves. With martnets, leech-lines, buntlines and clewlines, the sailors struggled with the ever-growing topsails which, as seamen began to see the desirability of carrying them in stronger winds, needed some form of reefing. (*Illus. 28*)

Bonnets were tried, but found to be impractible as the foot could not be conveniently stretched in the confines of the top. The solution was to attach reefbands and points, or *knittles*, across the head of the topsail so that the yard could be lowered, the reef-earrings hauled out and the reef-points fastened around the yard. To do this the sailors had to lay out on the yard with the sail often jumping and thrashing. Now those ancient sailors could have put an ape to shame aloft, but to attempt to crawl out on a topsail yard in a gale of wind with the wind spilling from the sail was dangerous enough; to attempt to let go with both hands and tie the reef-points would be suicide. So, from about the time reef-points were reintroduced, ships' yards began to be fitted with footropes. (*See Illus. 29 and 30*)

Bonnets continued to be used for quite a while on the courses, but gradually, towards the end of the

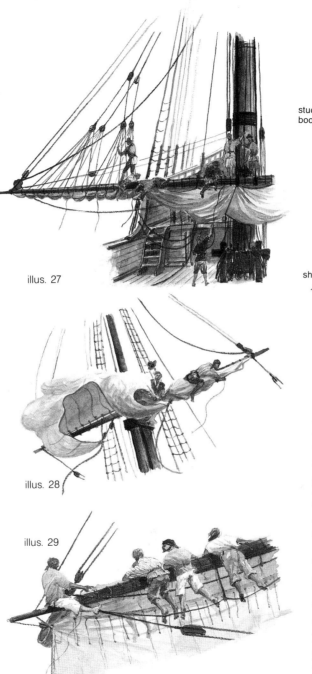

illus. 27

illus. 28

illus. 29

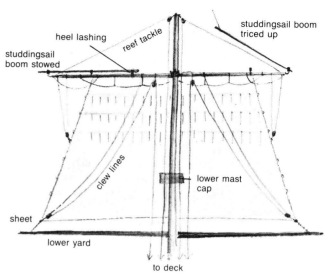

illus. 30

century, reefbands began to appear on the fore and mainsails in place of the bonnets.

The three-masted sailing ship, from the early fifteenth century, was in a constant state of change and improvement. Apart from the more apparent developments above, there were significant changes in construction, largely because of the use of heavier guns. The 'tween-deck, or second deck, became known as the gundeck and the enormous weight of the artillery resulted in a need for bluffer bows and a steep *tumblehome*, or curve inwards of the ship's side above the waterline.

Steering became a problem, sometimes needing teams of men in the large carracks. It was further complicated by the depth the tiller flat was buried by the huge aftercastles. No doubt relieving tackles were led and used for convenience, and perhaps on a warship such as *The Great Harry* steering orders were passed below by a pilot. In a sailing ship working as a merchantman, however, it is desirable that the helmsman has some visibility, if not to see outboard, then at least to see the weather leeches of the sails on the mainmast. Sometime during the sixteenth century the *whipstaff* was introduced. It could give small movements to the tiller by leverage, and greater movement by pushing the tiller with the staff. With the tiller coming inboard just below the upper-deck beams on large ships, a helmsman could stand on the upper deck, perhaps on a platform, or *traverso* in Spanish, with a view out at quarterdeck level. (*Illus. 31 and 32*)

The three-masted ship was not the only vessel engaged in transatlantic activities. Much of the detail of early small ships is lost, but no late-sixteenth-century expedition worth its salt would sail without a *pinnace*, a small craft larger than a ship's boat but small enough for inshore work and ducking up rivers and creeks. Often these had to make their own perilous way across the ocean, or were carried, knocked down, in the holds of the larger ships. How these were rigged is guesswork, but they will be depicted under some reasonable form of rig in illustrations. Likewise, knowledge is misty where records refer to such vessels as *frigates, patatches* and many other smaller vessels common in the sixteenth and early seventeenth century. During the

seventeenth century both 'pinnace' and 'frigate' came to refer to larger vessels. The former was a small three-masted ship used for fighting and trade; the frigate was a small warship with one complete gundeck but was not yet the swift and glamorous frigate of the eighteenth century.

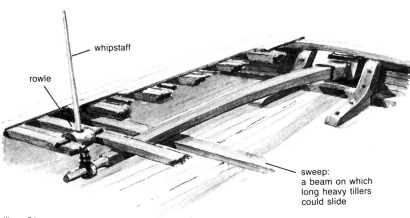

whipstaff

rowle

sweep:
a beam on which
long heavy tillers
could slide

illus. 31

illus. 32

THE NORSE VOYAGERS

It is highly probable that there were other Atlantic crossings long before the Norsemen settled Greenland and ventured further to mainland America. Some ancient Mediterranean peoples and, notably, the Irish have their proponents. They may be right, for there are many mysteries which historians, archaeologists and theorists are unable to resolve because of the lack of conclusive evidence. Whatever prior claims there may be, few would refute that the Norse made the first positively recorded transatlantic voyages. For over 300 years they sailed to their colonies in south-western Greenland, and somewhere in North America they

Prins Christians Sund

landed and made attempts to settle. The vexed question is where? There are arguable hypothoses on the location being anywhere between Hudson Bay and Cape Cod and beyond. Archaeological finds at L'Anse aux Meadows in Newfoundland confirm the Norse presence in that land, and seem to indicate that the site may have been a base for wintering and ship repair for voyages further south, but exactly where Leif Eriksson's elusive 'Vinland' is to be found, neither study of the *Sagas* nor modern research can resolve, and I am happy to leave this ongoing controversy well alone.

With reasonable certainty we can say that Iceland, the northern stepping-stone to North America, had been occupied for at least 60 years before the arrival

of the Norsemen. Irish monks, in their light and seaworthy *curraghs*, had found a quiet retreat on the island until about 860, when the first Norse exploratory voyagers arrived on the coast. These contemplative Irish religious were a tough and hardy people, and, perhaps like their counterparts today, well able to cope with rambunctious troublemakers, but the first wave of settlement by the Norsemen 14 years later proved too much and they left. A very interesting question is, for where? Back to their monasteries in Ireland? Into the bleak interior of Iceland? Onward to America? Or were they lost at sea in a vain search for mythical islands in the south?

During the last decades of the ninth century, the harrassed populations of France, Britain and Ireland

began to organise successful resistance to viking bullying, while, at home, Norway's King Harald was sorely infringing the people's freedom and independence in his campaign to unify the country. Throughout these years a steady stream of audacious but disillusioned Norse chieftains, freedmen and their slaves departed to settle in Iceland, where there was land and the independence they sought.

The south coast of Iceland is barren and a dangerous shore in a south-westerly blow. Consequently most of the early settlements were in the fjörds beyond the south-west headland of Reykjanes. The Norse mariners soon discovered that it was possible to approach the western fjörds north-about Iceland, and this route was sometimes used, for it avoided the dangerous south shore. The passage from Norway, either direct or by way of the Scottish Islands and Faroes, was not exceptional and cannot be considered transatlantic. However, taking into account the swiftly changing and often violent weather, the standard of seamanship and weatherliness of the ships is to be admired. From Stad in Norway to Iceland is 525 nautical miles, and from Ireland to Reykjanes 690 miles; records suggest that it was 3½ and 5 days' sailing respectively. This gives their vessels an average speed of about 6 knots – not bad for a single-masted, squaresail rig. Not that they could guarantee this passage time. The Norse seafarers were adept at weather forecasting, but a misjudgment could have them blown all over the place, and months could be spent on the voyage.

As the majority of Norse settlements were on the west coast of Iceland, it was not surprising that some worried sailor would overshoot Iceland to the west and sight Greenland while either driving before a storm or suffering from *hafvilla*, the Norse term for complete loss of position and direction due to fog or overcast skies, always an extremely unnerving experience for anyone at sea. Some time during the first 30 years of the tenth century, a mariner by the name of Gunnbjörn Úlf-Krakuson, either trying to make the Icelandic settlements from Norway or on

an exploratory voyage around the island, was driven west in foul weather and sighted some skerries and beyond them a high and unknown shore. The skerries, named Gunnbjarnarsker or 'Gunnbjörn's Skerries', cannot be satisfactorily identified today, but the land he saw beyond was undoubtedly Greenland.

Eirík the Red explores Greenland

Some years later, in the same century, the peace of Breidafjörd, in West Iceland, was shattered by scrapping and feuding, at the heart of which was one Eirík Raudi, or 'Eirik the Red'. Eirík was following a family tradition, for his parents had been banished from Norway for similar activities, which had resulted in a murder. Eirík likewise went too far, slew two of his enemy's sons and was banished overseas for 3 years. As Eirík's sentence was for *lesser outlawry*, one wonders what mayhem merited the term *greater outlawry* in the code of the Norsemen.

Eirík went into hiding while his loyal supporters fitted out a ship. As Norway was barred to his family, he determined to seek out the land that Gunnbjörn had sighted in the west, so, in early summer, he sailed out of Breidafjörd, escorted by his friends, and made his departure from Snaefellsnes. Sailing due west, he had about 450 miles to cover, aided by the seasonal prevailing easterly wind. Within a few days he would have made his landfall, probably in the vicinity of Greenland's Midjokull or 'Middle Glacier'. At this period the climate was warmer than at present, and ice, brought down from the north by the East Greenland Current, extended far offshore. Eirík steered south-south-west, well off the inhospitable coastline, which was backed by mountains crowned with the glistening ice-cap. Some days later he either rounded Cape Farewell or

navigated through Prins Christians Sund and stood on north-west up the western coast.

Before long, anxiety must have turned to relief as Eirík began to find everything a homeless Viking could desire; deep channels, safe anchorages, good pasturage, an equable climate and unoccupied land. He first put into what was later to become Eystribygd or 'The Eastern Settlement', wintering on Eriksey. The following spring he sailed up to the fertile plain at the head of Eriksfjörd and built a house. During the summer he explored; the next winter was spent at Holmar among the islands near Hvarf. Another summer saw him exploring northwards, possibly up the east coast, where contact may have been made with the Eskimo. After another winter at Eriksey, his exile was over.

Eirík and his shipmates safely navigated back to Breidafjörd, but here Eirík soon got into strife again. Finding his position untenable, he set about publicising his discoveries with the idea of returning to settle the new land. By naming the country Grœnland, or 'The Green Land', and extolling its virtues, he managed to raise a large number of followers who were prepared to try their luck. At that time famine had recently decimated the population of Iceland and there was a degree of social discontent caused by greedy and tyrannical landowners.

When Eirík once again set out for Greenland in the summer of 985 or 986, his fleet consisted of 25 ships loaded with families with all their livestock, (such as cattle, horses, sheep, goats, dogs and cats), their furniture, tools and all that was necessary to pioneer the new land. Sadly, 11 of the ships failed to make the passage. Their fate is unknown; they may have put back or been lost, but with the people and freight of the remaining 14 ships safely landed, the Norse settlement of Greenland was firmly established.

From the first settlement until the thirteenth and fourteenth centuries, when communications gradually declined, regular voyages were made to

Greenland, initially from Iceland and later from Norway direct. The latter were the first truly transatlantic sailings. Fourteenth-century sailing instructions direct that:

> From Hernar in Norway sail due west for Hvarf in Greenland; and then you will sail north of Shetland so that you can just sight it in clear weather; but south of the Faroe Islands, so that the sea appears half-way up the mountain-slopes; but steer south of Iceland so that you may have birds and whales therefrom.[1]

After making their departure from the Faroes, a thousand miles of ocean had to be traversed before landfall off Hvarf, with birds and whales the only navigational check as they passed between 100 and 200 miles south of Iceland. It is possible that the Norse used some form of latitude sailing, but there is no conclusive evidence and it is certain that they lacked the aid of the compass. If we consider the remarkable and uncanny skills of the Polynesian Pacific navigators and the use of these skills in the transpacific voyages of the double canoe, Hōkūlea, we should have more understanding of the Norse navigators with whom, in 'hands-on' seamanship, the Polynesians must nearly equate. Although the passage to Greenland was reckoned difficult and dangerous and there were many losses, the voyage was safely completed more often than not.

The colony was desperately short of timber. The only source available to them was driftwood, from which many of their small craft were built. They had no means of producing iron, and thus no weapons and tools could be made. Timber, iron and weapons, along with corn, clothing, malt and most of the refinements of European life, had to be imported. In return, Greenland's Eastern Settlement, and, 300 miles north-west, the Western Settlement,

exported sealskins and seal oil, walrus-hide cordage, the tusks of narwhale and walrus, falcons, polar bears, *wadmal*, and high quality woollens. Much produce of the country was won on extended summer voyages north, up the west coast to well within the Arctic Circle, and in 1266 a party got almost as far as the seventy-sixth parallel.

The first sighting of the American mainland

It was the son of Eirík Raudi who first pioneered the direct passage between Greenland and Norway, but before Leif Eríksson made his significant voyages, another experienced and successful sailor, Bjarni Herjólfsson, lost his reckoning and made an unexpected landfall.

Son of an Icelandic family, Bjarni Herjólfsson was a well travelled and respected young man who had prospered sufficiently to buy himself a ship. One year, on his return home from a voyage to Norway, he discovered his father had sold up and resettled in Greenland. Determined to spend the winter with his father, Bjarni reprovisioned his ship and without discharging his freight, immediately sailed on a voyage which neither he nor any of his crew had undertaken before.

For 3 days they had a fair wind, which took them out of sight of land, then a northerly set in, bringing with it fog. They were unable to steer a course and many days passed while they were driven southwards. At last the sun broke through and Bjarni was able to lay a course to the west and within a day had made a landfall. Closing the land, he saw low hills covered with forest, so without landing, and keeping the land on the port side, they sailed on until 2 days later they sighted forested, flat country. The wind died and the crew wanted to go ashore for wood and water, but Bjarni would have

none of it and ran offshore for 3 days before a south-west wind. After 3 days they raised another land, this time mountainous and glaciered and clearly not Greenland. Sailing on, they discovered they were coasting an island, so they turned seawards. After 4 days, during which the winds blew fresh, they saw land again. This time Bjarni was certain it was Greenland, and that evening as they came in under a cape they saw a boat which it turned out belonged to Bjarni's father who lived on that very headland.

What a superb example of navigational skill! If the account is true, Bjarni, after losing his reckoning far off course, found an unknown land. From there he confidently and doggedly kept the sea and stood on for his destination; not just coasting, but standing boldly out from his landfalls on three occasions, until he 'hit the target' with, to my mind, rather suspicious accuracy. Although it is not certain, the descriptions and distances fit his landfalls as being Newfoundland, Labrador and Baffin Island, in that order. Thus Bjarni Herjólfsson can be credited with the first recorded sighting of the American continental mainland.

Fourteen years later Bjarni went back to Norway, where he was slated for his lack of curiosity and enterprise in not making a deeper investigation of his discovery.

Bjarni's reports sparked an enthusiasm to follow up his discoveries. Eirík the Red bought Bjarni's knörr and gave command of the expedition to his son Leif. With a crew of 35 and, apparently, some cattle, Leif retraced Bjarni's course, naming the barren, mountainous island 'Helluland' and the flat, wooded land 'Markland'. Two days voyaging beyond Markland brought them to another shore where they landed on an outlying island before entering a sound which lay between the island and a cape projecting northwards from the mainland. Then, steering west around the cape, they sailed into shallows, finally running aground. At low tide they were high and dry on a large bank, far from the sea. Curious to get ashore, they left the ship to explore,

returning when the tide had refloated their vessel. They brought the knörr up a river and into a lake which they had discovered.

Leif decided to winter in this spot. Large houses were built and during the following months the explorers enjoyed the equable climate where it seemed unnecessary to store fodder for the cattle and the days and nights were of more equal length than in Greenland. At the winter solstice they noted that the sun was visible in the middle of the afternoon as well as at breakfast time.

Salmon, larger than any they had seen before, abounded in the lake, and in the course of their exploration of the surrounding countryside, vines and grapes were found. Leif had the grapes harvested and presumably dried, for, when they sailed homeward the following spring, the ship was fully laden with timber and grapes. Leif named the land 'Vinland'. Homeward bound, when in sight of the Greenland shore they were fortunate enough to be able to save the crew and some of the cargo from a wrecked vessel, and ever afterward Leif was known as 'Leif the Lucky'.

Immediately following Leif's voyage, the Greenlanders made a series of voyages to Vinland. Thorvald, Leif's brother, in the same veteran knörr which had been Bjarni's, spent 2 years exploring, wintering at Leif's camp. During the first summer he explored to the south-west and found no sign of human life except a wooden grain-holder. The following season was spent examining the land to the north-east, where, one stormy day, the knörr was driven ashore, breaking her keel. Making a new keel took quite a while and when they left they erected the old keel on a cape as a marker, naming the headland 'Kjalarnes', or 'Keelness'. Further north Thorvald found land to his liking and was making plans to settle when they discovered their first native people resting under three skin boats. In character

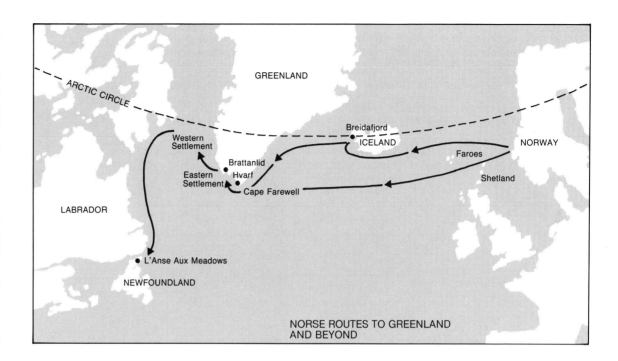

NORSE ROUTES TO GREENLAND AND BEYOND

with their murderous reputation, the Norsemen slew eight of the party; one, however, managed to escape. While sleeping back at the ship, Thorvald and his crew were attacked and in the fight Thorvald was fatally wounded and was buried on the headland he wished to make his home. His crew sailed back to Leif's winter camp, gathered a cargo and sailed home the following spring.

Another brother, Thorstein, with his wife Gudrid and 25 men, set out to retrieve Thorvald's body. In Bjarni's well tried knörr, he spent the best part of a summer knocking about the Greenland Sea and the North Atlantic in filthy weather without making a landfall. Before they succeeded in making land at Greenland's Western Settlement many of the crew had died, including Thorstein.

That same summer, a wealthy Icelander, Thorfinn Karlsefni, arrived in Greenland and married Gudrid.

The following summer he led a large expedition, consisting of 60 men and five women, along with all kinds of livestock, all apparently crammed into one ship. After two winters at Leifsbudir they returned to Greenland, probably considering their numbers were insufficient to defend themselves against attacks by the natives with whom they had been alternately trading and warring.

The last recorded voyage was in two ships, one commanded by two brothers, Helgi and Finnbogi, and the other by Eirík's virago of a daughter, Freydis. During the first winter Freydis incited her husband to slaughter the brothers and their crew, dispatching the women and children herself when her followers refused to do the dirty work.

The discoveries at L'Anse aux Meadows confirm Norse maritime activity in Newfoundland and significantly, the buildings and artifacts appear to belong to the first half of the eleventh century, 100 years or so later than the recorded Vinland voyages. Thus, as would be natural, it would seem that voyages from Greenland to the south did not stop with the murderous voyage of Freydis, but continued into the eleventh century and perhaps later. L'Anse aux Meadows seems to have been occupied for only a brief period – perhaps 30 years, and then only as a base for ship repair and wintering. No other Norse artifacts have been found beyond Newfoundland and the location of Vinland remains a mystery. It should also be noted that there are no records of any voyage direct from Norway to Vinland or, apart from Bjarni's accidental excursion, from Iceland. Vinland appears to have been solely a Greenland venture.

Large ships were difficult to build in the timberless fjörds of Greenland, and as the Greenlanders turned more from the sea and began to depend on Icelandic and Norwegian vessels for their communication with the outside world, their standard of seamanship declined. 'Markland' remained within the Greenlanders reach, and as late as 1347 Icelandic records state:

> A craft came from Greenland which was smaller in size than a small Icelandman. It came into the entrance of Straumfjörd. It had no anchor. There were seventeen men on board who had been on a voyage to Markland and later been driven by gales to this land.[2]

Although the sailing directions and will for voyages to Vinland were lost, transatlantic voyages to Greenland continued until neglect by the mother countries so reduced the sailings that the colony slowly faded out of the consciousness of Europe. By the end of the fourteenth century, contact had all but ceased. The colony, it seems, struggled on against increasing cold as the climate changed, and with the ice came the Eskimo to compete for the resources of the land. The last recorded contact with Greenland was in the late summer of 1410, when some Icelanders left after an extended and enforced visit when they were storm-driven to the Eastern Settlement and were unable to get away for 4 years. From this date nothing is known of the fate of the colony except that archaeological finds of clothing at grave sites suggest that it may have survived into the second half of the fifteenth century. A sad and lonely end.

The knörr

Thanks to the happy circumstance that it was the custom of the vikings to have their leaders buried along with a ship fitted out and stored for a last voyage to Valhalla, fine examples of their vessels have been unearthed, granting us today a deeper understanding of their architecture than of any other ship type until the sixteenth century. The Gokstad ship, discovered in the nineteenth century, is a graceful 80 ft (24 m), ninth-century example of maritime technology. It is a strong but flexible, truly seagoing craft, a replica of which was sailed to America in 1893. The Gokstad ship is a *langskip*, or longship, a warship of the type that sent coastal peoples all over Europe scurrying for cover. Until 1962, most other Norse finds were of this type of craft.

Superb as it was, the longship was not the class of vessel which transported heavy freight between Norway and Greenland with small crews, or crammed aboard 60 brawny Norsemen, their women, livestock and equipment as recounted in Karlsefni's voyage to Vinland. It was the merchantman of the north, variously designated as a *knörr, knarr, hafskip* or *kaupskip*, which made the epic Atlantic voyages and maintained communications and trade between Norway and her colonies in the bleak Western Ocean.

Since 1924 it was known that ancient wrecks lay in Roskilde Fjörd in Denmark, but not until the 1950s was it discovered that the remains belonged to the viking period. In 1962 a major archaeological excavation was begun which recovered some 50,000 pieces of what turned out to be five ships which, during the first half of the eleventh century, were deliberately sunk across the channel near the fishing village of Skuldelev with the intention of preventing seaborne attacks on the town of Roskilde at the head of the fjörd. Two of these ships proved to be merchant vessels. 'Skuldelev 3' was a small 43 ft 8 in. (13.3 m) merchantman capable of carrying about 3.5 tonnes and suitable for coastal work and, with her shallow draft, able to work far up any waterway. 'Skuldelev 1' was a true deepwater knörr, the class of ship consistently named in the Atlantic sagas and the first of her kind to be discovered.

Built of pine, oak and lime, 'Skuldelev 1' measured 54 ft 2 in. (16.5 m) overall, with a beam of 14 ft 9 in. (4.5 m) and depth amidships of 6 ft 3 in. (1.9 m). As it is thought that these ships could measure up to 80 ft (24.38 m), my reconstruction illustrates a knörr similar to but larger than 'Skuldelev 1', measuring about 65 ft (19.81 m). Unlike the longship, she is first and foremost a sailing vessel, only carrying sufficient sweeps for manoeuvring in confined waters. There is no continuous watertight deck, but fore and aft of a hold amidships there are halfdecks, under which there is considerable space which must have been used for smaller freight and storage. Although built more robustly than a longship, this knörr is still lightly built by later standards and ballast must have been carried to enable her to sail effectively. The laps of the planking are fastened with soft iron rivets and the ribs, fitted after the planking is complete, are lashed to carved cleats on the inner surface of the strakes with leather or withies.

A knörr must have been a miserably uncomfortable vessel in which to sail long distances. With all the livestock, families and chattels on board,

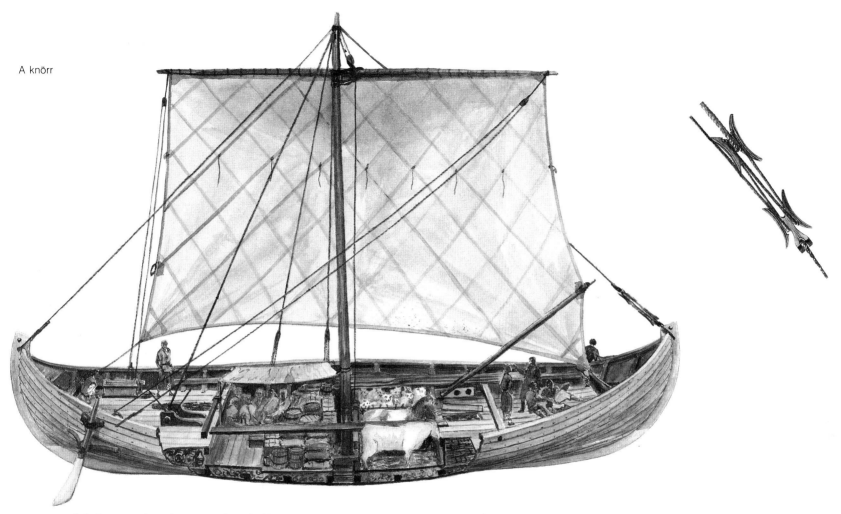

A knörr

some sort of shelter must have been rigged, probably in the way of a skin awning over part of the midship hold space. Part of the strength and seaworthiness of the knörr was due to her flexibility, always, within reason, an attribute in a sailing vessel. However, as she gave and worked with the sea, she would have leaked; so what with rain, spray, shipped green water and working seams, bailing would have been regular and imperative.

The simple single squaresail rig is basic but effective. Not a great deal is known of the details,

but some elegant cleat-shaped blocks and other pulleys have been found. The knörr in the illustration is equipped with a windlass as there are some indications that they may have been used in viking times. The luff of the sail, when sailing on a wind, is stretched by a pole known as a *beita*.

Sailcloth was made out of wool and stretched badly. To overcome this, strips of hide, probably walrus hide, were sewn on to the fore side of the sail, giving it a distinctive latticed appearance. One of the primary exports from Greenland, walrus hide

was in great demand, for it was very strong and rot resistant, and when laid up into a cable, made an ideal anchor warp. Anchors were of the *fisherman* type, with wooden stocks, equipped with several fathoms of lead chain, a sophisticated feature which greatly improved the holding power of the anchor and overcame the problem of chafe on a foul bottom.

Steering was by means of a side rudder on the starboard side. For this type of vessel, which was often beached, the side rudder had the advantage that it could be easily shipped.

CHRISTOPHER COLUMBUS

While the Norse settlements in Greenland were fading to extinction, Portugal was beginning her push south along the African coast. In 1434, Gil Eannes rounded Cape Bojador, and, half a century later, Portuguese endeavours were rewarded when, in 1488, Bartolomeu Diaz rounded the Cape of Good Hope and opened the seaway to the East. Forced by prevailing winds, calms in the Bight of Benin and adverse currents, the Portuguese pioneered the art of ocean sailing, striking far out to sea on their return voyages from the south to lay the north-east trades on the starboard tack and on through the horse latitudes to pick up the favourable westerlies in the latitudes of their homeland.

The volcanic islands of the Azores, 700 miles west of Portugal, which were inevitably discovered, could have been placed there by some sort of divine providence intent on benefiting the sea-weary, homeward-bound Portuguese sailors. Among other, more venal purposes, their voyages certainly were carried out for the glory of God, for it was the search for Prester John, the legendary Christian king in the East, which fired their crusading spirits. As each navigator pushed further south, he erected a stone cross or *padrão* on the African coast at the point he turned back, and each river he came to was considered a possible pathway to the lost kingdom.

Portugal, perched on the south-western tip of Europe, and facing seaward, was ideally placed to take up the challenge when Europe had its back to the wall. The foothold in the Holy Land, won by the Crusades, was long lost. The menace of the Moorish empire, the monopoly of Mediterranean trade by the Genoese and Venetians, the fall of Constantinople, and the relative poverty of the soil of their homeland all influenced the Portuguese, encouraged by the austere Prince Henry, to turn their faces seaward. The vessel they devised for their ventures was the graceful and weatherly caravel, and by the last decade of the fifteenth century their ships were to be found all over the eastern Atlantic, from Good Hope (or 'Cape of Storms' as it was then known) to Iceland, and they were on the verge of attaining their goal in the Far East.

While the Portuguese were at last beginning to approach the tip of Africa in their southern voyages, a Genoese mariner was impatiently waiting the decision of Queen Isabella of Spain. The life and background of Christopher Columbus are too well known to be repeated here. He was an experienced seaman; he claimed that he first went to sea at the tender age of 10 years. He had sailed about the Mediterranean, traded in West Africa and probably made a voyage to Iceland. In 1476 the armed convoy he was sailing in as a seaman was attacked by a French fleet, and the Flemish ship he was sailing in was sunk. With the aid of a sweep, he managed to swim the 6 miles ashore, landing near Lagos. He never returned to Genoa, and in the Portuguese caravels trading to Guinea he must have first grasped the notion of sailing westward.

It was a notion which soon became an obsession. After years of frustration, attempting to get first the Portuguese and then the Spanish Crown to back him, in 1492 Columbus's perseverance was

From the deck of the *Santa Maria*

rewarded, for Isabella finally relented. Columbus was now 41, reckoned to be approaching old age in those days. Before him lay a stupendous and magnificent challenge.

The first voyage

When, on Friday 3 August 1492, the three Spanish ships, *Santa Maria*, *Pinta* and *Niña*, weighed anchor at Palos and worked down the Rio Tinto to the sea, only their commander had clear in his mind what to expect during the coming months. For years Christopher Columbus had single-mindedly pursued his dream to sail west and raise the eastern shores of Asia. How many leagues it might be until these lands lay before him, Columbus was prepared to demonstrate to anyone who might further the voyage . . . 750 leagues or 2760 miles to Cipangu or Japan, the fabled outlier of Asia. Whether Columbus actually believed his own calculations, or they were bent to serve his purpose, is still argued. It is certain that Columbus made a monumental mistake, and if he had known the true distance, about 12,200 miles, even he might have hesitated before setting out. (The Portuguese had not believed him, for their figures were more accurate; also, they were already committed to extending their explorations in West Africa.)

That the brave sailors who signed on for the voyage thought they would sail off the edge of the world, I doubt. The expected long ocean voyage would have worried them, and this was apparent in their nervousness later. They would have been superstitious, and in those days their range of imagination was unlimited by science. All forms of horrors, natural and supernatural, might lie below the horizon. They were used to this, but considered that God was on their side. With faith and attention to prayer, they might win through – and what a prize! What must be always remembered is that the first voyage was based firmly on the science of the day, and all who sailed put their lives on the line, on the basis of a theory. The theory was right in principle but wrong in detail. Those who were bold enough to test the theory found a new world.

The ships were well found and provisioned for about a year, and much care was given to selecting their crews. We do not know whether Columbus and the other captains were swamped with volunteers or whether they had to drum up their crews. Seamen then possessed a degree of independence, and they were certainly not, as is sometimes made out, criminals and down-and-outs shanghaied for the voyage. They would have been told where they were heading, and most would have asked some pertinent questions before signing on. Simple and rough a number must have been, but they were good seamen and, on the whole, good men.

The 90 or so who made up the complements of the three ships were organised in much the same way as those in sailing ships engaged on long ventures during the following centuries. The two caravels, *Pinta* and *Niña*, had been demanded in reparation by the Crown from the citizens of Palos '. . . for certain things done and committed by you to our disservice . . .'[1] and many of the crews came from that area, including their captains and owners. The Pinzón brothers, Martín Alonzo, captain of the *Pinta*, and Vincente Yáñez, were prominent middle-class citizens of Palos, and it was Martín Alonzo who was to considerably vex Columbus during the voyage. A dubious case has been put forward that it was Martín who made the voyage possible and in reality led the enterprise. Whatever the truth, both brothers were good seamen, particularly the younger Vincente, and were keen to undertake the venture. It must have greatly assisted Columbus to have had the enthusiasm of the Pinzóns behind him when raising his crews in Palos. Other leading seafaring families also actively and willingly participated in the voyage. It is indicative of the communal effort of the voyage that the owners of the caravels were prepared to sail, Cristóbal Quintero accepting the lowly rank of seaman. Three of the Niño family embarked: the owner of the *Niña*, Juan; the gifted pilot of the *Santa Maria*, Peralonso; and 19-year-old Francisco, who shipped out as grommet.

All three captains were experienced seamen, which was not always the case in those days. They were in overall command but were expected to consult with, and respect the advice of, the other officers, especially the master and pilot. The master was responsible for the entire management of the ship and, although subject to the authority of the captain, had the same responsibilities as a nineteenth-century sailing-ship captain. It was on the master's judgment, experience and seamanship that captains short on sea-time relied, but on this voyage, with experienced captains, he may have fulfilled more the position of a first mate, except that he would have had charge of all shiphandling.

Next in line, the pilot, was responsible for the navigation of the ship. He kept the reckoning and his task became very important in later years when trans-ocean voyages became more regular. He was expected to guide the ship and be acquainted with the routes, and he became second in authority to the captain. On this voyage the pilot was under the command of the master and performed much of the duties of a mate, whose prime responsibility was navigation. It is indicative of the importance of the pilot that he was paid the same as the master. The only other officer who had direct dealings and authority with the men was the marshal, who combined the duties of policeman, jailer and executioner. How busy he was kept we do not know, but there is no evidence of punishments being meted out on the outward voyage, although there was some unhappiness and incipient mutiny before they made their landfall.

The boatswain's task has never changed. Even the Ark must have had a bo'sun; someone on whom the master could lean, and depend to supervise and lead in all the practical, hands-on work of a ship. A good bo'sun is a gem to be treasured. He should be able to tread the fine line between alienating his men and being too soft. Ever vigilant for the chafed line or rat in the sail locker, he must stay one jump ahead of the mate and master, and when the mate can't think of the next job – which is rare – the bo'sun will have a dozen lined up.

The steward, about equivalent in rank to the bo'sun, fulfilled all the duties one would expect of that position. Water, provisions, lamps and the galley firebox all came under his care. In addition, he was a kind of schoolteacher, and the grommets, or boys, took instruction from him.

The cooper, caulker and carpenter were petty officers of lesser rank, but their skilled tasks in the days of wooden ships and wooden containers were extremely important. The cooper had to be able to make, maintain and repair the multitude of wooden casks, tubs and buckets; it was the caulker's task to keep the water out of the ship. Interestingly, with a certain logic, it was the caulker who had charge of the pump, not the chippy. In any case, Chips would have had plenty to otherwise occupy him.

All through that first day at sea, while the crews would have been shaking themselves down to sea routine and getting their sea legs back, the ships sailed south, hard on the starboard tack. The watches were set and changed at 3, 7 and 11 – 4 hours on and 4 off. Each watch was in charge of an officer; the master would probably have had the starboard watch and the pilot the port. The only timekeeping instrument was a half-hour glass or *ampolleta* which was turned, promptly if he valued his skin, by one of the boys, who sang out a ditty to mark the time. Thus there were eight glasses to a watch, and this is the origin of the system of bells extant today. What means of 'dogging' or recirculating the watch times were used, if any, is unknown.

That night the wind veered through north-west to north, allowing the ships to work an offing from the coast and lay a course for their first destination,

the Canary Islands. Two very practical reasons led Columbus to take his departure from the Canaries. Firstly, the islands lay on the same latitude as Cipangu, and Columbus, equipped with a quadrant, would have considered that he would be able to roughly maintain that latitude. As it turned out, any attempts at getting a latitude using the Pole Star were failures. Secondly, the Portuguese had tried to sail west, out past the Azores, and failed because of the prevailing westerlies; also, Columbus would have observed on his voyages to Africa that, once clear of the Canaries, he would get a fair wind.

The stretch of water between Spain and the Canaries usually required a 10-day passage and, although it could not be termed rough, it is no millpond, with fresh winds and high seas often experienced. It was the ideal shakedown for the ships, and it is possible that Columbus had this in mind. (I have had personal experience of taking a sailing ship, after a major refit, offshore on a long trip with no time for a shakedown cruise to test both the ship and the crew. I was lucky with the crew, but the ship kept us anxiously on our toes the whole voyage; it is a practice to be avoided if possible.)

The crews of the three ships, apart from sorting out the problems which only the sea can find, soon got to know the idiosyncracies of their ships. The *Santa Maria* was found to be slow, so that the sleeker caravels had to reduce sail to keep station. As soon as the wind freshened and the sea got up, the lateen rig of the *Niña* proved unhandy. One can imagine the problem – the square-riggers happily rolling off right before the wind, but the little *Niña* always on the verge of a disastrous gybe, and at times having to run dangerously by the lee to maintain her station; meanwhile, without a lateral wind to steady her, rolling heavily, thus adding to the danger of a gybe and putting enormous stresses on the rig. To gybe a lateen, the whole yard and sail has to be brought round before the mast, a job requiring all hands, careful judgment, and a good deal of strength when the seas run high. On their own, the crew would

have brought the wind on the *Niña*'s quarter and tacked downwind, which can be faster and is what most fore-and-aft sailors do if they have room and want a peaceful ride.

It was the *Pinta* which was to give the most trouble. Four days out, with the little fleet making excellent progress, the *Pinta*'s rudder lifted clean out of its gudgeons in heavy seas. Unable to give any assistance, the *Santa Maria* and *Niña* hove to and stood by while Martín Alonzo, '... a man of energy and ingenuity' in Columbus's estimation, got some sort of temporary lash-up rigged on the heavy rudder. The next day, 7 August, they got under way for Lanzarote, only to heave to again the following day after *Pinta*'s rudder once more came adrift. To add to their frustration, the caravel had begun to take in more water than usual. There were murmurings that Cristóbal Quintero, *Pinta*'s owner, upset at having his ship requisitioned, had sabotaged the rudder; if true, this was a pretty desperate effort, akin to putting a bullet through one's foot, for he could easily have lost his ship. A decision was made to put in at Grand Canary to seek another ship, but the wind failed them the next morning when the island was in sight. Until the night of 11 August they drifted about in sight of the island, and when finally they got a wind, Columbus bore away for Gomera, leaving Martín Alonzo to take the *Pinta* into Las Palmas on Grand Canary, thus widening their search for a replacement for the *Pinta*.

On the evening of 12 August, the *Santa Maria* and the *Niña* anchored off San Sebastian, Gomera. No ship was available, but a start was made on provisioning and watering. There was a chance that Columbus might be able to charter a ship which was then at sea, on its way from Grand Canary with Doña Beatriz de Peraza y Bobadilla, the 30-year-old widowed Governess of Gomera, on board. In a small vessel bound for Las Palmas, Columbus sent one of his best men to assist with the repairs to the *Pinta* and inform Martín Alonzo of the whereabouts and intentions of the commander.

The days went by with no sign of the ship bearing the Governess. On the twenty-fourth Columbus could wait no longer and put out for Grand Canary. Either towing or using sweeps, they caught up with the little coaster, which had been becalmed between Gomera and Teneriffe for 10 days. They took their messenger off and carried on to Grand Canary. The volcano of Teneriffe was putting on a frightening show as they passed, but the terrified sailors, who had never seen an eruption before, were calmed by Columbus's explanation of the phenomenon. On the twenty-fifth they arrived at Las Palmas and were reunited with Martín Alonzo. Doña Beatriz, Columbus discovered, had left 5 days previously.

The *Pinta* had only got in the day before. For 2 weeks she had been struggling to make port with her damaged rudder. With the fleet reunited, every effort was made to ready the ships for the long haul to Cipangu. The *Pinta*'s rudder was repaired and new gudgeons fitted. She was trimmed less by the stern by shifting ballast, and the leaks were caulked. *Niña* was entirely re-rigged so that she carried the same rig as the *Pinta*. On 1 September they sailed to Gomera, where Columbus finally met up with Doña Beatriz. The story goes that he fell in love with her, but Columbus did not delay on this account. Early in the morning of 6 September, after confessions and farewells had been made, and when they were on the point of sailing, a caravel arrived from Ferro with the news that three Portuguese caravels were not far off, seeking to arrest Columbus. Unworried, he ordered the anchors weighed and the *Santa Maria, Pinta* and *Niña* put out to sea.

So began the voyage which was to put the whole of western civilisation on to a new track. It was a voyage with few parallels and literally opened up a whole new world to a rejuvenated, vigorous, renaissance Europe, now well able to gain a foothold and exploit a previously unknown continent. Greed and cruelty often overshadowed the more honourable aspirations of the Spanish, Portuguese,

French, Dutch and English who were later to settle the vast lands, but this does not detract from the stupendous significance of that first voyage when Columbus inadvertently stumbled on the outlying islands of the American continent.

For the next 2 days the ships flopped around between Gomera and Teneriffe in calms and light winds until, in the early hours of Saturday 8 September, the wind came in from the north-east and they were truly under way. The *Santa Maria* immediately began to hobbyhorse and pitch her bows under, reducing the speed of the ships to under one knot. By Sunday morning the flagship's behaviour had been improved, probably by redistributing some of her considerable load of stores, and the following 24 hours saw them averaging a respectable 5½ knots.

From the outset, Columbus, with a canny insight to the source of future trouble and the psychology of his crews, determined to supply the men with a short reckoning of each day's run, keeping what he thought was the true estimate to himself '. . . so that the crews should not lose heart or be alarmed if the voyage grew long.'[2] As it turned out, Columbus appears to have habitually overestimated his speed and consequently his broadcast distances were nearer but still somewhat greater than the truth. It seems no form of log for measuring speed was used and, as the assessment of speed relied on experience and a glance over the side, it is little wonder the pilots came up with wildly different conclusions; Peralonso Niño of the *Santa Maria* often proved to be the most accurate navigator. The speed of a ship in a seaway is always hard to judge. The fuss the ship makes, the acceleration when cresting a wave, and the commonly experienced feeling that a ship goes faster during the night, can all make even the most expert seaman overestimate speed. Each day Columbus knocked from his distance run whatever he thought he could get away with, thus on the tenth, when he recorded 60 leagues*, the crew were told 48, and on the thirteenth, when he reckoned

33, he only subtracted 3 or 4 leagues.

The *Santa Maria* must have carried some weather helm or an inclination to broach before the seas out of the north-east, and this took a bit of getting used to, for on the first day of clear sailing, on 9 September, Columbus had frequently to rebuke the helmsmen for letting the ship round up to the west by north, and even west-north-west. Due west was the course, and for Columbus it was imperative that this course was maintained. No more is heard of bad steering, so either the sailors got the feel of the ship or sail was trimmed to ease the helm.

Columbus did not realise just how lucky he was on that first voyage. He sailed at the tail of the hurricane season and missed that potentially disastrous experience, and he held the north-east trade winds nearly the whole way. The region of these winds varies north and south with the sun, and they are somewhat unpredictable. In the season he made his crossing, present wind charts lay down the northern limit of the trades south of his track for most of the way, yet he had to suffer no calms or storms, and only a few days of variable but not entirely unfavourable winds. On Sunday 16 September Columbus records:

> On that day and all succeeding days we met with very mild breezes, and the mornings were very sweet, with naught lacking save the song of the nightingales . . . and the weather was very like April in Andalusia.[3]

Idyllic sailing indeed, with only a whisper of anxiety as to how long it would last and what lay below the horizon. On that same day Columbus records the first sightings of sargasso weed, which he naturally thought may have been torn from some

* *Note:* The Spanish reckoned 17½ leagues to one degree or 60 nautical miles, therefore 1 league = 3·428 nautical miles.

nearby land. Continually throughout his log signs such as birds and clouds are interpreted as indications of land, and such *señas* did provide a significant aid to navigation in those days. All aboard the ships would in their hearts fear the loss of all contact with land, and these signs, although incorrectly interpreted, gave a reassurance they desperately needed.

Almost anything out of the ordinary was interpreted as a sign of land. The very next day, Monday 17 September, Columbus records a whole plethora of indications that land lay not far to the west. In the weed a crab was found '. . . a sure sign of land, because crabs are not found more than 80 leagues from land.'[4] The water of the sea was less

salt, and if they believed this false observation, they can only have interpreted it as a sign that a large river emptied into the sea not far away. Porpoises and birds all told them, quite incorrectly, that land was nearby.

Pinzón was clearly excited, for the next day Columbus writes of his anxiety, later to be justified, concerning the captain of the fast-sailing *Pinta*, who had ranged far out ahead in the hope of finding land.

He is a fine captain and very resourceful, but his independence disturbs me somewhat. I trust this tendency to strike out on his own does not continue, for we can ill afford to become separated this far from home.[5]

Santa Maria, Niña and *Pinta* at sea

The possibility of being dispersed while sailing west must have been a constant source of anxiety for Columbus. Every effort was made to ensure that contact was maintained, and signals were arranged to aid this purpose. At night the stern lantern of the *Santa Maria* provided a homing beacon for the other ships, and other signals must have been arranged to indicate distress, a wish to communicate, and changes of course and sail. The only signal we know of for certain was that for sighting land, when a lombard was to be fired. Normally, with a fleet sailing to a known destination, rendezvous could

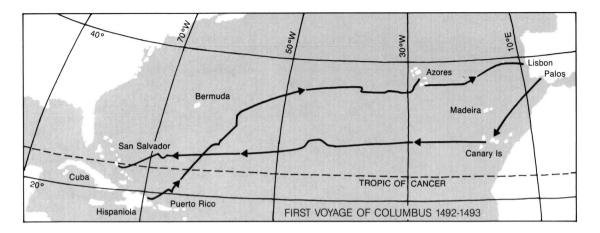

FIRST VOYAGE OF COLUMBUS 1492-1493

be prearranged in the event of separation. For Columbus, no such rendezvous was possible, and if the ships were dispersed, the likelihood of them meeting up again was remote. The security of the whole enterprise depended on staying together. In an era of seafaring when losses were to be expected among men and ships, each ship was the others' lifeboat, and in a strange land, three ships were far more formidable than one alone.

When, on 18 September, Martín Alonzo lay the *Pinta* to and the others had caught up, he reported that the previous evening he had seen land about 15 leagues to the north and Columbus was urged to alter course to search for it.

They may have thought that the signs of land they were seeing came from the islands of Antilla, thought to lie on the route to Cipangu, but this was not the goal of the commander and he refused to deviate.

On Wednesday 19 September the weather was calm and Columbus took the opportunity to take a cast with the deep-sea lead on a 200-fathom line. No bottom was found, but birds and another augury, rain without wind, still made them believe land was near. On this calm day the captains and pilots seem to have got together and compared their reckonings.

Columbus's pilot, Peralonso Niño, came up with a distance run of 400 leagues . . . nearly correct. Sarmiento of the *Pinta* estimated 420 and Ruiz, of the *Niña*, 440. Martín Alonzo continued to put pressure on Columbus to search for land to the north.

The following day the wind came in variable and sometimes calm so that Columbus was forced to leave his course of due west, steering sometimes west by north and west-north-west. The crews, already showing signs of restlessness and anxiety, were further dismayed by the rafts of sargasso weed which looked likely to entrap the ships. During the following days they lost the trades and for the first time suffered contrary winds. In a way this was a boost to the morale of the crews, for the continual easterlies were making their return voyage look extremely difficult, if not impossible. Columbus, who had other plans for the return voyage, seems not to have imparted these to the men. He had a very sound idea that they would find their homeward-bound winds to the north. On the twenty-third little wind, but a heavy swell, probably out of the south-west, encouraged the crew to think that stronger winds might at times favour them if they wished to return.

On the twenty-fourth the wind came fair again, but only light. Columbus recorded the first indications of serious trouble with the crew. He was told by a few of his trusted seamen that the men were considering throwing him overboard if he persisted in continuing to the west. Columbus quietened the sailors for a while by laughing and joking with them.

During the twenty-fifth Columbus and his pilot spent some time trying to plot their position on a chart showing some islands which they should have raised by then. They could only conclude that they had been set to the north by a current and they had overestimated the distance sailed. That evening Martín Alonzo, this time keeping close company, hailed the *Santa Maria* in some excitement and yelled that he saw land and claimed his reward. Prayers were offered in thanksgiving and, swarming aloft, the crews all agreed that land lay there to the south-west. Columbus estimated that their distance off was about 25 leagues and course was altered towards it. The next morning they found the land was an illusion. What they had thought was land was probably a cloud bank showing firm against the westering sun. They resumed course and for the next 10 days, at first in light wind but later in fresher winds, they rolled on westward.

During this period the pilots seem to have awoken to the fact that Pole Star observations to check their compasses were giving them some strange variations. One evening the observation showed a whole point (11¼°) westerly variation and the following morning the needle was right on the star. As Columbus rightly pointed out, it was not the compasses at fault or anything strange happening to the north pole. It was the Pole Star describing its path around the true pole which accounted for the error, and this was a phenomenon widely known at the time. However, the pilots, according to the commander, were mightily worried and confused, and the explanation only partly eased their minds. They had moved out of the zone of easterly variation to which they were accustomed, and now had a westerly variation of 7° which, added to the approximately 3½° of Polaris east of the true pole, gave a total of 10½°, just short of the 11¼° of a compass point.

The deflection of the needle entirely to the west must have become apparent to the pilots and incited some more careful checking than usual. As Admiral Samuel Eliot Morison points out in his book, *Christopher Columbus, Admiral of the Ocean Sea*, it was this westerly variation, which Columbus only later was to admit, that deflected the course of the ships to the south. Had they continued true west, they could have ended up in the Gulf Stream and on the American mainland.

On 1 October Peralonso Niño reckoned they had covered 578 leagues; Columbus told him his reckoning was 584 and kept his 'true' estimate of 707 to himself. Once again it was Peralonso who was nearly right.

On and on they sailed, sometimes making the very respectable speed of between 8 and 9 knots. If this is not another of Columbus's overestimates, the *Santa Maria* must have been on her hull speed. This is the maximum speed a displacement hull can be pushed through the water and depends largely on the waterline length and hull shape. The flagship's lines would not have enhanced these factors. It would have been grand sailing in any case, but it did not please the crew. As each league passed beneath their keel, they were further away from home, and it must have seemed that the ships were on a slipway to eternity.

Columbus frequently had to restate his intention to keep on and not go beating around for islands over the horizon but off his course. On 6 October Martín Alonzo told Columbus he thought it would be a good idea if they steered to the south-west for, if they had been set north and the island of Cipangu was at the distance laid down on the chart, it should not be far off in that direction. But no, the commander would not comply; he would stand on to the Asian

mainland, their final goal.

The days, as they often are in those latitudes, were somewhat hazy and the ships spread out to the limit of visibility so as to cover as much ground as possible in their search for land. To maintain communication, and probably to prevent Martin Pinzón taking off into the sunset after another chimera, Columbus had ordered the ships to assemble at dawn and dusk when the haze would clear and they had maximum visibility.

At dawn the next day, 7 October, while the ships were in close company, they thought they could make out land ahead, but after the last false sighting everyone was being careful. Ten thousand *maravedies* was to go to him who first sighted land. (This would be the equivalent of several hundred American dollars, and a fortune in those days.) A false 'Land ho!' from an over-keen lookout would disqualify him entirely. As everyone thought they could see the longed-for land, but were not prepared to commit themselves, the three ships cracked on sail and raced ahead to get first in a position to be able to confirm the sighting.

Niña, by far the best sailer, was quickly ahead of the fleet and someone, we do not know who, felt confident enough to put their chances on the line. From the *Niña* came the thud of a gun, and a flag was run to the masthead. In happy anticipation, the ships ran on, but by sunset gloom and disappointment had settled over everyone. There was no land. Columbus, always in search of hope in adversity, watched the large flights of birds flying towards the south-west and, keeping in mind that the Portuguese had discovered many of their islands by following birds, finally purposefully departed from due west and steered west-south-west, intending to stay on that course for 2 days.

The following day the ships maintained the new course and the weather held fine. On the ninth the wind fell light and variable, forcing the fleet to fall off to the west by north for a while. It was possibly on this day that some sort of conference was held,

for the crews, and probably the other captains, were ready to throw in their hand and turn back. Columbus also was becoming extremely anxious, for they had already overrun his estimated distance, even by his false reckoning, and the pilots knew this. An agreement was made to stand on for another 3 days. If land was not sighted, they would then turn back.

On the tenth, only 200 miles offshore if they had but realised, the crew of the *Santa Maria* came out in open mutiny, which was quietly put down by Columbus's determination and reassurances, possibly emphasising the 3-day limit which may not have been communicated to the men. It was not surprising that the sailors had reached their limit, and no one, sitting in an armchair, can accuse them of cowardice. They had sailed further, very much further, out of sight of land than any known person before them. Their hopes had been dashed time and again, and every day was taking them farther away from home. That day the wind began to freshen and the ships were tearing through the water to the west-south-west.

On the eleventh the winds became strong, stronger than at any other time on the voyage, and the ships began taking water over the decks. In spite of the heavy seas, they began to see flotsam which undoubtedly came from land nearby: a green reed and other land plants, what looked like a carved stick, a small board and a stick covered with barnacles. These signs gave some heart to the men, and prayers in thanks for the renewed hope were said that evening, and after sunset the course was brought back to due west.

Columbus took a risk. Caution and good seamanship would have had him lie to for the night, especially in the prevailing conditions, for the wind had freshened and must have been at gale, or near gale, force. While the night was clear and a land mass would easily be made out miles away, they could be running down on a lee shore. Coasts are frequently cluttered with offshore reefs and shoal water, and there was a very good chance danger would be seen too late and they would strike before being able to round up. Columbus urged the watches to be alert and vigilant and doubled the lookouts, reminding them of the reward for the first sighting.

No good captain would have left the deck in these circumstances, and Columbus was no exception. About 10 o'clock, his eyes, sweeping the dim horizon, picked up the merest glimmer of a light '. . . like a little wax candle bobbing up and down.'[6] He well knew that very human tendency, especially at night and when eyesight is strained with continual searching, to see things which were not there. He called Pedro Gutíerrez, the representative of the King's Household, and asked him if he could see anything. A very faint light can be seen first in the periphery of one's vision. Look directly at it and you will not see it. Look a little to one side and you will see it – but you will not be sure, for you will rather sense it than see it in focus. It must have been like that. After searching for a few moments, Pedro confirmed that there was a light. Pedro Sánchez de Segovia, the fleet comptroller, was called and failed to see it, as did the rest of the watch when they were asked. Columbus considered that what he had seen was too uncertain to act on. At that time they were still about 35 miles offshore, so it is more than likely the light was pure imagination.

Shortly before midnight the moon rose and Columbus estimated they were making an impressive 9 knots, carrying as much sail as possible in the conditions. At 2 a.m. the *Pinta*, as usual way out ahead, fired a gun. Land had been sighted. It had been first seen by one of *Pinta's* seamen, Rodrigo de Triana.

When the *Santa Maria* came up with the *Pinta*, Columbus estimated the shore was 6 miles off and had the ships shorten sail and jog on and off for the remainder of the night. When the sun rose, before them lay the island which was to become known as San Salvador.

In the West Indies

For over 3 months Columbus explored parts of the Bahamas, and the north coasts of Cuba and Haiti, firmly believing that he was on the doorstep of Asia. At first he was convinced that Cuba was the mainland and a mere 300 miles from China. Haiti, or an island near Haiti, might be Cipangu; certainly the gold they collected on the island encouraged them in this belief. The apparent abundance of the precious metal aroused the acquisitive interest of the Spanish and was the key factor in the swift occupation of the islands subsequent to their discovery.

The commander was ecstatic in his descriptions of the country and harbours they discovered, and the manner in which Columbus and his officers worked their ships to windward, often off a lee shore, is a tribute to their seamanship. The loss of the *Santa Maria* was an abberation, the result of a brief, uncharacteristic lack of vigilance.

On the coast of Cuba the ships were each in turn beached, hauled down and breamed, that is, the growth was burned off the bottom. This may have been done last in the Canaries; certainly the *Pinta* would have had some treatment there while work was being carried out on the rudder. The mixture of pitch and tallow used to protect hulls under water was not a very effective antifouling and in warm waters marine growth is prolific. No doubt shipworm, or teredo, was also beginning to work its insidious havoc. By the time they reached Cuba, the rapidly fouling bottoms of the ships would have been seriously affecting their performance.

Although a high standard of efficiency generally seems to have been maintained, all was not sweetness and light in the shipboard relationships. Martín Alonzo Pinzón, inwardly seething over his lack of independence, was the first to flout Columbus's overall command. On 21 November the ships were working back inshore to the Cuban coast

after failing in an attempt to reach the island of Babeque, or Great Inagua, where the islanders had led them to believe there was a wealth of gold. Without so much as a word to his commander, Martín Alonzo sailed away from the *Santa Maria* and *Niña*, apparently determined to reach the island and get first whack at the gold. In the words of Columbus:

> This day Martín Alonzo Pinzón sailed away with the caravel *Pinta*, without my will or command. It was thorough perfidy. I think he believes that an Indian I had placed on the *Pinta* could lead him to much gold, so he departed without waiting and without the excuse of bad weather, but because he wished to do so. He has done and said many other things to me.[7]

The smouldering resentment against the commander, frustration at having to creep along with the less weatherly *Santa Maria*, and plain outright greed must have provided the motive for this reprehensible desertion. No matter what excuses he may have had, Martín Alonzo must have known he was putting the whole success of the enterprise at risk. As it happened, he was rather reluctantly obliged to come up with *Niña* some time after the *Santa Maria* was wrecked and then gave some lame excuses for his behaviour, none of which Columbus believed, but he accepted them for the good of the venture. If it had been Drake or Magellan in command, Pinzón would have been hanged.

The grounding of *Santa Maria*

The *Santa Maria* was slower and less weatherly than the caravels and she also drew more water. She was not the ideal craft for exploration in coastal waters and her loss is often attributed to these failings. This is not the case and the accident could just as easily have happened to the *Pinta* and *Niña*.

On 20 December, while examining the north coast of Haiti, the *Santa Maria* and *Niña* came to anchor in Acul Bay, which they named 'La Mar de Sancto Tomás'. Here, among the overwhelmingly friendly natives, they passed an exuberant but exhausting few days and nights fraternising with the locals and finding out about the surrounding country. They learned that a great quantity of gold was to be found in a land called Cibao far to the east. Columbus was convinced this land was Cipangu and his eagerness to sail there, combined with a desire to spend Christmas Day at a large village a few miles eastward along the coast, led him to sail with what must have been an exhausted crew. Few had any sleep during those happy days. They sailed before sunrise on Christmas Eve and it was probably with some relief that at last they thought they could get some rest. The winds all that day were light, and working the ships through the numerous reefs required all the concentration of the commander and officers. As the after-guard was not getting much rest, I suspect the off-watch sailors were set to

The wreck of the *Santa Maria*

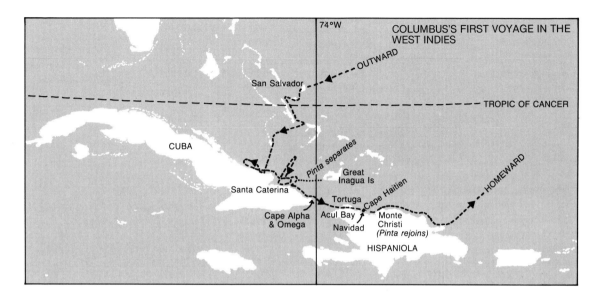

COLUMBUS'S FIRST VOYAGE IN THE WEST INDIES

OUTWARD

San Salvador

TROPIC OF CANCER

CUBA

Pinta separates

Great Inagua Is

Santa Caterina

Cape Haitien

HOMEWARD

Tortuga

Acul Bay

Cape Alpha & Omega

Navidad

Monte Christi
(Pinta rejoins)

HISPANIOLA

cleaning up the ships after the hiatus of the previous days.

At 11 o'clock that night they were 3 miles beyond Punta Santa (now Cape Haitien) after a tiresome day beating against wind and current. Previously Columbus had sent a boat to the village to which they were now bound, and its crew had roughly surveyed the course the ships must take. Now, with the *Santa Maria* on a port tack which would, they thought, give them plenty of sea room, creeping along through the silent night in calm and light airs, the middle watch reluctantly came on duty. Columbus, as any officer worth his salt would do, no doubt stayed around for a while until Juan de la Cosa, in charge of the watch, got his night vision and then, after giving out the night orders – the usual 'Call me if in doubt or the wind gets up' – the commander decided he could at last turn in, leaving the ship in the hands of the master.

What followed would never have happened if de la Cosa had fulfilled the first commandment of any officer in charge of a watch – stay awake. With the lookouts and helmsman on duty, the rest of the watch could find a comfortable plank on which to curl up and doze. There was nothing to do provided these few, and the boy who turned the glass, stayed alert. A glance around the quiet and innocent sea and a quick, 'You know where to find me', and de la Cosa vanished below. Without that watchful eye, the seamen relaxed. Although Columbus had expressly forbidden the helm to be left in charge of any grommet, the helmsman handed over the tiller to the boy, and it was not long before the whole darned lot were asleep. The youngster, left with the heavy helm, steered either by star or compass when the ship had steerage way at all. Beneath the quarterdeck he could not see outboard and, if he was not dozing quietly himself, the soporific but increasing sounds of surf would have been hard to hear below, over the slatting sails and creaks of the hull lifting to the low swell.

So gently did the *Santa Maria* take the ground that no one was awakened. The first the poor boy knew was the rudder striking and the sound of breaking water. His cry of alarm brought Columbus scrambling on deck with a clear idea of what had happened. A good captain is very rarely completely asleep; the slightest change in the usual rhythms and noises of the ship will wake him. Among the rest there was at first confusion. De la Cosa, quickly, and no doubt guiltily, followed Columbus on deck.

But for some very strange behaviour, again on the part of de la Cosa, there is little reason why the ship could not have been got off with only slight damage. The launch was towing astern, the anchors would have been cleared, and it is quite likely a kedge was kept ready aft with the cable flaked down on deck, ready to run out and veer the ship while at anchor or to use in just such an emergency as now happened.

De la Cosa was immediately ordered to get a boat's crew together and run out an anchor. He got his crew together – perhaps they were his northern Spanish shipmates, who may have been at the root of the discontent before landfall – but then pulled away for the *Niña*, 1½ miles to windward. Vincente Yáñez Pinzón demonstrated a bit more common-sense and loyalty and sent de la Cosa straight back, expressing himself somewhat forcefully I imagine. That 3-mile row would have taken them the best part of an hour, an hour during which the crew of the *Santa Maria* were engaged in cutting away the mainmast and otherwise lightening the ship as much as possible. The yawl was too small to run out an effective anchor, and without this the effort was futile, for the low swell and perhaps a light wind drove her further on.

Vincente Yáñez sent across the *Niña*'s boat, which arrived before de la Cosa, but they were too late. The *Santa Maria* had driven broadside far up the shelving reef and the ship had bilged and flooded. As there was a good chance of the ship breaking up, Columbus abandoned her, transferring everyone to the *Niña*. Uncertain of the extent of the reefs, he then stood off and on until dawn.

At dawn Columbus took the *Niña* in and

anchored near the wreck of the flagship, and a boat was sent ashore to seek help from Guacanagari, the *cacique* ('head man' or 'chief') of the village towards which they had been bound. In no time at all the friendly chief had a fleet of large canoes sent out and work began on stripping the *Santa Maria*, tearing up the decks to get at the more inaccessible parts of the ship. All Christmas Day the crews and natives laboured to save everything possible from the wreck and ferry the salvage ashore, where it was placed under guard by Guacanagari.

The next day the cacique visited Columbus in the *Niña* and offered everything he had to assist, and provided houses ashore for the now overcrowded complement of the caravel. The generosity and honesty of those Arawak islanders, whatever their motives, was remarkable. Columbus writes that 'not even a breadcrumb' was pilfered from the salvaged stores and equipment. The good relationship, and later indications that they were near a source of a good deal of gold, solved the problem of what to do with the now surplus crew. As it was obviously impossible for everybody to return to Spain in the tiny *Niña*, Columbus ordered a fort to be built, probably using timbers from the wreck, with the intention of settling some of his men. The settlement he named 'La Navidad' after the Nativity.

On 30 December came the first welcome news that the *Pinta* was not far away along the coast to the east. Columbus despatched one of his sailors to beg Martín Alonzo to rejoin him, but the messenger failed to find the *Pinta*. Without another ship Columbus had to give up any idea of exploring the islands further. It became more important that the news of the discoveries was got back to Spain, and with only one ship, this was chancy. On 4 January the *Niña* raised her anchors and left La Navidad, homeward bound. Ashore they left 39 officers and crew with weapons, a good stock of supplies, one of the boats, and a promise to return as soon as possible. While they waited they were to respect and treat kindly the natives who had aided them, and

collect and search for the source of the gold. Their hope of ever seeing another of their countrymen rested on the seaworthiness of one small caravel and the seamanship of one man. It cannot have been a happy parting, in spite of their commander's reassurances.

On clearing the outlying reefs off La Navidad, the *Niña* coasted eastward, literally rock-dodging in the nimble little caravel. On the sixth, the lookout, who had been sent aloft to watch for shoal water, spotted the *Pinta* running down towards them before the fresh easterly wind. As the water was too treacherous for them to either lie to or anchor, Columbus led the *Pinta* back into the harbour of Monte Cristi where he had anchored the previous night.

That evening Martín Alonzo came aboard the *Niña* and apologised for the separation, and gave his feeble excuses. He also reported that while he had discovered no gold on Great Inagua, plenty had been found further eastward along the Haitian coast. Columbus accepted the captain's excuses for the sake of peace and unity, but determined to make haste back to Spain to rid himself of Martín Alonzo and his followers. However, he decided, as they now had the security of two ships, it would be worthwhile taking the time to explore the remainder of the north Haitian coast. Two days windbound in Monte Cristi were spent in re-caulking the *Niña* and watering the ships from a river in which they found a quantity of alluvial gold.

On the ninth they left Monte Cristi and explored eastward until on the sixteenth they anchored in a large bay which Columbus named 'Golfo de la Flechás' or 'Gulf of Arrows', for it was here for the first time that they encountered belligerent islanders who attempted to capture seven sailors sent ashore to trade. The natives, upward of 50 strong, were soundly trounced in a determined attack by the shore party.

Columbus had learned that further to the east were more islands; one, named Caribe, was the

home of cannibals, fierce people who terrorised the more peaceful Haitians and Cubans; another, Matinino, was reputedly inhabited entirely by women. He suspected that the natives who attacked the shore party could be Caribes. Mistaking the eastern ranges of Haiti for the island of Caribe, Columbus put out to sea, intending to steer east by north for the island. Logically connecting the sargasso weed he had observed on the outward voyage with a similar weed he found along the coast, he considered that a chain of islands must stretch the best part of the way to the Canaries, but it was not his intention to island-hop in the teeth of the easterly trades all the way back to the Canaries. He decided to visit Caribe and then the island of women, Matinino, which was reputed to lie to the north-east; after that he would sail directly for Spain.

After they had covered about 48 miles, the natives he had with him as guides indicated to Columbus that the Caribe lay to the south-east and he altered course in that direction. The alarm of the crew over the diversion from a homeward course, the rapidly deteriorating state of the ships, which were beginning to leak badly, and a fair wind for Spain, all decided Columbus to give up the attempt to reach the island. Around came the ships to north-east by east, his estimated course for Spain.

The homeward voyage

When, on 16 January, Columbus gave up the idea of visiting the land he thought to be the island of Caribe and bore away for home, he hoped that he would, that same day, raise the island of Matinino. The natives he carried to sea with him indicated that it lay in the direction they steered, but Columbus had his doubts, which were soon confirmed, for by sunset there was no land in sight.

On 4 March Columbus thankfully and wearily brought the *Niña* to anchor at Restello, 4 miles below

Lisbon. The homeward voyage had given Columbus more than a fair share of anxiety and frustration. From the beginning the ships were leaky, and in the case of the *Niña*, underballasted. Pinzón continued to grate on his commander's nerves before the *Pinta* parted company one night during the first spell of foul weather some 120 miles south of the Azores. On Wednesday 23 January Columbus wrote:

> Last night there were many changes of the wind, and having been on the alert for everything and having taken the precautions good sailors are accustomed to take and must take, I went last night to the NE by north about 63 miles. I waited many times for the *Pinta,* which had a lot of difficulty sailing close to the wind because the mast was not sound and the mizzen helped her very little. If her captain, Martín Alonzo Pinzón, had taken as much trouble to provide himself with a good mast in the Indies, where there are so many good ones, as he did to separate himself from me with the intention of filling the ship with gold, he would have been better off.[8]

The weather which parted the ships rose to a savage gale and during the following day Columbus began to believe the *Niña* would not survive. She did, and in the evening the wind eased. The following morning they raised Santa María in the Azores where they put in for rest and repair. They got neither. The Portuguese Azoreans arrested five of his crew, along with his only boat. They were released after Columbus threatened to bring down the wrath of Spain on the islanders and he had finally managed to prove his authority. He had already been driven once, short-handed, from the poor anchorage, and with his crew and boat returned, he set out to seek another to take on ballast and wood. They anchored again on the south coast of the island, but it was not long before the wind swung, putting them on a lee shore, and Columbus decided to use what was a fair wind to set out for Spain.

It was on this last stretch that the *Niña* survived the greatest danger of the voyage. For 3 days they had fair weather, but on the night of 26 February the wind turned foul and they ran into another gale. Columbus, being so near home, was becoming understandably fed up and worried by the high frequency of storms he was encountering. All the twenty-eighth the *Niña* beat to the eastward in the teeth of the gale until the wind veered, allowing them to run off to the east-northeast. After dark on the twenty-eighth a front hit them and the accompanying squall blew out the low-set mainsail and the other sails clear out of their gaskets. They spent the next day scudding downwind under bare poles and in considerable danger from cross seas. Lots were drawn for those who would make future devotions but, a mixed blessing, they did observe signs that land was near. They were now running down on a lee shore in frightful conditions:

> . . . we thought we would be lost because the waves came from two directions, and the wind appeared to raise the ship in the air, with the water from the sky and the lightning in every direction.[9]

They were experiencing the elements of disaster for any sailing ship: night, winds of near-hurricane force and dangerously confused seas, with the vessel driving down on an unknown lee shore. An anxious watch was kept and, fortunately, the night must have been reasonably clear, for during the first watch, between seven and eleven in the evening, land was made out ahead of the ship.

To continue driving under bare poles was courting almost inevitable shipwreck. Vessels have been known to strike lucky and find a hole to dive into, but no good sailor would trust to his luck while there was still a chance to keep the sea. With what must

have been heroic effort, they managed to get the mainsail set and they brought her up, reaching on the starboard tack before the north-west gale, and fought their way off the land.

What superb seamen sailed the *Niña*, and what a captain! There was a bigoted tendency among the northern Europeans to denigrate Spanish seamanship, but whatever the failings of some later seamen and ships, this last battle against everything the elements could throw proved the mettle of *Niña* and her crew. Columbus passes over the ordeal in a few words:

> In order not to approach the land until we knew more about it and until we could find a harbour or place to save ourselves, I raised the mainsail, since there was no other remedy, and we sailed some distance with great danger, putting to sea. Thus God protected us until daylight, but it was with infinite labour and fright.[10]

The courage and seamanship displayed that wild and dangerous night can be better appreciated if we examine what had to be done. After the sails had been blown out the night before, a new mainsail was bent or the old one repaired as soon as was practicably possible. Now the mainsail without the bonnet was still a large sail, set on a yard the length of the keel, and it could not be reefed any further. To raise the sail, the gaskets were cast off, leaving the canvas contained by its gear, that is the martnets, clew garnets and buntlines. In the strong gale the sail at once began to thunder and threaten to shake the mast out of the ship. With the halyard fully manned, the heavy yard was swayed up, to about half-mast, while the lines containing the sail, braces and lifts were tended and overhauled. Any carelessness at this point on the wildly rolling ship would have the heavy yard out of control, yet speed was essential to get the gear steadied by the sail, let alone the fact

During the night of 3 March 1493, homeward bound on his momentous voyage, Columbus made a frightening landfall on the Portuguese coast north of Lisbon. The *Niña* was driving under bare poles before a ferocious north-westerly gale when land was seen to leeward. There was no alternative but to set the mainsail and try to claw offshore. This was done expertly but with some trepidation; for should the little ship not stand up to the wind and sea, or her sail blow out, nothing could prevent disaster. The *Niña* and her people proved their mettle that wild night and the next morning they entered the Tagus.

that they were tearing down on a lee shore at a rate of knots.

Once the yard was up and the halyard belayed, all hands went to their stations and the tacks and sheets were double manned. Now to set the mainsail. Shouted commands were useless in the screaming wind and teamwork was essential. Once the wind got in the sail, one good flap and they would lose the lot. The trick was to keep the sail full through the whole operation. First the tack was hauled down with both the tack rope and sheet as the clew, martnets and buntlines were eased off and the ship brought with the wind on the quarter. With the tack down, a good beefy team manned the sheet and got it aft sufficient to set the sail, which took on the attributes of a curved sheet of steel.

The ship now was tearing along, surfing off the crests and threatening to broach in the huge quartering seas. Carefully, and watching for a bit of a flat, the *Niña* was brought into the wind, and as she came round the lee sheet was hauled right aft, while both wind and sea appeared to increase in fury as the apparent wind changed. Her lee rail buried as she started plunging heavily into the sea, hurling great sheets of green water and spray over the decks.

Apart from her leaks, the *Niña* and her gear were in superb condition to have withstood the rest of that night and morning as she clawed offshore. That the sailcloth withstood the ordeal says something for the weavers of Brittany. I am fairly certain that, as is apparent on many illustrations, a middle sheet was hooked to the bunt of the sail and more than likely some form of quick-saver, or strapping, was also hauled around before the sail. The greatest danger was that lee shore and the caravel needed power to drive the ship to windward. Once, after what must have been heavy and terrifying work, and all extra support that was possible had been given to the mast, yard and sails, there was little to do but hang on and pray that nothing would carry away as the *Niña*, grossly overcanvassed, lay over and crashed through the monstrous seas.

Dawn showed them the Rock of Sintra, north of the entrance to the Tagus and Lisbon, under their lee. In the frightful weather the *Niña* must have been barely holding off the land, and to attempt to reach Spain, either north or south, was clearly tempting fate. Columbus squared away, rounded Cabo Raso, scudded across the bar and tore upriver to come to anchor at nine in the morning of 4 March. The Atlantic had been crossed and the voyage was all but over.

Columbus learned from the seafarers in the river that never had there been such a winter for storms.

Twenty-five ships had been lost in Flanders, and no ship had left the Tagus during the last 4 months. Columbus, the *Niña* and his sailors had weathered the winter storms, but now faced a tricky situation. They were in the realm of Spain's rival, Portugal, and, with the recent reception in the Azores in mind, Columbus was worried that his ship and crew would be arrested. Therefore he quickly got off a letter to Don Joao II, requesting to move up to the town for the safety of the ship, and explained that he had not come from Guinea, where the Spanish were forbidden to trade. Columbus's anxiety was soon put at rest. After a rather tight diplomatic tussle with the captain of a large, powerfully armed carrack anchored nearby, all difficulties were smoothed over and the Spaniards were given all the assistance they required. The captain of the royal carrack, by the way, was none other than Bartholome Diaz, the discoverer of the Cape of Good Hope and who was later in the fleet which discovered Brazil.

On the morning of 13 March the *Niña* weighed and stood down the Tagus bound for Palos. At noon on the fifteenth they crossed the bar at Saltes and worked up the Rio Tinto to anchor off Palos.

By some incredible coincidence, later on the same tide that brought the *Niña* home, Martín Alonzo Pinzón brought the *Pinta* to anchor off Palos. Sick, exhausted and bitterly disappointed, he had himself taken ashore without making any attempt to communicate with those in the *Niña*. Ashore, he took to his bed and died. The *Pinta* had first put into Bayona, near Vigo, in northern Spain where Martín had tried to steal Columbus's thunder by first getting the news of the discoveries to the sovereign, but King Ferdinand refused his request to come to court, saying that he would wait to hear from Columbus himself. Martín had then sailed from Bayona for Palos, probably hoping that the *Niña* had gone down, leaving him the prize of their discoveries.

The news that Columbus brought set Spain on the road to empire. Columbus, and those who sailed with him, for a while reaped the rewards of their courageous exploits, and for us, for all their failings, they surely remain true heroes.

Columbus made three more voyages across the Atlantic, during which he ranged almost the whole chain of the Antilles, explored the entire south coast of Cuba, discovered the straits between Trinidad and mainland South America, coasted the continent to the island of Margarita, and, on his last voyage, explored the coast from Honduras to Panama before his ships fell apart, leaving him stranded in Jamaica for just over one year. The voyages were remarkable and had all the elements of high adventure, but the perfidious machinations of his compatriots towards him and each other soured his achievements, and his fortunes as a governor declined dismally. The islanders who had welcomed and assisted Columbus were cruelly treated and finally exterminated by the colonists who, in their rapacious search for gold, initiated the era of the conquistadores, that brave but ruthless breed that went on to bring nations of Central and South America under the Spanish heel.

The *Santa Maria*

The *Santa Maria* must be the most renowned ship in the history of the western world, and yet her historical career was brief and she was rather unloved by those who sailed in her. The light of historical research which has brilliantly illuminated so much of the happenings of that burgeoning era, throws only a flickering glimmer on the famous ship, and indeed all the ships of that time. For those engaged in maritime research, the fifteenth century is truly a dark age as far as providing good, solid, factual information on the structure and rig of ships. More is certainly known of the viking longships and Hanse cogs than of the caravels and naos of the dawn of western expansion. Not one caravel or nao has been dredged from the mud, no manuals of operation, detailed descriptions, plans or careful

Two anchors attributed to the *Santa Maria* have been found on the north Haitian coast near the site where she was wrecked. The *Santa Maria* carried five anchors and two grapnels. Two bowers were stowed with the flukes to the rail and the shanks secured forward, level with the gunwale. I have shown only one anchor each side. There seems to have been some form of platform at this level, between the break of the forecastle and the hawse. This is logical, for to get the anchors aboard a fish tackle must have been hitched to the crown and some arrangement hooked on to secure the shank. Trying to do this by hanging over the towering forecastle with its whale-back sides would have presented some difficulty. A large, heavy, vertical clamp is featured in the Mataro model, where it is pierced by a sheave hole leading inboard. It may be that a shank painter or rope was led inboard through the clamp, by which means the shank of the anchor was hauled up to rest on the riding beam which protruded well out from the ship's side. One of these bowers weighed 460 kg (about half a ton) and beefy provisions must have been made for catting and securing for sea. The largest anchor, the sheet anchor, which was streamed when things looked grim, was stowed below in the hold.

The *Santa Maria*

studied drawings exist . . . if only Da Vinci or Michaelangelo had mucked about in boats!

We know that ships were swiftly changing and improving in design and rig, and we can generalise from earlier ships as represented by the Mataro model, from later, more evolved vessels, and from indirect sources such as manifests, shipping records and mostly rather poorly executed illustrations. From these we can piece together a fair idea of what the ships were like, but must be wary of accepting the composite impression as fact. Little is known of what must have been considerable regional differences in shipbuilding practice and style, and this applies particularly to detail. Our two dependable sources from that era consist of one remarkable model of a single-masted ship of about 1450, and a collection of drawings by an astute Flemish artist commonly

Mataro votive model

A fifteenth-century ship engraved by the Flemish artist 'W.A.' It is interesting for its detail, particularly the objects which hang about the stern. The pear-shaped article and the pole may both be buoys, and the barrels could serve a variety of purposes, one of them perhaps used for firefighting. Among official orders for English warships in 1568 was the suggestion that two hogsheads should be secured to the side of the ship for 'the soldiers and mariners to piss into that they may be full of urine to quench fire with and two or three pieces of old sail ready to wet in the piss.' What magic properties urine was considered to have over straight seawater is not stated.

known to us as 'W.A.'. The model is really too early and W.A.'s drawings, rich in detail, can often pose more questions than answers.

It is known that Columbus's flagship was built in Galacia, perhaps on the Biscay shores of northwestern Spain, and for this reason she was nicknamed 'La Gallega'. Her owner, Juan de la Cosa of Santona, a port near Santander, hired the ship to the Crown for the voyage. She was a *navio* or small

nao or carrack of the type developed in the Mediterranean but which had been adapted and had become the general freighter in Atlantic waters. That northern or local features may have been incorporated in her building is, in my opinion, almost certain, for there was brisk trade with Britain, Flanders and France from Biscayan ports, and it is known that then, and later, the ships and seamen of Biscay were considered a superior breed.

I feel that it would be a mistake to presume that, because the style of ships such as the *Santa Maria* was influenced by Mediterranean practices, we can assume she was a Mediterranean ship. The shipwrights and sailors of northern Spain would have had their own ideas and no doubt were as jealous and conservative of their own expertise as all such people. Studies by Michael Barkham of Basque shipbuilding contracts from the second half of the sixteenth century show that during this period the basic building practices and ratios of hull dimensions changed very little, and I think it is reasonable to extend this conservatism back to the time when the *Santa Maria* was built. In my reconstruction, some features of the later Basque whaler (see page 134), such as the ratio and configuration of keel and stem, have been incorporated.

Length of keel	45 ft (13.7 m)
Length at height of maximum beam, approximately at the bottom of the curve of the tweendeck wale	75 ft (22.9 m)
Length at upper deck	85 ft (25.9 m)
Beam	19 ft (5.8 m)
Depth of hold approx	15 ft (4.6 m)

When these are put together to produce a version of how the *Santa Maria* may have appeared, the result does not seem to be the cantankerous old tub complained about by Columbus, but a fairly graceful and seaworthy vessel.

The *Niña*. Many tentative reconstructions of this famous little ship have been put forward. Nearly all depict her with a full quarterdeck extending to just aft of the main mast, giving her, for modern eyes, an impression of clumsiness and excessive topweight for such a light vessel. This suggested reconstruction may incur the fair criticism that it shows, in the fairing of the after parts, elements of later ship design which are more agreeable to modern eyes. I am unrepentant and admit that I have taken advantage of the lack of evidence to illustrate the *Niña* as I would like her to be, even to the painted eye, or oculus, on the bow; evidently a feature of the Portuguese caravels. It has always been noted that some dhows might bear a fair resemblance to the old caravel, which certainly owes its origin to Moorish influence. However, features of ship design have also passed from west to east and the beautiful sterns of some *baggalas* and *kotias* are almost identical to eighteenth-century western ships. The smaller *sambuks* and *shu'ais*, so similar to how we imagine the caravels may have appeared, possess wings extending from the gunwale at the transom, purely, it is said, for decoration. It has been pointed out that the wings may be a relic of sixteenth-century European influence, when, on caravels and other ships, the wings were an integral part of the counter of the aftercastle. If this is true, perhaps other features may have come from the west at that time, including the graceful rise of the gunwale towards the stern which makes the Arab craft so attractive.

This version of the *Niña* conforms to the accepted measurements, being about 80 ft (24.4 m) on deck. From abaft the main mast the gunwale sweeps up with the superstructure rising above to give reasonable headroom under a small poop, where the space would be cluttered by the tiller. The high bulwarks aft would give protection to the relatively uncluttered deck where a capstan and companionway below might be situated. The foresail is small, set on a forward-raking mast as it would be necessary to place the centre of effort of the sail as far forward as possible. The mizzen mast is stepped on the transom beam and could be the only mast and sail which survived her conversion to a caravela redonda.

THE BRISTOL MERCHANTS

While no Atlantic discoveries were recorded from the early Norse voyages until the Portuguese started pushing south in the fifteenth century, traders and fishermen cruised the known European Atlantic seaboard with increasing familiarity, using an ever-diversifying assortment of craft. To the cog, doggers, balingers and barges can be added the hulk, successor of the cog, the navis or nef, crayers and farcosts among the larger craft. Spinaces, picards, row-barges, cokke botes describe some of the smaller, general-purpose craft. Cobles, trink-boats, and peter-boats for fishing, and keels, shouts, wherries and trows for transport, designate some of the smaller English craft. Haynes and foncets came from France, drumblers, pinks, corvers, smacks, plats and busses from the Netherlands, and there was another Dutch vessel, the hoy, which came late on the scene. From the Mediterranean, also latecomers, came galleys, the carrack and, refined by the Portuguese, the ship which opened up the world to Europe, the caravel.

The list is by no means exhaustive, even of northern-European vessels, let alone the possible comparable litany from Biscay southwards. Many of these vessel types were the progenitors of a long line of local craft, some of which survived almost unchanged to this century. The humber keel, with its single tall squaresail, has sailed right out of the Middle Ages. Named for an illustrious fisherman, the fourteenth-century, double-ended, clinker-built peter-boat, with a wet-well amidships, was until recent times still working the Thames. Nearly all the names above would have been familiar to any coasting seaman until the last days of sail and, although most of them do not concern our theme,

it was the experience gained knocking around the coast in such craft, combined with the burgeoning renaissance spreading from Italy, that enabled the first major voyages of European oceanic expansion.

The Bristol merchants

By the beginning of the second half of the fifteenth century most of the Atlantic islands were known to mariners. The Portuguese had raised and were using the Cape Verdes, Madeira and Azores; the Castillians were in the Canaries, and Iceland had been a settled country for almost 500 years. Greenland was an enigma beyond the bounds of European civilisation, though possibly visited by Dutch or English fishermen. Because of the politics of the time, and perhaps jealous of their fishing-grounds – are not all fishermen – they kept a closed mouth.

Stories of mythical islands to the west abounded. 'St Brandan's Isles', originating from the legendary voyages of that saint, and faithfully represented by cartographers, had gradually cruised south and west. Antillia, identified with a legend of an 'Island of Seven Cities' and reported to have been settled by eighth-century Iberian refugees from the Moslems, was a large island placed far out to the west. The travels of Marco Polo sparked the glimmer of an idea that one could sail west to the fabulous East, and the land of 'Cipangu', or Japan, began to be located far in the west. In 1474 a Florentine physician, Paolo Toscanelli, wrote to Afonso V of Portugal a letter proposing that a voyage westward was feasible, and

placed Antillia about 1500 miles out, Cipangu 2000 miles beyond Antillia, and China a further 2000 miles on.

With our ingrained world concept and slick communications, it is easy for us to ridicule the theories of past geographers. The mathematics and astronomy necessary to calculate a realistic value for the circumference of the Earth were only then beginning to be recovered from the ancients by way of the Arab world. For people whose fastest mode of transport was the horse, and to whom the world beyond the limits of knowledge could be only

Distinctive for its straight raked stem and clencher construction the more capacious *cog* superseded the knörr in northern Europe during the thirteenth and fourteenth centuries. It may have been the first class of vessel to hang a stern rudder, and it voyaged as far afield as Greenland and the Mediterranean.

guesswork, Toscanelli's idea was brilliant, even if his distances were vastly underestimated. King Afonso, probably more concerned with following through the African ventures, did nothing, but a copy of the letter later came into the hands of Columbus.

One last chimerical island should be mentioned, as it became the objective of some early Bristol ventures. As late as the nineteenth century, people from the west coast of Ireland believed – or said they believed – that once every 2 years, out on the western horizon, an isle could be seen. This was the 'Isle of Brasil', shown in late medieval maps as lying not far off the coast. As this island would have clearly been discovered very early, the Bristol merchants were not taken in, but did consider that

About the end of the fourteenth century, another step in the evolution of the ocean-going sailing ship took place when the *hulk* began to replace the cog as the all-purpose carrier in the north. Very little is known about these vessels. They may have been precursors of the northern carrack and at a later date the terms *hulk* and *carrack* may have been synonymous. Experts suggest they may have featured clencher construction, a curved stem, fenders and wales and a proper hawse. Possibly they were clencher versions of the Mediterranean carracks of the fifteenth century.

'Brasil' lay far out and was well worth a search. The Portuguese also had reason to believe that sizable land lay to the north-west of the Azores and, in 1452, may have set out on a deliberate search, but were driven back by adverse winds.

Bristol emerges as a major port

Northern Europe, just beginning to emerge from the murky Middle Ages, leaves us sparse records, but it is apparent that shipping activities were vigorous and expanding, with a multitude of vessels engaged in commerce and fishing. Bristol had become second only to London as a port, with trading connections from Iceland to the Canaries, the Azores and the Mediterranean. It is hardly surprising that, on the polyglot waterfronts, tales were swapped and conjecture hardened into belief that some great land was westward over the horizon. Before 1498 we only dimly know of a few voyages that tried to locate 'Brasil'; what unrecorded lands fishermen came upon, historians would dearly like to discover. The merchants and fishermen of Bristol were faced with competition with the Dutch in the north and gradual expulsion from Icelandic waters. Continental Europe was already over-serviced, and southern trade depended on the goodwill of the Portuguese and Spanish. The men of Bristol began to look west into the Atlantic, chiefly, it seems, to find a new source to provide the lucrative stockfish.

The first Bristol enterprise westward

The first recorded Bristol enterprise westward occurred in 1480*. John Jay and other merchants fitted out an 80-ton ship to sail to 'The Island of Brasil'. She was placed under the command of 'Thloyde', or John Lloyd, who was considered the most knowledgable master in the whole of England, and sailed on 15 July. Nine weeks later the ship was in Ireland undergoing repairs and resting the crew after having been driven back by storms.

Another expedition was sent out the following year, this time with two ships, the *George* and *Trinity*. They sailed on 6 July and the *Trinity*, at least, returned, for she appears in records at a later date. A merchant named Thomas Croft, an eighth-owner of the ships, had loaded 40 bushels of salt, as he explained, 'for the reparacion and sustentacion of the said shippes'.[1] This could be an indication that the voyage was intended to fish the coast of 'Brasil', and if they succeeded in reaching the Newfoundland Banks they would have indeed bought home a rich harvest. Of the success or failure of the venture, we are left in the dark.

There is no evidence of further voyages until 10 years later, when it seems that the Bristolians began to send out yearly expeditions involving two to four ships, and in 1494 it is quite likely that two Bristol merchants, Robert Thorne and Hugh Elyot, discovered the North American continent, although evidence for this is confusing. What can be claimed with some certainty is that, at some time before John Cabot's voyages, a landfall was made from ships operating out of Bristol. In 1956 a letter was discovered in the Spanish archives at Simancas. It was written by an Englishman named John Day in the winter of 1497-8, and quite possibly was addressed to Columbus. Day was reporting on the Cabot voyage of 1497, and when describing the land that Cabot had found, stated:

> It is considered certain that the Cape of the said land was found and discovered in the past by the men from Bristol who found Brasil, as your Lordship knows. It was called the Island of Brasil, and it is assumed and believed to be the mainland that the men from Bristol found.[2]

* For the voyages out of Bristol and the expeditions of Cabot I have relied almost solely on the work of James Williamson in his book *The Cabot Voyages and Bristol Discovery Under Henry VII* (Hakluyt Society, London 1961). His suggestions as to the extent and direction of the Cabot voyages most nearly fit the few known facts.

45

When this discovery was made depends on the interpretation of the Spanish phrase *en otros tiempos*, which may mean 'a long time ago' or just 'formerly', but taken in conjunction with the efforts made by the Bristol merchants during the two decades before the letter was written, it seems reasonable to suppose they had found something, otherwise why the persistence? Could it be that the canny entrepreneurs had found the Newfoundland Banks and were quietly fishing them? This would account for the numerous ships sent out west year after year with apparently nothing to show for their endeavours. What could be more human than for these merchants and fishermen to make the most out of an enormously rich resource before the cat inevitably got let out of the bag.

The voyages of John Cabot

Where and when John Cabot was born is unknown, but it is likely that he was from Genoa. Sometime between 1471 and 1473 he was granted Venetian citizenship, which required 15 years prior residence in the city, where, before 1484, he married Mattea, who bore him two sons. Employed either as a merchant or a merchant's factor, he may have travelled to Mecca in 1483-4, inquiring into the spice trade and eastern caravan routes. This could have sparked his interest in seeking a westward route to China. In 1492-3 there is a record of a 'John Cabot Montecalunya' working on harbour improvements at Valencia. If this is so, he was likely to have witnessed, in the spring of 1493, the triumphant procession of Christopher Columbus along the coast to Barcelona. During these years it is possible that Cabot sought support for his ideas in Seville and Lisbon, but failed; he may also have visited England for the same purpose. However, the first positive record of John Cabot's presence in England is in 1495, when he was seeking the backing of Henry VII.

Cabot realised that Columbus, in spite of his claims, had not reached the Indies. He seemed to have had some knowledge of the Bristol discoveries and considered that if the 'Brasil' of the Bristol merchants trended south and west, it may well take him to the island of Cipangu and thus to China. As he was a map- and globe-maker of some skill, he was well able to expound his ideas to Henry, who granted him Letters of Patent on 5 March, 1496. This gave Cabot permission to annex for the Crown any territories 'which before this time were unknown to all Christians'.[3] It stipulated that Cabot, his heirs or deputies, maintained the sole rights to the lands, and that one-fifth of the revenue should go to the Crown. The provision limiting his authority to lands 'unknown to all Christians' was inserted to avoid conflict with Spain.

Cabot's first voyage

Thanks to the letter of John Day, it is now known that John Cabot made an abortive attempt in 1496. Briefly (and this is all that is told) '. . . he went with one ship, his crew confused him, he was short of food and ran into bad weather, and he decided to turn back.'[4] His next attempt the following year was successful. From various sources, including the letter of John Day, a reasonably clear account of this voyage can be gathered, although many questions remain unanswered.

Whereas Columbus recorded his first voyage in letters and journals, there is absolutely no evidence from anyone who sailed in Cabot's navicula, the *Matthew*, in 1497. The most immediate sources are the letter of John Day, a brief mention in a letter sent from England to the Duke of Milan, a more extensive and rather lighthearted report by Raimondo de Soncino, ambassador to the Duke of Milan, and a letter to his family from a Venetian merchant, Lorenzo Pasqualigo. In addition, there is a much disputed map made by Juan de la Cosa dated 1500, and a few entries in the royal daybook which tell us next to nothing about the voyage. There are other sources, but these were written considerably after the event and are less reliable.

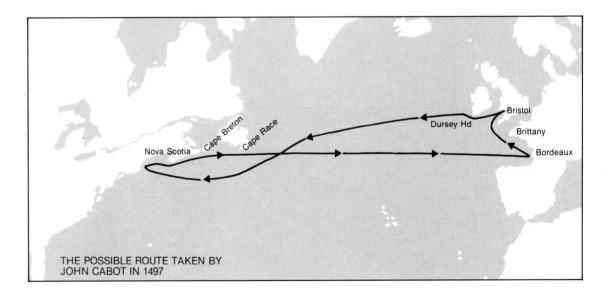

THE POSSIBLE ROUTE TAKEN BY JOHN CABOT IN 1497

Nova Scotia · Cape Breton · Cape Race · Dursey Hd · Bristol · Brittany · Bordeaux

John Cabot makes a landfall, 1497. His ship, the *Matthew*, is being brought-to to lie *a-try*, or hove to, while the coastline is examined.

Although there are various theories as to where Cabot actually made his landfall and the extent of his coasting, there is a basic outline of his voyage which is generally accepted.

Cabot fitted out one small ship, a navicula or bark of 50 ton, with a complement of 18 or 20, including some Bristol merchants and two friends of Cabot, a Burgundian and a Genoese. They sailed from Bristol either on 2 May or late in May; about 20 May is more likely. They passed south of Ireland and then turned north to make a departure from land on a particular parallel on which they were to run their westing down, which seems to indicate that somebody knew where they were going. Most of the voyage of 35 days was made in east-northeast winds and smooth seas. They came into a region where there were two points westward variation of the compass and 2 or 3 days before landfall on 24 June they had heavy weather which lasted only 1 day. Cabot may have named the first land they sighted 'Prima Tierra Vista', and near there Cabot and a party went ashore and ceremoniously took possession, erecting a cross and the banners of Henry VII, the Pope and St Mark of Venice.

They went no further than a bowshot inland, and saw no one. There was evidence of inhabitants, for they found a track leading inland, the ashes of a fire, notched or felled trees, snares for game, and a carved stick like a netting needle. The weather was fine and hot, and it was considered that brasil-wood could grow there and silkworms breed, also there was tall grass and trees suitable for masts. Being only a small party, they did not linger, but filled their water casks and returned on board. They 'spent a month discovering the coast'[5], remarked on the enormous quantity of fish, and left, homeward bound, from 'the cape nearest to Ireland'[6], 1800 miles west of Dursey Head. After leaving the coast they passed two islands. Cabot made the passage to Europe in 15 days, making a landfall in Brittany, to the southward because 'the sailors confused him'[7], saying that he was heading too far north. From Brittany he sailed around Lands End, up the Bristol Channel, arriving in Bristol about 6 August.

In his book, James Williamson puts forward an hypothesis as to where Cabot might have voyaged and as this author leans heavily on the letter of John Day among other sources, it is worth noting the content of the relevant parts of the letter. After an introductory sentence, Day wrote:

I am sending the other book of Marco Polo and a copy of the land which has been found. I do not send the map because I am not satisfied with it, for my many occupations forced me to make it in a hurry at the time of my departure; but from the said copy your Lordship will learn what you wish to know, for in it are named the capes of the mainland and the islands, and thus you will see where the land was first sighted, since most of the land was discovered after turning back. Thus your Lordship will know that the cape nearest to Ireland is 1800 miles west of Dursey Head which is in Ireland, and the southernmost part of the Island of the Seven Cities is west of the Bordeaux River, and your Lordship will know that he landed at only one spot of the mainland, near the place where land was first sighted . . .[8].

There follows a description of the land and the voyage, and then, 'They spent about one month discovering the coast and from the above mentioned cape of the mainland which is nearest to Ireland, they returned to the coast of Europe in fifteen days'.[9]

According to Williamson, Cabot intended to find the coast of Asia and, as he knew from the Bristol merchants where to find Brasil, instead of running westward he struck off much further to the south. The purpose of this single-ship expedition was to reconnoitre the route to the East by making the coast further to the south and westward, then to follow the coast back eastward to connect with the already discovered Brasil. The landfall was made either in Maine or southern Nova Scotia . . . the 'Island of the Seven Cities' in Day's letter.

Near his landfall Cabot landed and took possession, and then coasted north-eastward. From his latitude of 45½° north, or the latitude of the Bordeaux River, to the latitude of Dursey Head, 51½°, even allowing for a one-degree error in each, involves an improbable amount of coasting within a month. It also implies that they rounded Cape Race where the coast turns north-westward. Therefore one of these must be in error, and it is more likely that the northernmost latitude is incorrect. If Dursey Head was the jump-off for the fishermen bound for Newfoundland, then it is logical that the swift Labrador Current would set them south to the region of Cape Race and the Banks. Returning, due east, from Cape Race or Cape Breton, the set would once again be southward, magnifying the error in the return voyage. For his point of departure from the coast, either Cape Breton or Cape Race would serve. In favour of the former are the two islands sighted after leaving. These could have been the islands of St Pierre and Miquelon, or projecting headlands of Newfoundland. If Cabot made his departure from Cape Race – 'the Cape nearest to Ireland' – there is no accounting for the islands.

This theory fits nicely to the detail of Day's letter and to my mind seems to be the most logical of the various suggestions which have been put forward. Williamson himself stresses the uncertainty of his conclusion, but whatever the true facts may be, an historical beginning was made in the discovery of North America, and Cabot and his merchants were eager to go further. Perhaps, beyond the Island of the Seven Cities, lay Cipangu and then China?

Cabot's voyage of 1498

John Cabot's first voyage is spiced with historical uncertainty, but his second is downright mysterious and can only dubiously be traced by subsequent changes in thought and certain reactions on the part of the Spanish in the Caribbean.

On 3 February 1498 John Cabot was granted a new patent by King Henry VII which allowed him to impress six English ships of not more than 200 tons each. Only five were fitted out, one of which was hired and equipped by the King. The other four ships belonged to merchants of London and Bristol, and loaded 'slight or gross merchandises'[10] suitable for trade. The King's ship apparently carried no such cargo and was probably a merchantman belonging to London merchants Lancelot Thirkill and Thomas Bradley, and chartered for the voyage.

All the ships were prepared for a one-year voyage. We do not have any names for the vessels and it is uncertain whether the *Matthew* sailed again. It is likely that some friars and clerics were included in the company, and one of these, Giovanni Antonio de Carbonariis, seems to have been of some importance. The most likely date of departure was early in May, and the only other evidence concerning the voyage is that one of the ships, probably Cabot's, became damaged and put into an Irish port, from which, after making repairs, she continued her voyage.

Nothing more is ever heard of Cabot or his ships, but some conclusions can be inferred. Firstly, it is unusual for five well-found ships to completely vanish; this rarely happened, and it is more likely that one at least returned. More evidential, but still conjectural, is that in the following years North America is no longer identified with mainland Asia, nor is there any further search for a route thence to the south. The 'Brasil' and 'Island of the Seven Cities' became the 'New Found Land' and subsequent searches for a passage to the Far East were in the north-west, as in Sebastian Cabot's voyage of 1504 and 1508-9. The 1501 expedition of Gaspar Corte-Real obtained from the Indians a piece of a broken gilt sword and a pair of silver earrings, both of which appeared to have been made in Italy. There is no indication as to where they were found, but the expedition visited Labrador, Newfoundland, and possibly Nova Scotia.

During these final years of the century it is pertinent to remember that Columbus believed that Cuba was a promontory of Asia and the Spanish exploration of the Caribbean was not complete. In 1501 Alonso de Ojeda was instructed to follow the north coast of South America '. . .towards the region where it has been learned the English have been making their discoveries . . . so that you may stop the exploration of the English in that direction.'[11]

Therefore, not only is it possible that some of the ships of Cabot's second voyage did get back home, but one or more of them may even have reached the Caribbean. Finally, although it proves nothing, it is interesting to note that there is a Cape Carbonear in Newfoundland.

No passage to the fabulous 'Spice Islands' had been found by the determined merchants of Bristol and their Venetian leader, John Cabot. What had been gained was a bountiful fishery, large enough to cater for, without competition, the needs of any European nation who had the ships capable of making the voyage. The coasts of the continent were hesitantly explored during the following decades, but not until over 100 years later was there a successful attempt to colonise the new lands.

The map of Juan de La Cosa, dated 1500, is compiled from two maps drawn on a different scale to each other. A pre-Vasco da Gama map served as the model for the Old World, while the New World is drawn from the then recent discoveries. The coastline from Greenland to Central America is continuous, with a portion marked by English flags which have been attributed to the explorations of the Cabot expeditions. The map shows Cuba as an island, a fact unknown to the Spanish at that time, and is non-commital about whether South and North America are joined. A framed picture of St Christopher neatly leaves the option open.

The eastern seaboard of the continent is shown lying east-west, as it would by compass, not allowing for variation. Under the westernmost flags is the title *mar descubierto por inglese* or 'sea discovered by the English'. The map is considerably distorted and many arguments have been put forward for various interpretations of the locations, but it is generally agreed that part of the flagged area, at least, depicts the coast of Nova Scotia, and the easternmost point, entitled 'Cavo de Ynglaterra', is either Cape Breton or Cape Race. A great deal of study has been devoted to this map and because of such contradictions as the representations of Cuba as an island before it was circumnavigated in 1508, it was argued that the map was a hodge-podge compiled at a date later than 1500. However, there are good reasons for considering that the date is valid and the map represents the endeavours of the Bristol ventures. (Museo Naval, Madrid)

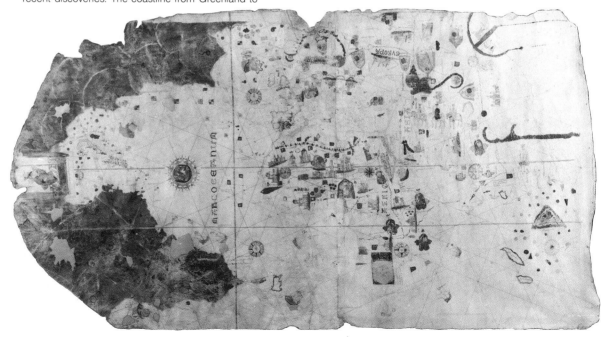

EXPLORATION OF THE
NORTH-AMERICAN EAST COAST

During the years immediately following John Cabot's second and uncertain voyage of 1498, continued interest in the new lands to the west was shown by the Portuguese and the English. The Treaty of Tordesillas spurred the former to seek out any territory which might lie to the west and north on their side of the line of demarcation, but the ultimate purpose of the voyages made by the two nations was the search for a north-western route to China.

By the end of the fifteenth century the Azores had become well settled and Angra on Terceira a popular port of call for homeward-bound Portuguese East Indiamen. It followed naturally that the Azoreans, with a head start in any transatlantic venture, were initially at the forefront of explorations across the Western Ocean. Bristol merchants, for years closely associated with the Azoreans, also grasped at the possibility of finding their own route to fabulous Cathay and engaged in several voyages, sometimes in partnership with Azoreans. The records of these early voyages are scanty and confusing, so that historians' conclusions are contradictory and uncertain.

Portuguese voyages

In October 1499 a patent was granted by King Manuel of Portugal to João Fernandes of Terceira, a *lavrador* or farmer, to seek out islands which might lie on the Portuguese side of the line of demarcation. His voyage took place during the summer of 1500,

and it is likely that he sighted Cape Farewell, the southern tip of Greenland. Certainly, for years Greenland was known as 'Labrador', the name being transferred to its present locality when the old Norse name was revived later in the century.

Gaspar Corte-Real

The same summer that João Fernandes was beating about the bleak Greenland shore, another Portuguese, Gaspar Corte-Real, the youngest son of João Vaz Corte-Real, the hereditary governor of Angra, whetted his appetite for exploration by raising Newfoundland, which he named 'Terra Verde'. Gaspar would have been about 50 years of age when he made his first recorded voyage of discovery, but it is fairly certain that he had made earlier attempts. Financing the expedition himself, and bearing letters from King Manuel, Gaspar sailed in one ship from Lisbon early in the summer of 1500, and was possibly joined by another vessel at Terceira before striking out to the west. He returned in the autumn of that year.

In May the following year, 1501, Gaspar set out once more from Lisbon, this time with three ships. Steering further to the north, they sighted Greenland and were stopped by ice from continuing up the west coast. That they experienced icebergs there is no doubt, for the narrative describes their watering from a berg where

> owing to the heat of the sun, sweet and clear water is melted on their summits, and

> descending, by small channels, formed by the water itself, it eats away at the base where it falls. The ships now being in want of water the boats were sent in, and in that way as much was taken as was needed.[1]

Field ice prevented further progress up the Davis Strait, so they crossed to the west or north-west and coasted south-west, perhaps briefly entering Hudson Strait. Their long coasting voyage took in the shores of Labrador, eastern Newfoundland, Nova Scotia and perhaps Maine. Either of the two last would have fulfilled their descriptions of the land as wooded with fine timber fit for masts and, 'when they landed they found delicious fruits of various kinds and trees and pines of marvellous height and girth.'[2]

Somewhere along these coasts they acquired from the Indians the broken gilt sword-hilt and Venetian earrings, possible relics of Cabot's second voyage, as there was no contact with the natives in the 1497 venture. From this region the Portuguese kidnapped a whole Indian community of some 50 people to sell as slaves on their return to Portugal. Two of the ships then returned to Lisbon, where they arrived in October.

Gaspar remained on the American coast to pursue his exploration to the south-west, but nothing more was ever heard from him. His brother, Miguel, set out with two ships the following year to search for Gaspar, but although one ship returned, the flagship and Miguel were lost and no new knowledge was gathered of the American coastline. The eldest brother, Vasqueanes, who had inherited the governship of Terceira and St George, was refused permission by King Manuel to set out in search of his brothers in 1503.

The Bristolian-Azorean voyages of 1501-2

In 1501 while Gaspar was making his second voyage, King Henry of England awarded a patent to three Bristol merchantmen, Richard Warde, Thomas Asshehurst and John Thomas, along with three Azoreans, João Gonsalves, Francisco Fernandes and, determined to improve on his earlier discoveries and probably engaged as captain and senior pilot, João Fernandes. Their 1501 voyage was successful enough to merit a reward to those 'men of bristoll that founde th'isle'[3], and another attempt in 1502. It is possible that João Fernandes and Richard Warde may have been lost in a third ship during this voyage, for in September only João Gonsalves and Francisco Fernandes received royal pensions of ten pounds a year 'in consideracion of the true service which they have doon to us to oure singler pleasure as Capitaignes into the newe founde land'[4], and Warde's name is omitted from other documents. Whether this may have been modern Newfoundland is uncertain, but in the records pertaining to the Bristol-Azorean voyage of 1502 the title appears for the first time. Among the items of interest which this voyage brought back to England were three Indians 'Clothid in beastys skinnys and ete Rawe Flesh'[5]. Two more Bristol voyages followed, in 1504 and 1505, supplying more curiosities for the king but apparently adding little to the geographical knowledge of the 'New Found Land'.

Apart from a dubious voyage made by Sebastian Cabot around 1508, no further voyages of discovery are recorded for nearly the next 2 decades. There is still a very big question mark over Sebastian's voyage, for which the only evidence comes from secondhand sources of a later date. If it did take place, the son of John Cabot may have discovered Hudson Strait and entered Hudson Bay, then ranged the whole of the North American coastline from Davis Strait to Florida, a voyage which must have involved two seasons' sailing.

Grand Banks fishing development

The new discoveries were not neglected and the Grand Banks fishing was swiftly exploited, with the fishing fleets of Brittany, Normandy and Portugal, joined later by the English, frequenting the waters off Newfoundland in ever-increasing numbers from 1504. Starting as early as 1508, Thomas Aubert, in a ship named *La Pensée* owned by Jean Ango of Dieppe, made several voyages in an attempt to found a colony in Newfoundland. The Portuguese, from Terceira in the Azores and Aveiro and Vianna in Portugal, were sufficiently well organised and profitable for the king to impose a tax of one-tenth of the profits of fish landed in Portugal, to be paid to the Crown. Although no permanent settlements were established, fishing bases were used annually around the shores of Newfoundland and Cape Breton.

João Fagundes

One of the first to visualise the benefit of curing fish ashore was a Portuguese shipowner named João Alvares Fagundes. Around 1520 he made a voyage along the south coast of Newfoundland and named Penguin Island 'Isla de Pitigoen' for the thousands of flightless great auks there. He also named the islands of St Pierre and Miquelon the 'Archipelago of the Eleven Thousand Virgins' and bestowed the names of the saints John and Peter on the island of St Paul. Many of these places were new discoveries, and on his return Fagundes succeeded in obtaining a patent granting property rights and privileges for the region.

During one of the summers between 1521 and 1525 João Fagundes returned to Ingonish on Cape Breton Island. Here, with the colonists he brought from his hometown, Minho, and from the Azores, he set up a colony to serve as a fish-curing base. Unfortunately, hostile Indians and equally bellicose Breton fishermen, who persistently sabotaged the Portuguese fishing-lines and buildings, drove them to look for more peaceful pastures. In their search they discovered the Bay of Fundy, but with no support from home, the brave efforts of the Portuguese settlers here faded out.

Verrazzano

Spain, England and France all possessed first-class seamen, but for men of ideas, versed in cosmography, they turned to the sons of the Italian renaissance. Columbus broke down the barrier of the Atlantic for Spain and Cabot did likewise for England. Now France, who for 2 decades had been sending her fishing fleets from Dieppe, St Malo and La Rochelle to work the foggy Grand Banks and Newfoundland coasts, leaned on a Florentine, Giovanni da Verrazzano, to attempt to find the elusive western passage to China.

Perhaps because of his successful privateering on behalf of the French monarch, Francis I, and an immaculate maritime record, Verrazzano was permitted to borrow a French warship, *La Dauphine*. Taking the southern route, *La Dauphine* and another vessel, *La Normande*, left Brittany in the autumn of 1523, snapping up a few prizes as they cruised down the Spanish coast. For some reason, perhaps to escort the prizes back to France, *La Normande* did not accompany *La Dauphine* when, on 17 January 1524, Verrazzano took his departure from the Madeiras

Giovanni da Verrazzano's ship *La Dauphine*. Built in the new Royal Dockyard at Le Havre in 1519, this French warship measured 100 tons, with a crew of 50. She probably flew the royal ensign of azure sprinkled with gold fleurs-de-lys.

La Dauphine anchored during the spring of 1524 in the narrows of the harbour which was to become New York. The half-mile channel is now spanned by the Verrazzano Bridge.

Verrazzano's brother, Girolamo, sailed in *La Dauphine* and later produced a world map. On this map he showed an ocean, which he described as *el mare orientale*, on the other side of the Carolina Banks. The mistake was understandable, for the mainland is often out of sight when viewed from seaward across the banks. On Girolamo's map there is pictured a ship sailing westward, very likely a representation of *La Dauphine*. Although she was described as a warship, she was not large and differed little from the usual run of merchant ships of her day. She clearly has a curved back stem and my reconstruction in the painting is based on this drawing.

to make a landfall about 1 March near Cape Fear in North Carolina.

Verrazzano, with the object of searching for a passage, was determined to cover all of the hitherto unexplored coastline from Florida northwards, so from his landfall he turned south to somewhere north of Charleston where he turned back, not wishing to become involved with the Spanish. His subsequent voyage took him the full length of the coastline to Cape Breton, but his survey was somewhat hurried and sketchy, and he made a monumental error when he mistook the waters inside the Carolina Banks for the Pacific Ocean. He was the first to enter New York Harbour, anchoring for a while in the narrows now spanned by the Verrazzano Bridge.

Verrazzano named Block Island 'Luisa' after the French Queen Mother, but likened it to the Rhodes; possibly this was the origin of Rhode Island, the Union's smallest state. He also made friends with the Wampanoag Indians in present-day Newport Harbour. The remainder of his voyage took him along the coasts of Massachussetts and Maine, into the Bay of Fundy. From the bay he sailed up the Nova Scotian coast without coming into land, before he took his departure from Cape Breton for home, to arrive in Dieppe in July 1524. On another voyage in 1528, which may have been launched to find a strait in the region of the Gulf of Darien, Verrazzano made his landfall on Florida and then followed the Caribbean islands to Guadaloupe. Here, while attempting to land from a boat, he was slaughtered by the Caribes as his brother, Girolamo, and the boat's crew watched helplessly from beyond the line of breakers.

Esteban Goméz

At the end of the same year that Giovanni Verrazzano returned from the American seaboard, another expedition set out from Corunna intent on finding a northern route to the Pacific. In command was Esteban Goméz, a Portuguese who, like Magellan, had offered his services to Spain. Indeed, Goméz, an able and experienced navigator, had urged the dispatch of an expedition to the south-west to seek a passage, but the command was given to his fellow countryman, Ferdinand Magellan, while Goméz was relegated to the role of pilot. Exceedingly jealous of Magellan and smarting because he had not been given command of the *San Antonio*, Goméz successfully led a mutiny against Captain Mezquita while they were negotiating the straits and sailed back to Spain. Although thrown into jail along with Mezquita, Goméz managed to talk his way out of trouble and back into favour with his king. Thus Esteban Goméz had good reason to prove he could find a more practicable strait than his now deceased but still detested rival, Magellan.

Nothing from the hand of Esteban Goméz has come down to us and the course of his voyage can only be garnered by later writings and map references based on his report, which must have been sent to the king on his return. In fact, no one is sure whether he cruised from north to south or vice versa, although, as he left Corunna either very late in 1524 or early in 1525 it would seem incredible for an experienced navigator to start in the icy waters of the north. It is known that he sailed in one ship of about 50 tons, provisioned for a year and well fitted out. His instructions were 'to examine all the coast from Florida to *Bacallaos* [Newfoundland]' and specified he was not to go north of Cape Race into Portuguese territory. He was away for about 10 months, during which he sailed 'by day because the land was unknown to him, and so he could see into every bay, creek, river, and inlet, whether it extended over to the other side'[6]. Among the many geographical features discovered by Goméz was the Gut of Canso, and it was he who ascertained that Cape Breton was an island. The Penobscot River, which he sailed up believing it may be the strait, he named 'Rio de las Gamas', or 'Deer River', and the largest island at the mouth of the Penobscot is still named Deer Island. Cabot Strait he traversed, considering that it was a bay. Altogether, Goméz filled in many of the gaps left by Verrazzano, although many of his discoveries were not followed up and had to be rediscovered by later navigators.

Further English voyages

Robert Thorne, the younger son of Robert Thorne of the Bristolian-Azorean ventures described on page 45, was a prosperous merchant who lived in Seville. In 1527 he proposed to the English Crown that a way to China should be sought through the north, even over the Pole as there is 'no land uninhabitable, nor sea innavigable'.[7] Perhaps because the news of Verrazzano's 1524 voyage was circulating, Thorne's propositions were followed up by Henry VIII, who quickly organised a voyage, wisely not to attempt the polar route, but to search for a passage in the north-west. Two ships were prepared, the *Mary Guildford* and the *Sampson*.

The *Mary Guildford* was a King's Ship of 160 tons whose normal occupation was to go once a year to Bordeaux to load the new vintage wines for the King's table. All through the summer she was usually laid up under the care of a maintenance crew, and considering the extensive voyage she was to successfully complete, she must have been well found. Her captain, a very experienced seaman, employed by the Crown, was John Rut, who had commanded vessels as far back as 1512. Nothing is known of the *Sampson* except that she was also a King's Ship and was nicknamed '*Dominus Vobiscum*', and was commanded by a Master Grube.

They left the Thames on 20 May 1527, and Plymouth on 10 June. Once clear of the Scillies, they steered north-west until, on 1 July, off the coast of Labrador, a storm blew up and during the next 2 days those in the *Mary* lost sight of the *Sampson*. They may have been at 53° or 58° N, for huge icebergs and the inability to find soundings so unnerved them that the ship was turned southwards.

On 7 July they came in with the mainland and dropped anchor at Cap de Bas, which may have been Lewis Inlet at 52°20'N. Here they spent 10 days putting the *Mary* in order and fishing, before sailing south to St John's in Newfoundland. Twelve French and two Portuguese fishing vessels were in port drying their catches, and John Rut sat down to write the first letter from an Englishman in North America, sending it in the care of one of the returning Frenchmen. His letter, 'in bad English and Worse Writing'[8] according to a later commentator, was dated 3 August, the date they were ready to sail and keep a prearranged rendezvous with the *Sampson* at Cape Spear, which may have been the centre of English fishing activities at that time. No English fishermen were in St John's.

The *Sampson* never arrived at Cape Spear and after the time of rendezvous had passed, John Rut sailed the *Mary* southwards, coasting and occasionally landing until they left the mainland before entering the Florida Strait, to arrive at Mona Island in the Mona Passage between Puerto Rica and Haiti. Gines Navarro, a Spanish captain, was quietly loading cassava when the large, well armed English ship rolled in and spoke him. Later the *Mary* anchored off the town of San Domingo and for an account of what happened there the reader should turn to pages 62-3, for all the details of her voyage from Newfoundland have come from Spanish sources and there is still some doubt that the ship they reported was indeed the *Mary Guildford*. Nothing exists to show when John Rut brought her home to England, but the following year both Rut and the *Mary* were back in harness, freighting fine red Bordeaux wines for the King.

While dealing with English voyages of about this time we should not omit an entertaining if unfortunate voyage in two ships undertaken by Richard Hore, a leather merchant of London. The *William* was to fish, while the 140-ton *Trinity* was to take some 30 gentlemen of the Bar on a sightseeing tour around the shores of Labrador and Newfoundland. According to Richard Hakluyt, they sailed in 1536 and the *Trinity* visited Penguin Island, where the defenceless great auks suffered more losses. The ship then ran out of provisions on the coast. Hunger drove the party first to eating 'raw herbes and rootes in the fields and deserts'[9] and then one of the sailors, while searching for food, slaughtered his mate and stayed out alone while he boiled him up and ate him. Another forager, savouring the aroma, but not realising it was 'boiled sailor', tracked down the source and abused the cook for not sharing. The guilty murderer burst out, 'If you want to know, this boiled meat is a piece of – buttock.'[10]

Finally many of the party were driven to casting lots for who should be eaten. Hore preached a sermon denouncing the wickedness of what they were doing, and, providentially, that same night a French ship came to anchor nearby. The English immediately seized the ship, marooned the French fishermen, and sailed for home, arriving some time in October. The irate French fishermen arrived home safely after a few months, having lived quite comfortably off the land without resorting to eating each other. Their claim for compensation to Henry VIII was liberally fulfilled.

EXPLORATION OF THE GULF OF ST LAWRENCE

The Italian wars which had inhibited Verrazzano's attempts to follow up his discoveries were over by 1526 and France began to recover from her losses. In 1532 the Duchy of Bretagne became a part of France. In 1533 Pope Clement VII declared that the bull of Pope Alexander VI, which divided the world between Spain and Portugal, applied only to lands that had already been discovered, thus opening the way for France to follow up and consolidate the discoveries of Verrazzano, seek once more for the passage west to China, and perhaps establish colonies in the New World.

Jacques Cartier

Promoting the efforts towards discovery and placing the possibility of colonisation before King Francis I was Phillipe de Chabot, Seigneur de Brion, Admiral of France. To lead the expedition and receive the Royal Commission, the Admiral selected a master-mariner of St Malo, Jacques Cartier. Cartier was born in the Breton port in 1491 and in 1520 married Catherine des Granches, the daughter of a leading shipowning family. He had made voyages to 'Brasil', perhaps in Portuguese vessels, for he could speak Portuguese. It is also likely that he had made previous voyages to Newfoundland and the Strait of Belle Isle, and it may well have been Cartier who convinced Phillipe de Chabot that the strait was well worth following up. Jacques Cartier's commission authorised him to sail 'beyond the strait of the baye des Chaseaulx' (as the Belle Isle Strait was then known), and to find a passage to China. Secondly, he was instructed to search for precious metals.

Jacques Cartier was given two vessels, each of about 60 tons. Unfortunately we know nothing more about these ships, not even their names. Raising some of his crew of 60 presented an initial difficulty, as the merchants of St Malo, anxious not to lose their fishermen, prevented them from signing on, but an embargo prohibiting any of the Bank fishing fleet to sail until Cartier's complement was complete soon solved the problem. On 20 April 1534, the two ships stood out of St Malo on a voyage that was to lay the foundations of the nation of Canada and set France on the road to colonisation.

Cartier made his landfall on Cape Bonavista after a voyage of only 20 days, averaging about 4¼ knots before what must have been an unusually favourable wind. April and May are bad months for ice on the Newfoundland coast, especially when easterly winds drive the ice inshore to block the harbours. Cartier would have expected this, but must have considered an early start weighed favourably against the chance that he might find his path barred by ice. He was obliged to seek shelter in Catalina, a harbour 5 leagues to the south-south-west and clear of ice. Ten days were spent here, preparing the boats and making repairs after the ocean voyage.

On 21 May the wind came offshore from the west, clearing the ice and enabling Cartier to put to sea and work up the coast. North-north-east from Cape Bonavista Cartier hove to off Funk Island, or 'L'Isle d' Ouaisseaulx' as he named it, and, although it was surrounded with field ice, a party managed to get ashore from the boats. The tiny islet was completely covered with nesting great auks, razorbill auks and gannets. Within 2 hours his crew had killed enough great auks, or *apponatz* as Cartier called them, to fill two boats. While the boats were approaching the island, they had seen a polar bear jump into the water and swim away. The next day they saw it again, swimming towards the mainland 14 leagues (32.2 nautical miles) from the island as fast as they were sailing. They gave chase in the boats, killed the bear and found the meat was as good 'as that of a two-year-old heifer'.

Five days later, on 27 May, they were at the entrance to the Strait of Belle Isle but put into Quirpon Harbour as their passage was cluttered with ice, which bottled them up until 9 June. While waiting for the ice to clear, they occupied themselves examining the lie of the land and surveying the harbour. Sailing on, they rounded Cape Degrat and stretched across the strait towards the Labrador shore. From Château Bay Cartier turned south-west into the strait, following the mountainous coast of Labrador, passing Black Bay and then Red Bay, later the scene of the wreck of the Basque whaler *San Juan*.

Continuing on, Cartier noted and carefully described the harbour of Blanc Sablon, even then well known to fishermen. Rounding Long Point, he entered Bradore Bay, another fishing harbour, but did not anchor, instead continuing along the island-studded coast to the harbour of Brest, where he anchored to take in wood and water. He was now at the limit of previous discovery. Leaving the ships at anchor, Cartier explored for 10 leagues further, finding innumerable islands along the coast. On one of these they camped and feasted on the large quantity of duck eggs they found there. The whole of this shore he named 'Toutes Isles'.

Still in the boats, they explored the coast as far as Shecatica Bay where, lying becalmed, they came up with a large fishing vessel from La Rochelle which had overshot Brest during the night, putting her master into some doubt as to where he was. Cartier went aboard and had his boats tow the ship into a harbour a little further west along the coast. This was probably Cumberland Harbour and Cartier describes it as being 'one of the good harbours of the world'.[1] He was much less enthusiastic about the coast of Labrador when he wrote 'Were the soil as good as the harbours, it would be a blessing; but the land should not be called the new land, being composed of stones and horrible rugged rocks; for along the whole of the north shore [of the Gulf], I did not see one cart-load of earth and yet I landed in many places. Except at Blanc Sablon there is nothing but moss and short, stunted shrub. I am rather inclined to believe that this is the land God gave to Cain.'[2]

The fishermen from La Rochelle weighed for home or to return to Brest, while Cartier took his boats back to the ships. On 15 May they got under way and steered towards what were apparently two islands far away on the southern horizon.

Half-way across the strait, before fog rolled in, they made out a cape and beyond, what they had taken for two islands, two hills rising to 1500 and 1600 feet respectively. They named it 'Cap Double' and it is now named Cape Riche on the west coast of Newfoundland. Beset by foul weather which prevented close examination of the shore, Cartier coasted the western shore of Newfoundland until 24 June when, in blowing and foggy weather, they made out a cape to the south-east. This was Cape Anguille, one of the capes on the south-western tip of Newfoundland.

Leaving the coast, they ran west-north-west until the evening of 25 June, when they hove to. During the second watch, about midnight, the wind swung north-west and they made sail to the south-west,

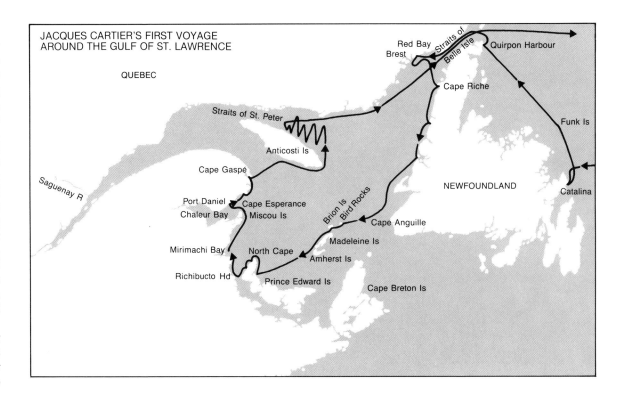

JACQUES CARTIER'S FIRST VOYAGE AROUND THE GULF OF ST. LAWRENCE

QUEBEC

Saguenay R

Straits of St. Peter

Anticosti Is

Cape Gaspé

Port Daniel
Chaleur Bay
Cape Esperance
Miscou Is

Mirimachi Bay
North Cape

Richibucto Hd

Prince Edward Is

Brion Is
Bird Rocks

Madeleine Is
Amherst Is

Cape Breton Is

Red Bay
Brest
Straits of Belle Isle
Quirpon Harbour

Cape Riche

Funk Is

NEWFOUNDLAND

Catalina

Cape Anguille

sailing 15 leagues (34.5 nautical miles) before they raised three small islands. Two of them were so steep it was impossible to land. These were Bird Rocks, and despite their inaccessibility, Cartier's sailors managed to scramble on to a lower ledge of North Bird and slaughter over 1000 auks and other birds for the pot. Cartier named the group 'Isles de Margaulx' for the thousands of gannets nesting there.

Five leagues further west they raised another island, which Cartier named Brion after the admiral and the name still survives. He found a good anchorage on the east side of the island and anchored overnight to take on wood and water. After the bleak coasts he had been ranging Cartier was full of praise for the comparatively lush island: 'one *arpent* of it

is worth more than the whole of Newfoundland'[3]. They also saw bears, foxes and walrus, which they described as 'beasts large like oxen, which had two tusks in their mouths like elephants'[4]. Cartier now made a significant remark. Realising he was between Newfoundland and a mainland, he was still uncertain whether the former was a peninsula or an island, but he said, 'I am rather inclined to think

A Norman or Bretagne ship perhaps similar to *La Grande Hermine* and other vessels in which Jacques Cartier sailed. Drawings of Norman ships from as early as 1525 show ships of the galleon type and seem to be distinctive from other nations' vessels only in the large amount of rake given to the main mast.

from what I have seen that there is a passage between Newfoundland and the Bretons' land. If this were so, it would prove a great saving both in time and distance, should any success be met with on this voyage.'[5] He was absolutely right, but for some reason, probably because some doubt still remained, he did not attempt this route until homeward bound on his second voyage. The passage is now known as Cabot Strait, although the *Matthew* never entered its waters as far as we know.

After leaving Brion on 26 June, Cartier crossed to the Magdalen Islands and spent the next 2 days sailing along the west and south coast of Great Magdalen, which he apparently considered to be part of the mainland. Unable to land on the exposed shore, on the twenty-ninth, close-hauled on a southerly wind, he stretched to the west-south-west, raising Prince Edward Island around New London Bay. Until the morning of 1 July they coasted the lovely shore of the island, and when fog rolled in they lay-to. When it cleared, they made out Cape Kildare and North Cape to the north-west. Using the boats, they made several landings, including one at Malpeque Bay, which Cartier named the River of Boats, observing many Indian canoes which had probably been portaged across the 2 miles from Northumberland Strait.

An offshore easterly wind called a halt to further explorations and the two ships clawed around North Cape to the west coast which Cartier examined carefully but found no harbour or anchorage, although he described it as the 'most temperate land one could ask for'[6]. Not realising that he was coasting an island, when he saw Richibucto Head 10 miles away across Northumberland Strait he crossed and turned northward, discovering Miramichi Bay. After dark on 2 July the weather worsened and they lay-to for the night until the wind came fair on the third, when they rounded Miscou Island and entered Chaleur Bay.

In the distance to the north they could see the Gaspé Mountains and, stretching away to the west, seemingly with no end, the sunny, sparkling waters of the bay. On that bright day one can understand the explorers' hopes that at last they had found another strait, one which might lead them to China. Naming the northern point of Miscou Island 'Cap d'Esperance', or 'Hope Cape', Cartier crossed to the Gaspé shore and coasted westward, looking for a harbour. He found a rather exposed, shell-like bay which he named 'la Conche St Martin', now Port Daniel.

Noting that the New Brunswick side was beautiful arable land and the Gaspé coast steep and clothed with forests of cedar and fir, some fit for masts for ships over 300 tons, Cartier named the bay 'la Baye de Chaleur', comparing its warmth with that of Spain. While the ships remained at anchor, the boats set off to explore up the bay, but their hopes were dashed when they found it ended in lowlands backed by high mountains. All along the way they had contact with Micmac Indians, who were initially over-friendly, surrounding the boats and causing some anxiety to the Frenchman, who first warned them off with a couple of rounds from the swivel guns, fired over their heads. When this was insufficient, they hurled a couple of fire lances among the Indians. However, they later became more confident and set up a brisk trade for furs. On 12 July they were back at the ships and despondently got under way, disappointed that the bay was not a strait and probably regretful at leaving the warm bay and friendly natives.

After sailing 18 leagues (41.5 nautical miles) along the Gaspé coast to a cape Cartier named 'Cape Pratto', or 'Meadow', the ships ran into very rough

In 1535, on his second voyage, Jacques Cartier worked his three ships, *La Grande Hermine*, *La Petite Hermine*, and *L'Emerillon*, up the St. Lawrence to the site of the future city of Quebec.

water with strong tides running over a shallow bottom. Cape Pratto is now Cape Despair and the origin of the name is curious. Over the years the name of Cartier's Cap d'Esperance was transferred to Cape Pratto as 'Cap d'Espoir' which was unconsciously but appropriately corrupted by the English to 'Cape Despair'. To keep out of the rip they hugged the shore and anchored that night between White Head and Bonaventure Island. The following day they made sail again, but could make no progress against strong currents and a heavy sea, so they returned to their anchorage. Setting out the next day, 14 July, they managed to work 5 or 6 leagues (11.5 to 14 nautical miles) along the coast to the mouth of a river, whereupon the wind turned foul and fog rolled in. They ran into the river and anchored to wait for a fair wind, but two days later, on 16 July, the wind increased so much that one of the ships lost an anchor. While lying there the boats had found excellent shelter further in at the head of the bay, so Cartier moved his ships in and anchored there from 16 to 25 July. The 'river' which Cartier had found was Gaspé Bay into which flows the Dartmouth River, and the secure anchorage at the head of the bay was the Gaspé Basin.

At the mouth of the basin Cartier set up a 30-foot cross with a crest bearing three fleurs-de-lys and an inscription 'Vive le Roy de France'. Earlier, a great number of Indians had arrived from upriver, intent on mackerel fishing. These were different in language and nature from the Micmacs he had previously encountered and were Hurons from the region about Quebec. They were friendly, welcoming the French with singing and dancing, and were keen to trade for the beads, knives, combs and bells, barrels of which Cartier must have had stowed in the hold. There were only two or three young girls among the crowd, so Cartier presented each of them with a little bell. This so delighted them they showed their appreciation by rubbing the captain's chest and arms, while a couple of dozen more young females, eager to win a bell, poured out

of the bush from where they had been discreetly hiding.

Watching the incomprehensible ceremony accompanying the setting up of the cross, the Indians realised that the French might be claiming possession of the land. Later, their chief, Donnaconna, dressed in an old black bearskin and accompanied by his three sons and a brother, came near the ship in his canoe and indicated by signs that the French had no right to do this, for the land was theirs. Cartier held up an axe, pretending to offer to swap it for the bearskin. Tempted, Donnaconna went alongside, only to be hustled on board by the French sailors. Cartier managed to pacify Donnaconna and his party with presents and told them that the cross was merely set up as a navigation mark, and even managed to persuade the chief to allow two of his sons, Taignoagny and Domagaya, to remain with the French, promising to return them in the future with many more gifts. The youths were delighted when they were rigged out in fancy European clothes and happily gave away their own furs to their friends.

When Cartier put out from Gaspé on 25 July he steered east-north-east, 'because, from the mouth of that river the coast ran back forming a bay, in the shape of a semi-circle, of which we could see the whole coastline from our ships. And holding our course, we drew near that coast, which ran south-east and north-west.'[7] This coast was the southern shore of Anticosti Island. Fog has been put forward as a possible reason why the French did not realise they had crossed the main channel, but Cartier clearly states that the whole coastline was visible. Mirage, a not uncommon phenomena in the Gulf, seems to be a more likely explanation. Logically, on arriving off the coast of the island, Cartier turned and coasted south-east, and on the twenty-ninth he rounded East Cape. At dawn on 1 August they saw the hills of the Quebec shore across the Mingan Channel.

Slogging against a strong headwind, the ships

beat backwards and forwards, examining both sides of the strait until 5 August, and making only 25 leagues (57.5 nautical miles) during all that time. At the narrowest part of the strait, with the land clearly visible on both sides, unable to make further progress against wind and current, Cartier ordered the boats away to examine a cape on Anticosti some 5 leagues (11.5 nautical miles) distant. Cartier's description of the point identifies it as High Cliff Point. Carried to windward on a swift inshore counter-current, the captain's boat ran on a rock. All aboard, including Cartier, went over the side into the cold water and managed to shove her off, and they continued until the tide turned, when even 13 oars with practised, lusty Frenchmen laying back could not make any headway. They beached the boats and Cartier, with a party of sailors, made his way overland to the next headland where they saw that the shore trended away to the south-west and were satisfied that they were in a strait. They then returned to the ships which, even though under sail, had been driven 4 leagues (9.2 nautical miles) to leeward.

Cartier was now convinced that there was a sea to the west and as 1 August was the feast of St Peter in Chains, he named the new strait after the saint.

Cartier called a council of all the masters, pilots and gentlemen to discuss what should be done next. They could not at present make headway against the strong winds and tides, the season was late, and the time of stormy weather on the Newfoundland coast was approaching. They had a choice to winter where they were or to head back before the north winds filled in and prevented them from working out the Strait of Belle Isle. It was wisely agreed to return. With a strong and fair wind they barrelled eastward along the Quebec coastline. From Cape Whittle the two ships laid across to Newfoundland and then, with a fierce east-northeaster blowing, north to Blanc Sablon, coming to anchor on 9 August. They sailed for home on 15 August and, after riding out a severe mid-Atlantic blow, they came into St Malo on 5 September 1534.

This first voyage of Jacques Cartier was quite remarkable. He had circumnavigated the whole outer Gulf of St Lawrence, safely navigated through murky, rock-strewn, often stormy waters and not lost one man. He had every reason to believe that beyond the Strait of St Peter a way lay open to China. Justifiably he was lauded by the citizens of his home port and praised by his sailors, who appreciated his skill and humanity. This voyage was a reconnaissance; his next, it was hoped, would take him all the way to China.

The later voyages

On 30 October the same year, Jacques Cartier received a new commission from Admiral Chabot de Brion, empowering him to employ three ships, equipped and provisioned for 15 months, to follow up the discoveries of the first voyage. These vessels were:

La Grande Hermine (Ermine), (flagship), 100 to 200 tons. 12 guns. Thomas Fromont, master. Several gentlemen volunteers were aboard, including the Dauphine's cupbearer, Claude de Pontbriand, and also the two Hurons, Domagaya and Taignoagny.

La Petite Hermine, about 60 tons. 4 guns. Macé Jalobert, captain and pilot; Guillaume le Maryé, master.

L'Emerillon (Merlin), galion of about 40 tons. 2 guns. Guillaume le Breton, captain and pilot; Jacques Maingard, master.[8]

They sailed on 19 May 1535 and during the course of this voyage Cartier named Pillage Bay on the Quebec shore 'Baye Sainct Laurens' as it was that saint's feast day. For some incomprehensible reason the name has spread until it now refers to the entire gulf and river. Cartier explored the Saguenay River, renewing his acquaintance with the Indians, and then worked up the St Lawrence until he arrived under the Rock of Quebec. After exploring upriver as far as a hill Cartier named Mont Royal, the present site of the city of Montreal, he built a fort and wintered over in a small river now known as the St Charles, just west of the rock. Twenty-five were lost to scurvy before the Indians showed them a remedy. (During the following centuries countless lives would have been saved if European sailors had grasped this wonder cure). In the spring there were insufficient hands to work the three ships, so *La Petite Hermine* was stripped of her sails and gear and given to the Indians as some compensation for 10 Indians Cartier had kidnapped to take back to France.

On the return voyage they affirmed that Magdalen was an island and sailed through the Cabot Strait, rounded Cape Race and anchored at Renewse to wood and water. Their return voyage across the Atlantic before fair winds took them 3 weeks to arrive in St Malo on 15 July 1536.

When Cartier arrived home France was again in a turmoil and Francis I was too preoccupied to attend to Cartier and listen to the tall stories of Donnaconna. All the Indians died except for one little girl who had been gifted to Cartier by an Indian chief up the St Lawrence. It was 1540 before Cartier received a commission for another voyage to the west. This was to be more for the purposes of settlement rather than discovery and is outside the scope of this chapter. Briefly, although Cartier was initially given the command of the expedition, in 1541 Francis I placed Jean-Francois de la Roque, sier de Roberval, over Cartier. The venture was comparatively ambitious, involving a large number of people and all the necessary equipment and skills to found a colony. The rumours flying around Europe caused consternation among the Spanish, who believed the fleet was destined for the Caribbean.

In May 1541 Cartier sailed in five ships, without Roberval, whose contingent were not ready. The fleet came to anchor at Quebec on 23 August and Cartier selected a more defensible site for his winter camp, 4 leagues upriver at Cap Rouge. Two of the ships were sent back to France on 2 September, and while the majority of the crews built two forts and prepared for the winter, Cartier explored once more upriver, intending to reach the Kingdom of Saguenay. However, he was baulked by the Lachine Rapids and gave up.

That winter the natives became hostile and killed 35 of the French, and Roberval never arrived. In June 1542 Cartier sailed back to Newfoundland where he met Roberval, outward bound with three new merchantmen packed with hopeful settlers, both men and women. Cartier tried to persuade Roberval to give up; Roberval wanted Cartier to accompany him back to Canada. Cartier solved the difficulty by slipping out of port one night and sailing back to St Malo. Roberval sailed through the Strait of Belle Isle and up to the site of Cartier's forts. Here he built a more formidable fort which he named France-Roy and planted vegetables to help the colonists through the winter. Two ships were sent back to France during September. Although Cartier had probably told Roberval of the cure for scurvy, about 50 died that winter. In spring Roberval led a party up the St Lawrence, but after eight men were drowned he turned back at the Lachine Rapids. Another party explored the Saguenay River but appears not to have got as far as the Chicoutimi Rapids.

About July in 1543 Roberval gave up and returned to France, and so ended the first attempt to settle in Canada. Jacques Cartier lived on in St Malo, a convivial and respected citizen. An amusing record of a baptism at which Jacques was a witness gives his name *avec d'aultres bons biberons* ('with other good tipplers')[9]. He died in an epidemic during 1557 and was survived by his wife. Jacques Cartier never lost a ship on his exploratory voyages and he seemed to be able to work the difficult and dangerous sailing around the Gulf and River St Lawrence with as much confidence as he would have the equally treacherous waters of Brittany. He must rank among the most skilful and expert mariners of his time.

ENGLISH TRADING VOYAGES TO THE CARIBBEAN

Off the West Indian port of Santo Domingo, towards the evening of Monday, 26 November 1526, a large, three-masted ship, with two decks of brass cannon cleared for action, smartly hove to and put away a well armed, single-masted pinnace. The pinnace entered the rivermouth and was pulling upstream under the wondering gaze of the inhabitants when she was hailed from the house of Alonso Zuazo, a judge of the city. The boat steered to the riverbank, disembarked three men, and then hauled off to lie in midstream, where the oarsmen rested on their sweeps while they shouted replies to the curious citizens ashore and afloat. Meanwhile, their three shipmates, one of whom was the captain of the strange vessel, vanished into the house of the judge.

Apparently quite candid, the strangers claimed they were English, who, under orders from their king, had sailed from England about 9 months before to seek out a passage to Tartary in the regions of Newfoundland and Labrador. They had sailed beyond 50°N, where one of their pilots and a number of other men had died of cold, and their other ship had been lost. From the north they had followed the American coast south-westward, struck out to the south and east and passed through the Mona Passage to call at Santo Domingo to revictual. In the hold of their ship they had linens, woollens and other articles with which they were willing to pay for their requirements.

The events which followed were later typical of the rather quixotic relations between the Spanish colonials and interlopers in their waters. On the one hand, explicit orders stated that there was to be absolutely no trade or refuge for vessels not sanctioned by Seville. On the other, many of the colonials, desperately short of the products of European civilisation supplied to them through the expensive and over-regulated Casa de las Indias (see page 92) were only too happy to oblige if it could be made quite clear to the inevitable later inquiry that they had had to choose between trade or a disastrous assault.

It was not a happy compromise. The traders, initially either English or French, were never certain of their reception or that the authorities were not playing along with the game to lure them to drop their guard, while the Spanish were never quite sure they were not letting a wolf into their fold. Although most of the visitors were only interested in profit on their merchandise, only by a powerful display of force by the foreigners, sometimes even to the extent of a mock attack, could the Spanish be brought to trade. In an atmosphere of mutual mistrust, with both parties playing war with loaded guns, it is little wonder that their theatricals sometimes escalated into the real thing.

Alternatively, business was done under cover of darkness at quiet anchorages and, as everybody except the Crown participated and benefited, officials could do little to uncover clear proof of conspiracy. Diego Ruiz de Vallejo, the distracted accountant to the Crown Treasurer of New Segovia, wrote, in 1568:

> These corsairs come fully supplied with all lines of merchandise, oils and wines and everything else which is lacking in the country. The colonists' needs are great and neither penalties nor punishments suffice to prevent them from buying secretly what they want. As a matter of fact they make their purchases, but nothing can be learned of them, for they buy at night and cover each other, and no measures suffice to prevent it . . .[1]

The unnamed captain of the first English ship to arrive in the West Indies must have been aware he was in forbidden territory. His ship stood off the port with her guns run out and the pinnace itself came in fairly bristling with armament. What the final intentions of the Spanish really were we do not know. There was bold talk of letting the ship in so as to arrest her and hang the heretics, but this may have been merely for the benefit of Seville. Whatever the Spanish secretly planned, the English captain was told he was welcome and returned to his ship with Diego Mendez, the High Sheriff of the island, and two pilots to guide the ship into port. Left as security were two English seamen, who wandered around the town quite freely, no doubt enjoying their spell ashore.

It was dusk, and with the offshore wind and approaching dark it was too late to work the ship in. The Sheriff returned to shore but the Spanish pilots remained on board to be entertained by the English. The next morning the ship was sailed into the mouth of the river, where she was brought to anchor so that preparations could be made to warp her into the anchorage. It was 10 o'clock and apparently time to eat, so work stopped while the whole company settled down to their meal. The English were in a happy mood, looking forward to a rest after their long and difficult voyage. The captain, officers and the pilots were sociably swapping yarns at a table spread under the quarterdeck awning when a gun thumped out from the fort at the mouth of the river. The stone shot smacked into the water close under the stern. The English captain 'turned colour', leaped up and claimed there was a plot to betray him. The pilots tried to calm him, saying it was only a salute of welcome.

'Why the devil was it loaded then?' retorted the irate captain, who then roused out his crew and set them to weighing anchor and making sail. The pilots were unceremoniously bundled into a boat alongside and sent ashore, and the ship cleared out on the offshore north wind.

As the pilots passed by the fort they hailed the warden and asked him why he had fired. The warden had, it turned out, been sick, and no one had thought to keep him informed. He knew about the English visitors, but had not been told they had been given permission to enter, so, doing his duty as he claimed was the usual custom, he had put a shot close to the ship to encourage her to identify herself.

The English left for Europe, never to be seen again, although they may have got their victuals, for it seems the pinnace made a raid a little down the coast – as it happened, on Judge Zuazo's estate.

Who these English were is uncertain. It could be, that, as discussed earlier, the vessel was the *Mary Guildford*, one of two ships in which John Rut set sail in 1527 for northern America. He too was driven back by cold and sailed south, but the dates given by the Spanish and their description of the ship do not reconcile with Rut's expedition. Alternatively, the first recorded English ship in the Caribbean may

have been some other rover who never got home.

In the Caribbean, the activities of the English, French and Dutch increased as the century passed. Most came with the intention to trade, but were not adverse to a little piracy on the side if they could get away with it. Traders or not, they were all deemed corsairs, or '*los corsarios luteranos*', and if found at a disadvantage, they were treated as such by the Spanish. This was to be the fate of John Hawkins's venture at Vera Cruz in 1567.

John Hawkins's most disastrous voyage

John Hawkins, with two lucrative voyages to Guinea and the Caribbean behind him, was a wealthy shipowner with influence in London and at Elizabeth's court. His father, William Hawkins, had made successful slaving voyages to Africa and Brazil, pioneering the various triangular trades of later years in which one leg was employed in shipping slaves out of Africa. Apart from needing manufactured goods such as ironmongery, the Spanish colonials depended for their survival on the importation of slaves to work their plantations and mines. Legitimate shipments were meagre and, by the time Seville had extracted her cut, expensive. Foreign ships could circumvent the duties and supply cheap labour in return for the gold and produce of the colonies – an arrangement whereby all except Seville benefited.

It was with the intention of lifting a cargo of slaves from Guinea for the Caribbean that Hawkins put out to sea from Plymouth in October 1567. His flagship was the large and matronly 700-ton *Jesus of Lubeck*. She belonged to the Queen and had been bought from the Germans by her father many years before. In spite of the vessel's age, Hawkins must have been fond of her, for he had sailed her on a previous voyage to the Caribbean. As an officer in

the *Jesus* sailed young Francis Drake, who had only just returned from the Indies in a fleet of Hawkins's ships under the command of John Lovell. Five other ships made up the new venture, one of which, the sizable and well armed *Minion*, also belonged to the Queen. In Biscay a severe storm scattered the fleet, sank the larger accompanying boats, and strained the *Jesus* so badly that she was turned for home. However, the wind came fair and spirits brightened along with the weather, so the old lady was once more put on course for the Canaries.

At Gomera the fleet was reunited and sailed on to arrive at Cape Verde on 18 November. Here they landed, hoping to capture some slaves, but were fought off with poisoned arrows, losing a number of the crew. Gathering the slaves went slowly until a local chief in Sierra Leone asked Hawkins's assistance in an attack on a neighbouring town. It was a hard-fought and bloody business, and more casualties were suffered by the English before the town fell, but their tally of slaves mounted by another 260 men, women and children. Now, with between 400 and 500 captives crowded into the ships, they set out for the Indies, leaving the African coast on 3 February. Four ships had been added to the fleet, one of which, the 50-ton *Judith*, became Francis Drake's first command. Two French ships, one named the *Grace of God* under a Captain Bland, were chartered by the company and a third, described as a caravel, was seized as a 'pirate' on the excuse that she carried no cargo.

The voyage along the South American coast from Margarita Island to Cartagena illuminates what the 'traders' could expect from the Spanish. Margarita presented no trouble and a roaring trade went on for 8 days, exchanging English cloth and African slaves for produce to revictual the ships. The fleet left Margarita in an atmosphere of goodwill and friendship, to coast for 300 miles westward to the port of Borburata, in the province of New Andalusia, now Venezuela. Governor Don Diego Ponce de Leon was away on tour, but received a letter from

Hawkins requesting permission, not to trade, for he knew this was forbidden, but only to be allowed to sell some of his wares and slaves so that he could pay his soldiers. He added that 'inconveniences' could happen to those who adhered too firmly to the letter of the law – a scarcely veiled threat. Meanwhile, Hawkins opened shop at Borburata, doing a fine trade which was not even interrupted by a regretful refusal by the distant Ponce de Leon.

From Borburata the fleet sailed eastwards around Cabo de Vela towards Rio de la Hacha. Drake was sent out ahead with two ships, his *Judith* and another small ship, the 33-ton *Angel*. His instructions were to feel out the response at Rio de la Hacha, where they were not certain of their welcome. Drake came to anchor in front of the town and requested water from the King's Treasurer, Miguel de Castellanos. Their doubts were confirmed when the battery ashore opened fire. Drake, true to his character, replied by putting two shots neatly through the Treasurer's house, and then waited for the rest of the fleet to arrive.

Castellanos was not intimidated by the fleet when it came to anchor, and refused a request to be allowed to sell 60 negroes in the town, because Hawkins claimed he could not feed them. The Treasurer warned Hawkins that he was ready to fight. Covered by the ships' gunfire, Hawkins led a landing party. After one volley from the defenders, which killed two of the English, the Spanish fled practically unharmed, leaving the English free to occupy the abandoned town. What happened next may have resulted from Hawkins's frustration at Castellanos's obduracy, or by accident, for a good part of the town went up in flames, including the Governor's house. In reply to a message from the Treasurer to the effect that he could burn the whole town if he wished, Hawkins told the messengers that it was all right for him, Castellanos, to make a bold stand, for he had got all his property and the Crown's treasure to safety.

The reluctance of the citizens to support

The *Jesus of Lübeck*. In 1544 this 700-ton carrack was bought by Henry VII for the English navy from merchants of the old Hanseatic port of Lübeck. Over the years she was often chartered out to merchants and was loaned by Queen Elizabeth to John Hawkins for his highly profitable voyages shipping slaves to the Spanish Main. In 1568 Hawkins lost her when he was attacked by the Spanish in the New Spain port of San Juan de Ulua where he had been forced to put in for repairs, particularly to the aging *Jesus* which had sprung a leak so bad that '. . . living fish did swim upon the ballast . . .'.

John Hawkins seems to have been fond of the old ship and her sailing ability may have belied her high-charged clumsy appearance. She survived decades of knocking about the Baltic, North Sea and Channel and successfully carried out two voyages of extensive coasting in the Caribbean. Her final loss on the second voyage was due to force of arms, not shipwreck. The *Jesus* had the distinction of being the first Queen's ship to be captured by Spain during the reign of Elizabeth I. Only one other ship, Sir Richard Grenville's *Revenge*, suffered the same fate.

There is an illustration of her contained in Antony Antony's Roll of the Navy and, although the drawing needs some interpretation, it does give authority to this representation.

Castellanos, hostages, and Hawkins's luck in having the whereabouts of the bullion disclosed to him by a runaway slave, thawed the Treasurer's resolve and the door to trade cracked open. Permission was first given for Hawkins to sell his 60 slaves, and then, although more clandestinely, the market was wide open. By the time Hawkins was ready to leave he had made a huge profit on his slaves and merchandise, and collected 4000 gold pesos as ransom on his prisoners and the remaining part of the town. The English must have had difficulty in coping with the elderly and very young captives from the African town they had assisted in seizing, for, when they departed Rio de la Hacha, a number of these unfortunates were left ashore in the care of the Spanish.

Cruising further westward along the coast, Hawkins had no trouble bringing the citizens of Santa Marta to the table after an initial, mutually arranged, show of force. However, at Cartagena the English gave up after spending over a week testing out the Spanish forces and failing to threaten the obdurate governor into submission. By now the voyage had made more than sufficient profit to enable the ships to sail for home and clear the Caribbean before the fast-approaching hurricane season.

The fleet left Cartagena on 24 July and was just entering the Florida Strait on 12 August when they ran into a severe storm, probably an early hurricane. For 4 days the ships battled the weather and suffered considerable damage, particularly the *Jesus of Lubeck*, which got so knocked about that Hawkins wrote '. . . that we cut downe all her higher buildings, her rudder also was sore shaken, and withall was in so extreme a leake that we were rather on the point to leave her than to keep her any longer.'[2] Another account told that all the planking on either side of the sternpost had started and was working, and that the leak was '. . . as big as the thickness of a man's arm, the living fish did swim upon the ballast as on the sea.'[3]

Before attempting to cross the Atlantic it was imperative that the ships be repaired, particularly the *Jesus*, but nowhere on the Florida coast could they find a suitable haven. Then another storm, this time from the north, drove the ships across the Gulf of Mexico. All except one, that is – the *William and John* managed to beat to windward and cleared the Caribbean for England. Hawkins, on the advice of a Spanish captain, reluctantly made for the port of San Juan de Ulua, situated on an island opposite Vera Cruz. On the way they took three Spanish ships loaded with passengers, which Hawkins included in his fleet '. . . the better to obtaine victuals for our money, & a quiet place for the repairing of our fleete'.[4]

Hawkins was in a difficult situation. From the Spanish he was made aware that the New Spain flota was due to arrive at San Juan de Ulua. Apart from the political mayhem any attack on the prestigious flota would cause, the English ships were in no condition to do battle, nor was Hawkins's complement of men up to strength. With luck he could be in and out before the Spanish arrived; it was a gamble which had to be taken, for there was nowhere else to go. The English now had eight ships, and, with the three Spanish in company, when they appeared off the port on 16 September the inhabitants of Vera Cruz took them for the expected flota. Their ensigns were so worn and faded that it was not until the welcoming officials had boarded the ships that they found out their mistake. The Spanish were horrified, but Hawkins reassured them that all he wanted was to enter and refit his ships and that he had no offensive designs. Permission was given and Hawkins led the fleet into the shelter of the port, where they moored along the inshore side of the island, with their cables made fast to the land and two anchors out astern. So close were they to the built-up embankment that it was possible to step ashore from the beakhead. To ensure good faith from the Spanish, Hawkins kept some of the influential officials in his ships, but released all the passengers from the captured three ships, and was careful not to interfere with other ships already in port.

The very next morning Hawkins's worst fears were realised when the 13 ships of the New Spain flota arrived off the port. He had two choices, both of which could result in calamity. It would not be difficult to prevent the flota from entering, but with the prevailing and often fierce northerly winds, all the Spanish ships would be at risk while they hung around outside. If, by forbidding them to enter, Hawkins caused the loss of any of the flota, he would create an international incident which would bring down the wrath of his own queen, let alone the Spanish, who would slam the door to any hope of future trade in the Caribbean. Alternatively, Hawkins could allow the flota to enter, knowing that, if they were given any chance at all, the Spanish would throw any mutual agreements out of the window and attempt to destroy him.

The first choice would bring inevitable trouble, so, after 3 days of negotiating, the flota was allowed to enter. Hawkins had the assurance in writing from Don Martin Enriquez, the new Viceroy of Mexico who had arrived in the fleet, that the English would be allowed to complete their repairs and victualling in peace. Ten hostages were exchanged, and for good measure Hawkins insisted on being allowed to occupy the island with its fort, for, as he remarked, '. . . with the first North winde they had cut our cables and our ships had gone ashore'.[5]

On the evening of Monday, 20 September, the New Spain flota entered to the accompaniment of salutes from the English and Spanish ships, and a start was made in arranging and securing the fleets in the now overcrowded little port, which was hardly more than a quarter of a mile in extent. Apart from a gap between the English and Spanish fleets, the ships were brought to their moorings so close to each other that it was possible to step from one vessel to the other.

During the 2 days it took to accomplish all the towing and warping, Hawkins began to suspect that an attack was imminent when he saw large numbers of men being brought out to the Spanish ships. On Thursday morning the activity increased. Guns seen to be moved from ship to ship and on to the island, and other warlike preparations, spurred Hawkins to send to the Viceroy for an explanation. The smooth assurance from Don Enriquez that nothing was afoot, and that anything which worried the English would be removed, counted for little when a large,

900-ton merchant ship in ballast was brought to moorings between the fleets and not far from the *Minion*. Hawkins was absolutely certain that a large force had been hidden in the ship during the previous night.

The Viceroy had never had any intention of permitting English heretics, already considered outside the laws of Spain, to reside peacefully in his port. Plans for an attack on Hawkins's ships had been laid before the flota had even entered. These called for reinforcements from Vera Cruz and preparations in the ships for an attack on Thursday morning. In the dark of Wednesday night, 150 arquebusiers and targeteers, together with General Francisco de Luxan and Admiral Juan de Ubilla of the flota, were to hide themselves on board the large, empty merchantman. During the morning it was intended that the apparently empty hulk should be innocently warped into the only possible berth between the English and Spanish fleets. Once her lines were ashore and the anchor laid out astern, it would be a simple matter to sheer her alongside Hawkins's *Minion* and board. Once alongside, General Luxan was to wave a white cloth as a signal to the Viceroy that he was ready, then a blast by the trumpeter in the Spanish flagship, or *capitana*, would herald the general action. Landing parties from boats and from the ships of the flota were to make a concerted attack on the island. With the island in their hands, the Spanish could then turn the guns on the English ships, which, as they were moored bow on, would be unable to answer, or fire at the Spanish ships, for by this time the *Minion*, the only ship with a clear field of fire, would be in Spanish hands. The plan was simple and effective, but depended on the preparations being kept secret. Even with the English suspicions thoroughly aroused, it would seem that the Spanish could hardly fail to capture the whole English fleet, but it did not turn out quite as easy as the plotters had expected.

As the huge Spanish merchant ship let go her stern anchors and was hauled into her berth,

Hawkins recognised the Spanish Admiral, who was hardly likely to be engaged in merely shifting an old hulk of a merchantman. He called out that he had been tricked and the behaviour of the Admiral was not that of a gentleman. Juan de Ubilla retorted that 'he was following his calling like a captain and a fighter'. Hawkins response was to let fly an arrow at de Ubilla, while a companion at his side opened fire with an arquebus, killing a soldier next to the Admiral.

It was too soon. Half an hour or more had been allowed for the hulk to be worked alongside the *Minion*, and already the first shots had been fired. Juan de Ubilla frantically tried to find General Luxan and get instructions as to what he should do, but the General could not be found. He then made a decision which was entirely justified but roundly criticised later. It was obvious the English were aware of what was going on and were already clearing for action, therefore de Ubilla took it upon himself to signal the flagship, and the trumpet faithfully rang out across the harbour. With the cry of 'Santiago', the Admiral led the attack on the *Minion*, his men hauling for all their worth on the headlines and port stern anchor cable so as to lay the hulk alongside.

The overwhelming Spanish attack on the island immediately put the English defenders to flight and most of them were slaughtered. A few managed to scramble aboard the *Jesus*, berthed next to the *Minion*. Hawkins wasted no time. Fighting off the initial attack from the hulk, he managed to cast off the headlines and haul the *Minion* out to her stern anchors. From this position he opened fire on the Spanish. Luxan and de Ubilla then had the merchantman hauled up to the *Jesus*. The *Jesus* was now beset by two other Spanish ships which had worked themselves around offshore but, in a very hot engagement, all three attackers were fought off and the English sailors managed to cut the headlines of the *Jesus* and warp the ship out to join the *Minion*. From this position, about two ship's lengths away, they pounded the Spanish in a fierce fire-fight.

The Battle of San Juan de Ulua.

When, in 1567, John Hawkins was forced to enter the Mexican port of Vera Cruz he had only one aim in mind; to repair his ships and leave. The harbour was small and the ships made fast to the island of San Juan de Ulua with a Mediterranean moor, headlines ashore and anchors out astern. The water was deep enough for it to be possible to step from the bows of the vessels to the shore. His force of eight ships was too powerful for the Spanish to protest and all was going well until the New Spain flota of 13 ships arrived with the new Viceroy of New Mexico, Don Martin Enriquez. Obliged to permit the fleet to enter port, he obtained a promise from the Viceroy that he would be left in peace, but, as extra security, Hawkins took over the island and its fort.

All day was spent in reorganizing the ships in the now overcrowded port; the English fleet to one end of the shoreline and the Spanish to the other. Moored nearest the Spanish was Hawkins's large ship, the *Minion*, with Queen Elizabeth's even larger, 700-ton carrack, *Jesus of Lübeck*, next in line.

During the night the English, observing the Spanish preparing their ships for battle, began to suspect that the Spanish were planning an attack. The next morning a very large hulk of a merchant ship was warped into the narrow gap between the English and Spanish fleets. Hawkins recognised an officer on board as General Luxan and, knowing that it was very unlikely that this illustrious Spaniard would be overseeing the berthing of an old merchant ship, accused the general of treachery and opened fire with a crossbow and arquebus. Luxan was then forced to signal the assault before the Spanish forces were ready. During the night a large force had been smuggled into the hulk, and now the Spanish tried to warp the ship alongside the *Minion*. Hawkins immediately had the *Minion*'s headlines cut. The ship was hauled out to its stern anchors and from this position opened fire on the Spanish ships.

During the first hour of the battle, luck and good gunnery made it appear that the English would win the day. A fortunate shot ignited a powder barrel in de Ubilla's ship, the *almirante*, which blew up in an enormous explosion, scattering debris and bodies far and wide. The English gunfire then set the *capitana* ablaze and it seemed she also was finished, thus obliterating the two most powerful of the Spanish

ships. However, the *capitana* sank in shallow water and, although immobile, was able to continue the battle.

Meanwhile Luxan had taken over the shore batteries on the island, trained the guns on the English and opened fire. His Admiral, having failed to capture either the *Minion* or the *Jesus*, set about organising a fire-ship to launch against the two ships, but had trouble getting it alight and abandoned the attempt to assist the Viceroy, who seemed to be in difficulty in the distressed *capitana*. Finding that the Viceroy was in fact holding out bravely, de Ubilla returned to shore and persuaded the captain of one of the Spanish merchantmen to sell him his ship so that it could be prepared and sent as a fire-ship.

The English were congratulating themselves that they had put the two Spanish warships out of action when Luxan opened up with the batteries from the island. They were soon in trouble. All the smaller ships except Drake's *Judith* and the French *Grace of God* were sunk before they could get clear. The gunfire carried away the *Jesus*'s foremast, crippled the mainmast and holed her so badly that there was no hope of getting her out to sea. Hawkins ordered the *Minion* and *Judith* in behind the *Jesus* and used his battered flagship as a shield from the murderous and unanswerable fire from the fort. Hawkins realised he would have to sacrifice the *Jesus* and a start was made on transferring the treasure and victuals she carried to the two other ships, with the intention of sailing out of the harbour at nightfall, which was not far off. Captain Bland, in his *The Grace of God*, attempted to work around to windward of the Spanish and then send his ship down on the enemy as a fire-ship. Unfortunately she was dismasted and Bland left her after setting her afire.

It was now that de Ubilla's fire-ship appeared out of the smoke, bearing down on the three rafted English ships. While some kept their heads and were prepared to see whether the blazing ship might go clear, it seems the men in the *Minion* panicked and, without orders, cut themselves adrift and made sail.

Hawkins tried to get all the men from the *Jesus* into the *Minion* and barely had time to get aboard himself before the ships drifted apart. Unknowingly, among those he was forced to abandon in the *Jesus* was his terror-stricken 11-year-old nephew. (The boy was captured by the Spanish and finally married and settled down in Mexico.) As many of the others who could, crammed themselves into a small boat and followed the *Minion* and *Judith* as they sailed out of the harbour. The Spanish could only let them go. Without their *capitana* and *almirante*, the only ships serviceable were the merchant ships still laden with their cargoes from Spain. A north wind was blowing and the risk of losing more of the flota through shipwreck was too great.

It was dusk. In a battle which had lasted the best part of a day, Hawkins had lost his flagship and all the smaller vessels of his fleet. The two surviving ships were ill provided, battered and strained, overcrowded with weary and wounded survivors, and they were far away from home. That night the *Minion* came to anchor only 'two bow-shootes' away from the Spanish, and rode there until the morning. Drake in the *Judith* put out to sea and, as Hawkins described it, 'the same night forsooke us in our great miserie'. There is some question as to what actually happened to explain that rather bitter comment of John Hawkins. It is quite likely that he ordered Drake to take the more lively and weatherly little *Judith* clear out to sea to wait for him to work out the next day. However, the following morning Hawkins only managed to get near a small island a mile clear of the port when he was forced to anchor as a northerly gale set in. This same gale would have made the *Judith*'s position off a lee shore untenable and Drake set her on course for home. Hawkins nearly lost the *Minion* in the gale. Three cables and two anchors were sacrificed but the ship survived and followed the *Judith* out to sea on the next day, Saturday.

Desperate, the English in the *Minion* wandered about the inhospitable shores of the Gulf of Mexico, seeking a place to repair and provision the ship. The men were starving and there was no hope that all 200 survivors could make the voyage to England in the overcrowded vessel. At their request, Hawkins found an exposed beach where, given good weather, he could land 100 volunteers who were prepared to take their chance ashore, and also where he could get water for the ship. The day after landing the men, Hawkins took 50 of his remaining crew ashore to get water, but while they were filling the casks a gale sprang up and for 3 days Hawkins and his watering party could only sit on the beach and hope that the ship would ride it out. Once more the *Minion* survived, and with a fair wind she set out for home.

On the voyage to Europe the hundred or so remnants of Hawkins's venture barely survived. Everything was eaten – cats, dogs, rats and leather – and by the time the ship was driven by adverse winds and weakness to Ponte Vedra, near Vigo in Spain, many had died and those who remained could hardly work the ship. The survivors of that terrible voyage were further decimated by overindulging themselves in the Spanish port. It was clear they were not welcome in Ponte Vedra, so they made for Vigo. Here they got help from some English ships before sailing the *Minion* to England, where they arrived in Mounts Bay on 20 January. Drake, in his *Judith*, had arrived in Plymouth 5 days before.

Of the 400 men who left England in October 1567, only 70 returned. To the English the behaviour of Don Martin Enriquez was treacherous and unforgivable. Drake never forgot his experiences in San Juan de Ulua; doubtless they fired the spirit of vengeance in his later attacks on the Spanish.

ENGLISH VOYAGES OF SETTLEMENT

From the disastrous voyage of Richard Hore in 1536 until the 1570s, the English, in the absence of historical records, appear to have lost interest in the New World. The dearth of exploratory and colonising ventures, backed by merchants and sanctioned by the Crown, is apparent and understandable, for during those years England was preoccupied with other matters close to home. However, English fishermen in increasing numbers continued to make annual voyages westward, working the Grand Banks and the inshore fishing off Newfoundland. To these intrepid tradesmen an Atlantic crossing was no great adventure and by the time of England's first efforts at colonisation they must have had considerable local knowledge of the American continent's north-eastern seaboard, possibly as far south as the coast of Nova Scotia. Perhaps if Sir Humphrey Gilbert had drawn on the fishermen's expertise, his venture might not have failed so miserably.

Sir Humphrey Gilbert

Humphrey Gilbert was born either in 1537 or 1539, the second son in a family of five of a wealthy Devon landowner, Otho Gilbert. When Otho died in 1547, his wife, Katherine, remarried another of the Devonshire gentry, Walter Ralegh, and had three more children; a girl and two boys, one of whom was named for his father. Walter Ralegh Junior, at least 13 years younger than Humphrey, became closely involved in his half-brother's ventures and later took over the reins and attempted to establish England's first colony in Virginia.

At the age of 17 or 18 Humphrey entered the service of Queen Elizabeth. His first commission took him soldiering to France, where he may have met André Thevet, a French geographer. He returned from France in 1562, the year that Jean Ribault came home from a colony he had established in Florida, and when Jean visited England the following year, interest in North America was awakened. From the time Humphrey returned from France his enthusiasm was directed at arousing support for a search for a north-west passage, and in 1566 he wrote a 'discourse' in which he showed evidence for the existence of the strait and expounded on the benefits that would accrue to England. The first Englishman to do so, he suggested founding a colony, 'and settle there such needie people of our Countrie, which now trouble the common welth, and through want here at home, are inforced to commit outragious offences, whereby they are dayly consumed with the Gallowes.'[1]

Gilbert was knighted for his zeal in ruthlessly suppressing rebellions in Ireland between 1566 and 1570, and on his return he married Anne Aucher (or Ager). Throughout the following years he undertook a variety of occupations, including, during 1572, another spell of campaigning in the Netherlands. In 1576 his *Discourse* was published, but it seems that Martin Frobisher's voyages and the preparations for Drake's Pacific enterprise inspired Sir Humphrey to forego his main goal of a north-west passage and, in 1577, put before the Queen a more belligerent proposal. War with Spain, he considered, was inevitable, therefore England should strike first to cripple the Spaniards' seapower. Under the cover of colonising ventures, fleets could be sent out, firstly

to raid the Iberian fishermen off Newfoundland; the prizes could be brought back and surreptitiously disposed of on the Netherlands or English coasts and knowledge of the enterprise disavowed. Secondly, again under cover of letters patent for a colonising venture, an alliance could be made with the many successful rovers in the Caribbean and, using Bermuda as a base, a joint attack made on the Spanish treasure fleets. Finally, Gilbert proposed that Cuba and Santo Domingo should be captured preparatory to an assault on the Spanish mainland.

In 1578 Gilbert was granted letters patent, but the expedition which set out that year failed, possibly because of the privateering tendencies of many of his subordinates, and all the ships were back in Dartmouth the following spring.

After the shambles of this 1578 venture, Sir Humphrey's fortunes were at a low ebb, but he persisted with his schemes for a colony. In 1580, using what was probably the only ship remaining to him, he sent out a reconnaissance voyage to America. The ship was the *Squirrel*, a tiny, 8-ton frigate which had been included in the fleet of '78. Command was given to a Portuguese, Simon Fernandez, who had been master of Ralegh's *Falcon*. Fernandez was almost certainly once a pilot for the Carrera de Indias, but for some reason had an abiding hatred of the Spanish. He had been involved in privateering or outright piracy in the Caribbean, and had an unrivalled acquaintance with the American coast. He was a forceful and intolerant character, and while he was either liked or despised by his shipmates, Ralegh and Gilbert got along with him and valued his skill and knowledge. The Portuguese pilot's predilection for piracy was well known and

Gilbert had to put up a bond of £500 to guarantee Fernandez's behaviour on his voyage in the *Squirrel*.

After fitting out at Dartmouth, the *Squirrel* sailed in April 1580, crewed by about 11 men. She was back before the end of June. All that is known about the voyage is that they observed that the inhabitants of the lands they visited lived in round houses, and the *Squirrel* brought back some hides, perhaps from bison. It is suspected that they landed somewhere on the coast of New England. The voyage is quite remarkable and speaks well for the skill of Fernandez and the *Squirrel*'s seaworthiness. I calculate the little frigate was not much over 40 feet on deck, not much larger than Slocum's *Spray*, but probably not as handy.

Another voyage the same year was made by John Walker, who explored the River of Norumbega (Penobscot?) some 30 miles inland, claimed to discover a silver mine, and returned with 300 hides. Walker made the passage back in the remarkable time of 17 days. If Sir Humphrey was not directly involved with this voyage, he certainly knew of its results.

Sir Humphrey's fortune was still at a low ebb and it was 1582 before preparations for founding a colony got under way. Two prospecting voyages were planned in that year, one under Gilbert and another commanded by Anthony Brigham on behalf of a Catholic group seeking freedom from the restraints placed upon them in England. Gilbert's venture never sailed, but it is possible that Brigham made the voyage. In the same year a corporation was founded in Southampton titled 'The Merchant Adventurers of Sir Humphrey Gilbert'. Its members were guaranteed free trade and contributed funds in the hope of acquiring huge tracts of land within the radius of the 200 leagues specified by Sir Humphrey's patent. To encourage investors, wide publicity was given to the venture. Richard Hakluyt, the younger, published *Divers Voyages* that year, expounding the attributes of North America, and a public inquiry was conducted by the Queen's Secretary, Sir Francis Walsingham, and other notables. Apart from the information gathered by Hakluyt and the voyages of Fernandez and Walker, a 40-year-old sailor was brought before the committee to tell his incredible story.

David Ingram's story

David Ingram was none other than a survivor of the 100 men who had volunteered to be marooned on the shores of the Gulf of Mexico to relieve the crowding in Hawkins's battered *Minion*. In the course of a year, accompanied by two others named Richard Browne and Richard Twyde, he claimed to have walked from the Gulf to somewhere near Cape Breton, a distance of some 2000 miles. What an astonishing epic journey through the pristine heartlands of eastern America. He was guided and assisted, it seems, by a chain of amicable Indian peoples.

It is apparent that the native Americans, in spite of their interminable intertribal wars, were not commonly hostile to those who offered no threat. Verrazzano, Cartier and many others all attest to the initial friendliness and generosity of the Indians. Only when their resources were threatened, or when they were maltreated, did they understandably turn hostile. David Ingram's account, given before the commission, is a confusion of reasonably accurate observation and fabulous tales, the latter probably gathering gloss over the 12 years since his return. Plants, people and animals, including bison, are described fairly faithfully, but one must draw the line at, among other fantasies, vast quantities of gold and silver, elephants, a 'strange Beaste bigger than a beare' with its eyes and mouth in its breast, and another 'monstrous beast twise as big as an Horse', like a horse except its hinder parts were more like a greyhound and it had 2-foot-long horns growing out from its nostrils. This last could, of course, have been a walrus, but Ingram added for good measure that 'they are naturall enemies to the Horse'[2]. The three overlanders came out either on Northumber-

This little *pinnace* or *frigate* in which Sir Humphrey Gilbert lost his life seems to have been his favourite. By the last decades of the sixteenth century the details of larger ships were beginning to emerge from the murk. This was not the case for most of the small craft. The term *pinnace* had come to describe a range of vessels from over 100 tons down to the larger ships' boats and the term *frigate* was equally ill-defined. What differentiated Sir Humphrey Gilbert's *Squirrel*, apart from size, from other pinnaces and frigates is unknown, and rig can be discounted as it was the practice to re-rig smaller vessels for specific purposes. For her deep-sea voyages, the *Squirrel* was almost certainly square-rigged. Vessels as small as 40 tons often sported a ship rig but, at 10 tons, three masts are unlikely. The illustration of the *Squirrel* shows her with fore and main topsails, which, if they were carried, may well have been set flying, rather than with the lifts and braces shown.

The most difficult consideration is the question of tonnage. Tonnage measurement was based on the number of wine *tuns*, or *pipes* a vessel could stow. This could be determined by actually stowing the barrels, but by the last quarter of the sixteenth century, methods were being used to calculate a vessel's tonnage from her keel length, breadth and depth. Applying these rules, the *Squirrel*'s burthen gives a vessel of only 30 ft (9.14 m) on deck, surely too small for her achievements. Apart from the extensive voyages she made, her complement under the command of the Portuguese pilot Fernandez was about 11 men, and manning under the command of Sir Humphrey would have been about the same. Sir Humphrey, the general of the expedition, would require his own accommodation and in addition, space had to be found for stores, weapons and equipment.

It is much more likely that the *Squirrel*'s tonnage was arrived at by experience — in other words, it was found she could stow from 8 to 10 tons depending on the size of the casks. Her stowage space would be in the hold, where room would also have to be found for cables, equipment and crew. Aft there would also be accommodation of some sort for the master. As the size of a vessel reduces, the space taken up by these factors increases in proportion. Sailors, except in number, are not scaled down with the ship. The smaller ship's curves are tighter, making it more difficult to stow the casks efficiently. It would be fair to say that the rules become less accurate as the size of the vessel diminishes.

The *Squirrel* depicted here is 42 ft (12.2 m) on deck. She has a 30 ft (9.14 m) keel, 12 ft 6 in. (3.81 m) beam and 5 ft (1.52 m) depth. She is fully decked and could

almost be described as a scaled-down galleon. As she belonged for a number of years to Sir Humphrey, she would be well appointed and decorated. She is provided with six sweep ports each side and a raised poop deck, beneath which there is room for some modest accommodation for the admiral. Sir Humphrey, described by Queen Elizabeth as 'a man noted of not good happ by sea', was also criticized by his fellow captains for cluttering her up with boarding nettings, bases and swivel guns to the extent that the little vessel was put at risk. None of this is shown in the illustration and it can be left to the imagination how obstructive head-high boarding nets would be between the masts, and *fights* or waistcloths rigged above the gunwales.

land Strait or the coast of Nova Scotia, where they were picked up by a French ship and taken to Newhaven (Havre de Grâce), and from there they made their way home. Both Hawkins and Hakluyt appear to have confirmed the veracity of their journey, but Hakluyt, wary of the taller parts of the story, scrubbed it from the second edition of his *Principal Navigations*.

A sense of urgency now begins to hurry along Sir Humphrey's venture. The 6-year term of his patent was fast evaporating and Gilbert's entire fortune was dependent on the success of his colony. In February 1583 Queen Elizabeth gave him a fright and also somewhat hurt his pride. He heard through Walsingham that she had 'especial care for his well being and success', and desired him to stay at home, as 'a man noted of not good happ by sea'[3]. Gilbert wrote a piqued letter in reply, defending his seamanship, ability to survive on sea fare and immunity from seasickness. The Queen relented.

Sir Humphrey's fleet sails

By June 1583 Gilbert was ready to sail from Southampton with a fleet of five ships. These were:

Delight; 120 tons; flagship or admiral, in which sailed Sir Humphrey with William Winter, captain and part owner, and Richard Clarke, master.
Barke Ralegh; 200 tons; vice-admiral; supplied by Walter Ralegh. M. Butler, captain, and Robert Davis, of Bristol, master.
Golden Hinde; 40 tons; rear admiral. Edward Hayes, captain and owner, and William Cox, of Limehouse, master.
Swallow; 40 tons; a ship with some doubt over her ownership. Gilbert had not long before defeated a pirate, John Callis, in the Channel. The *Swallow* was Callis's ship and Gilbert took it over for the American voyage. She had belonged to a Scottish merchant before being pirated by Callis, and the Admiralty disputed Sir Humphrey's right to her. Her captain was Maurice Browne.
Squirrel; 10 tons; more than likely the same *Squirrel* that undertook the reconnaissance voyage. William Andrewes, captain, and Cade, master.

The total complement of all five ships was about 260, including shipwrights, masons, carpenters, smiths, minerologists and refiners. For entertainment and for the 'Allurement of the Savages', the usual orchestra was provided along with 'Morris dancers, Hobby horsse, and Maylike conceits to delight the Savage people'[4].

In early June they sailed from Southampton after delays which caused them to eat into their sea-stores. The season was rapidly slipping by, and before their departure there was some controversy as to whether the course should be laid north by way of Newfoundland or south by way of the trades and West Indies, so as to explore the coast north of Florida. This was favoured in view of the late season and the chance of finding a site to winter over in a kindly climate. Unfortunately, it seems that funds were unavailable to replace the quantities of provisions consumed before sailing and what was left was insufficient for the long haul through the trades. The northern route was decided upon as it was quicker and stores could be replenished from the fishermen in Newfoundland before steering south 'untill we arrived at places more temperate to our content'[5].

The first night out the weather turned foul, but the ships hung together until 13 June when *Barke Ralegh*, making her regulation evening report, hailed that they had many men sick. At midnight she turned about and sailed back to Plymouth, where it was later said they arrived in some distress, owing to some contagion, while other commentators indicated that she may have had insufficient stores. Whatever the cause, Sir Humphrey was furious that the vice-admiral had deserted when the wind was fair and the voyage going well. The *Golden Hinde* now became vice-admiral and Captain Hayes was quick to move his 'flagge from the mizon unto the foretop'[6].

From 15 to 28 June they had continuous fog and rain, with the wind varying between west-north-west and west-south-west, forcing them to make long boards as far south as 41° and, later, as far north as 51°. On 20 June those in the *Delight* and *Golden Hinde* lost sight of the *Swallow* and *Squirrel*. On the twenty-seventh, through the mists, they saw icebergs and then they came into soundings over the Banks. On 30 June, far to the north, they made an uncertain landfall in foggy weather, and became

embayed, they suspected, in Grand Bay. The description of the 'hideous rockes and mountaines, bare of trees'[7] fits the Labrador shore of the Strait of Belle Isle. Following the Newfoundland coast south, they saw and identified Penguin Island or Funk Island and sailed on to Conception Bay where, on 3 August, they found the *Swallow*.

All hands were elated at the reunion, but those in the *Delight* and *Golden Hinde* were amazed at the extravagant exuberance of those in the *Swallow*, who 'cast up into the air and overboard, their caps and hats in good plenty'[8], and saw that her sailors had somehow acquired new duds. It will be recalled that the *Swallow* was a late addition to the fleet, having been captured as a pirate. Her crew had remained with her but had not given up their old ways. Short of stores, and with her crew shivering in disintegrating rags, the *Swallow* had come across a fishing vessel homeward bound from Newfoundland. The crew, promising to behave themselves, persuaded Captain Browne to allow them to go aboard the fisherman to 'borrow' the provisions and clothing they needed. Once aboard, they proceeded to pillage the Newfoundlander of everything not nailed down. Sails, tackle, food and clothing were pilfered and, 'like men skillfull in such mischiefe'[9], they tortured the poor fishermen to extract the whereabouts of anything else worthwhile. Returning to the *Swallow* in the overloaded cock-boat, they were swamped. Some of the reprobates were drowned, but most were rescued, incomprehensibly, by the sailors they had just robbed and left, thousands of miles from home, without victuals, tackle and sails.

On the same day that the *Swallow* rejoined, they came up with the *Squirrel* anchored off the entrance of the harbour of St John's. At this time the Newfoundland fishermen were well organised and the different nationalities worked amicably together. The English, as their ships were the best armed and perhaps because of the tradition of Cabot's discovery of the island, had become dominant over other nations fishing south-east Newfoundland. English skippers took turns to fill the post of admiral at St John's and ruled the port for the benefit of all, including, on occasion, the defence of other nation's ships against the depredations of Englishmen.

Sir Humphrey was not prepared to be frustrated by the fishermen when he learned that the *Squirrel* had been refused entry into St John's, perhaps on account of the recent activities of English privateers. He readied his ships for battle, sent in a boat to declare his peaceful intentions, and, with the wind light, stood in for the narrow and spectacular entrance of St John's. The Narrows are about a half-mile in length and from 200 to 300 yards wide, with hills rising to about 700 feet on either side. The *Delight* ran aground by holding too far to the port-hand side of the Narrows. Her pilot, probably her master, had either failed to see or clear in the fluky wind an outlying rock – more than likely the Pancake lying about 50 yards offshore just before the Narrows open into the harbour. Fortunately the English fishermen came to the flagship's assistance with a number of boats and managed to tow her off. The four ships came quietly to anchor among 36 fishing vessels, 20 of which were Spanish and Portuguese and the remainder French and English.

The English claim St John's

As soon as the ships were anchored, a meeting was called in the flagship. All the expedition's captains and masters attended, along with the skippers of the English fishing vessels. Sir Humphrey displayed his patent and signified his intention of taking possession on behalf of the Crown. On the strength of this and, one imagines, his well displayed firepower, the General demanded that the fishermen should supply his captains' needs, and indicated that he wished to sail further south that season. Apparently the fishermen, of all nationalities, readily assented, and during the following days the expedition's officers, at least, fed royally on salmon,

trout and lobster accompanied by wines, marmalades, biscuits and 'sundry delicacies' generously supplied by the Portuguese.

On 5 August Sir Humphrey set up his tent ashore and, before all the assembled crews and fishermen, formally took possession of St John's and all the land within a radius of 200 leagues. He then proceeded to lease to the fishing captains parcels of shoreline for dressing and drying their fish. Edward Hayes claimed that this was appreciated, as the English often arrived too late to claim a site on a first-come, first-served basis. One imagines, also, that the fishermen quietly considered that it was unlikely that the rents would be collected often. While the ships were repaired, trimmed and stored, the next 2 weeks were spent examining the land, mapping and prospecting for ore. Of the latter, the General's mineralogist, a Saxon named Daniel, found iron and a sample that he swore on his life was silver. Sir Humphrey recommended caution in case the news got out among the French, Spanish and Portuguese; proof of the sample could be made after the ships had got back to sea. Captain Hayes was certain that Daniel had not found silver.

While 'the better sort' worked on refitting the ships, others of the expedition decided they had suffered enough. One party stole a ship laden with cod from a nearby harbour and sailed away with her, and others were caught plotting to make off with ships from the expedition. Many hid ashore, waiting a chance to work their passage home in a fishing vessel. Apart from the disaffected, many died and others were so sick they were given permission to go home. Among those who were not prepared to continue were the captains of the *Delight* and *Squirrel*, William Winter and William Andrewes.

So depleted did the company become that it was decided to dispense with the *Swallow*. She was provisioned to take home the sick, while her captain, Browne, and his piratical crew were transferred to the *Delight*. Whether Captain Maurice Browne was given command over the *Delight*'s master, Richard

Clarke, is not clear. The ex-*Swallow*'s captain was a little under a cloud owing to his lack of control over his crew and, although nominally in command, especially if it came to fighting, he could have well been subordinated to Clarke in nautical matters. This would explain why the blame for what was later to happen was placed on Clarke rather than Browne. Sir Humphrey chose to take over the *Squirrel*, either to avoid the *Swallow*'s unpleasant crew, or, as he claimed, because she was a handier ship for inshore exploration. Captain Hayes was highly critical of the General's nautical judgment in fitting the little frigate out with 'nettings & fights, and overcharged with bases and such small Ordinance, more to give a show, then with judgement to foresee unto the safetie of her and the men'[10]. Perhaps Elizabeth's protest that Gilbert was 'of not good happ by sea' had some justification.

On 20 August the *Delight*, *Golden Hinde* and *Squirrel* sailed from St John's. Their immediate destination was Sable Island, which was to become a veritable graveyard for shipping off that coast. They had heard from a Portuguese in St John's that he had been in a ship which had landed cattle and pigs on the island, and that since then the stock had multiplied considerably. It was Sir Humphrey's intention to provision with fresh meat before seeking his destination on the coast further south. After a calm spell off Cape Race, during which, in 2 hours, they caught 'fish so large and in such abundance, that many dayes after we fed upon no other provision'[11], they made some landings on the south coast before leaving Newfoundland for the island. Eight days out, in fickle winds and thick weather, they were in some doubt as to their position. On the evening of Tuesday, 27 August, soundings gave them white sand at 35 fathoms and they considered themselves close to Sable Island.

The *Delight* goes aground

Although it has been proposed that Sir Humphrey's ships were off Cape Breton, rather than Sable Island, at this time, their pilots' dead-reckoning had obviously placed them somewhere north-east or east of the island. All Wednesday they stood to the south-west. When the wind swung south in the evening, the ships closed up to discuss what course to lay. In the aftermath of what was to happen, explanations for the cause of the disaster conflict. Edward Hayes claims that the *Hinde* and the *Squirrel* were forced to follow the *Delight*, which remained the admiral, on an ill-advised course to the west-north-west, her master Richard Clarke claiming he could make no more to windward, regardless that the wind was south, a full 10 points free.

Clarke, in his defence later, insisted that Sir Humphrey had ordered the course to the west-north-west, and when the *Delight*'s master pointed out that the island lay in that direction 'but 15 leagues off, and that he should be upon the Island before day, if hee went that course', the General ordered him to obey 'in her Majesties name'[12]. Fearing Gilbert's authority, he did exactly what he was told. Although this is not anywhere stated, if the *Delight* remained the admiral, she was obliged to lead. But why, then, did not Clarke keep a better lookout? Hayes's account, apparently supported by Hakluyt, could be a cover-up for a disastrous decision made by Sir Humphrey, while Clarke was concerned with defending his reputation. Both stories could be slanted and what happened a combination of errors made by Gilbert and Clarke. The following interpretation of the causes and actions leading to the disaster is conjecture.

On the evening of Wednesday, 28 August, the weather was pleasant and fine, but high cirrus and perhaps a southerly swell portended that these conditions would deteriorate. The wind had veered to the south, putting the ships hard on the port tack, and it was likely to veer further. Both Clarke and Cox reckoned that Sable Island lay 45 to 50 miles to the north-west. With night approaching, Gilbert in his *Squirrel* closed up with the *Delight* and asked her master, Clarke, what course he considered the best to follow. Clarke proposed west-south-west, a course which would maintain a good offing and keep clear to windward of Sable Island should the weather turn foul, as appeared likely. At this time the ships were probably not making more than 3 knots, and Gilbert, anxious to get this diversion for stores behind him, calculated that at their present speed they would make their landfall during daylight on the following day, and they could stand directly in for the island, and so ordered Clarke to steer west-north-west. Clarke argued for caution but was overruled and brought his ship off to the west-north-west as commanded.

Gilbert now approached the *Golden Hinde* and spoke to Captain Hayes and Cox, who both suggested west-south-west as the better course. The General now realised that he may have made a mistake, but was not prepared to admit just then that he had ordered Clarke to the west-north-west. Instead he instructed Hayes to follow the admiral which, with a free wind, was by now some distance off in the dusk, with her crew, according to Hayes, whooping it up to the accompaniment of 'Trumpets, with Drummes, and Fifes'[13] and 'winding' the cornets and haughtboyes.

The southerly wind began to freshen and the *Golden Hinde*, sometime before midnight, came within hailing distance of the *Delight* and called for her to come round to west-south-west. Over the wind and sea, Clarke's reply was misheard to the effect that he couldn't point higher, or 'lie otherwise', whereas he had in fact answered that he was following orders and could not steer another course on the instructions of Hayes. Continuing to lead the way as was his duty, Clarke stood on, followed by the *Hinde* and then the *Squirrel* which, with the wind aft of the beam, would have been slower than the two larger ships.

Further communication was not possible as the weather worsened, with a strong wind from the south by east, rain and fog. At any time, at least until the weather really shut in, Gilbert could have fired a gun, the signal that a ship was in danger. This would have brought both the *Delight* and the *Golden Hinde* up to him. That he didn't could indicate either that he wished the course to be maintained, or that he was not prepared to admit his mistake to Clarke.

Shortly after dawn the *Golden Hinde* found herself in shoal water and started sounding, finding alternately shoal and deeps every four ship's lengths or so. Cox then claimed he could see what looked like white cliffs, but Hayes reckoned Cox had seen breaking water. Signals were straight away made to the admiral to come about and make out to sea, but it was too late. At 7 am the *Delight* struck.

Why, if the *Delight* was some distance ahead of the *Golden Hinde*, did not Clarke, or any in the admiral, realise they were running through shoals? Perhaps Clarke, having spent an anxious night on

The *Delight* was stranded in a welter of breaking seas and on a lee shore, so it was impossible for the other vessels to offer assistance and they could only beat up and down as close as they dared and hope the men in the *Delight* might be able to get off in boats or rafts. Fortunately for some of the complement, the largest ship's boat, the pinnace, had been left towing astern. Sixteen crew, including the master Richard Clarke, managed to swim to the boat before it was swept away. With only one oar, it was impossible to get to windward and the safety of the other ships; instead they were driven to leeward across the banks. After 7 days, 14 of the survivors in the overloaded boat managed to make the coast of Newfoundland where, after another 5 days, they were taken aboard a Basque vessel in which they sailed to Spain. They were smuggled across the border into France and were home in England by the end of the year.

There are some historians who consider that the wreck may have been on Cape Breton rather than Sable Island and this possibility can not be excluded. However, the navigators' dead-reckoning position on the eve of the wreck did place Sable Island to the north-west and they certainly found shoal water as expected.

deck, relaxed with the dawn and nipped down below for a break. Many of his sailors were not what one might call conscientious, for a good number were made up from the larcenous crew of the *Swallow*, and the watch may well have relaxed their vigilance when Clarke left the deck. Clarke would have refrained from blaming his watch, as the ultimate responsibility remained with him, and all he writes is that 'about seven of the clocke in the morning the ship stroke on the ground'[14]. There does appear to be a certain casualness about Clarke; for example, his stranding in the Narrows, and, if I am correct, his blind acceptance of Gilbert's dangerous decision. Ironically, it was this trait that was to save his life.

Those in the *Golden Hinde* and *Squirrel* were appalled to see the *Delight* come about and, in stays, drive aground stern first where the pounding quickly smashed the after part of the ship. Frantically the *Hinde* and *Squirrel* were 'cast about', which presumably implies that they wore or came about on to the other tack. As the wind came forward of the beam, the full force of the gale made itself felt as the ships plunged to windward over and through the heavy, steep, breaking shoal-water seas. Anxiously retracing their course, hard on the wind to the east-south-east, they gradually clawed their way clear and had time to turn their attention to the *Delight*. Through the murk to leeward they could see the wreck, but in the high seas off that grim lee shore there was no way in which they could render assistance.

During that day and part of Friday, they beat up and down, approaching as near as the shallow water and breaking sea would allow, hoping the weather would ease and watching for those in the *Delight* to attempt to get off in the boats or possibly a raft. Some time on Friday they gave up, but still continued to fetch up and down, hoping the weather would clear so that they could see land. Instead, it continued thick and blustery, and it got colder. Those in the diminuitive *Squirrel* began to suffer from lack of warm clothing, the wet, and short rations. They

begged the General to turn for home 'before they all perished'[15].

The men of the *Hinde*, weary of the poor conditions, sympathised and also opted for home. Hayes and Cox were for continuing but, on Saturday afternoon, 31 August, Sir Humphrey called them all together and, claiming he had seen enough this trip and would set out again next year, ordered the ships on a homeward course. As they came round on to their course, what was apparently a walrus, 'a very lion' with his head turning 'to and fro, yawning and gaping wide, with ougly demonstration of long teeth, and glaring eies' came alongside the *Hinde* and bade them farewell in a 'horrible voyce, roaring or bellowing as doeth a lion'[16]. The General took this as a good omen.

Loss of the *Squirrel*

With a fair wind but high sea they made good time and raised Cape Race on the second day. The same day Sir Humphrey, who had driven a nail into his foot, came aboard the *Hinde* to have the wound dressed. He was entreated to stay on the larger ship for his own safety, but would have none of it and returned to his *Squirrel*. Later on the passage, the weather being fair, Sir Humphrey came once more on the *Hinde*, where he stayed all day, making merry but also lamenting the loss of the *Delight* and his books and notes which had been in her. Suddenly turning upon his boy in fury, he beat the poor lad, berating him for failing to obey his orders when, on the Newfoundland coast, he had sent him across to the *Delight* to recover some items he had left there. On the boy's return one item was missing and Hayes conjectured that it was the sample of ore Daniel, now lost in the *Delight*, had found in St John's. They also discussed plans for the following year, Gilbert stating that he now favoured Newfoundland and would return there, while the *Hinde* should explore to the south. Once more the General was entreated to leave the *Squirrel*, but Sir Humphrey again refused

to 'forsake my little company' and returned to his ship in the evening.

Somewhere in the outer Western Approaches the weather turned foul with an enormous, confused swell, heavier than any of the experienced sailors had ever seen, and St Elmo's fire played around the mainyard of the *Hinde*. On the afternoon of Monday 9 September, they saw the *Squirrel* nearly overwhelmed, but she survived. When she was settled down, Hayes tells us that the General was sitting aft with a book in his hand, and each time they managed to work within hailing distance, he called out, 'We are as neere to heaven by sea as by land'[17]. Some critics have expressed doubts that it would have been possible to sit and read a book on deck in those conditions, and that the ships would have been unable to approach each other. I see no reason to disbelieve the story on this account. With a following wind and sea, however stiff, it can be quite comfortable to sit in the lee of a bulwark, or in the case of the *Squirrel*, a weather cloth stretched across the poop rail, and with careful handling the *Hinde* could get within hailing distance, but probably not hold her position.

About midnight that same night, those in the *Golden Hinde*, which was following in the wake of the *Squirrel*, saw the latter's lights go out suddenly, and the watch sang out that the General was lost. All the next day and during the following gruelling, stormy 12 days as they worked into the Channel, they kept a careful watch for the *Squirrel*, but the little ship was never heard of again. On Sunday, 22 September, narrowly escaping going ashore in fog, they made Falmouth, and later sailed on to Dartmouth, where Hayes reported the loss of the *Squirrel*. To get the crew, now weary, disgruntled and demanding their pay, nearer home, the *Hinde* was sailed on to Weymouth. It may be just a coincidence that about this time a French ship was taken, robbed and sailed into Poole 'by an English ship retorrning from Terra Florida & newe lande'[18].

To return to the *Delight*, stranded and being

pounded to pieces on Sable Island or, alternatively, perhaps on some strand of Cape Breton Island. The day before the disaster had been calm, and during the evening a soldier had bagged a bird of some sort which was lying in the water not far from the ship. The sailors got permission to swing out the pinnace, a large boat measuring about 1½ tons, to recover the game, but when they returned they took out the oars and equipment and left the boat in tow. Clarke neglected to hoist in the boat or chose to leave it astern for the night, and it was well that he did. When the *Delight* struck she must, as I have suggested, have done so stern first, for the boat survived. Exposed to the breakers, it would have been smashed under the stern of the *Delight* if it was to seaward. Some of the company who could swim managed to get aboard the pinnace and began to haul as many survivors as they could out of the water, including Clarke. Although they watched for Captain Browne, they never saw him, but according to Hayes one of the survivors told him that the Captain, true to the best tradition of the sea, refused to leave his ship until the last man had left.

In all, 16 made it to the boat before it parted company with the wreck. With only one oar left in the boat, they could do little but drift before the heavy seas. After 2 days, with the boat overloaded and barely able to stay afloat, one of the men suggested that lots should be drawn for who to be cast overboard to lighten her, but Clarke refused the suggestion, stating that 'we will live and die together'[19].

Seven days after the wreck, during which two men had died, the starving sailors came ashore in Newfoundland. They had no idea where they were, but were grateful that the country was well stocked with peas and berries, on which they lived while they rowed their boat along the shore for 5 days. In a river they came upon a Basque ship which landed them in Spain, not far from the border with France. The kindly Basque captain covered for them when the Spanish authorities came aboard, and that

night put them ashore to make their way into France. The 14 survivors of the *Delight* got back to England at the end of 1583.

Roanoke

Walter Ralegh, undeterred by the loss of his half-brother Humphrey Gilbert, picked up the baton in the effort to plant a colony at Roanoke on the North Carolina seaboard. In 1584, Queen Elizabeth granted her aspiring favourite a patent to continue with Gilbert's plan to settle a colony, provided that he did not infringe on the territory extending 200 leagues southward from Newfoundland, which had been annexed by Gilbert. Although this limited his search for a site to the coastline between the Spanish and French settlements in the south, and southern Maine in the north, he was still left with an immense region in which to find good land and, most importantly, a secure and accessible harbour.

A leading motive for founding the colony was to be its use as a base for operations in the West Indies and for forays against the homeward-bound flotas. This may have influenced the Portuguese pilot, Fernandez, to take them to Roanoke instead of the more secure harbours of the Chesapeake. He may have known that, in 1570, the Spanish had already tried a missionary settlement in the region. The Jesuits had been massacred by the Indians, and vicious Spanish reprisals made the Chesapeake unsafe for Europeans. Not only would it be unsafe, but the Chesapeake was the first place the Spanish were likely to search, should they suspect an English base to the north. Among many other causes, it was the impractical, shoal and exposed nature of the American terminus of their Atlantic lifeline among the outer banks of North Carolina, to which Fernandez guided the first settlers, that caused the failure of repeated settlement attempts and the final loss of the colony by the English.

The art of colonisation was then in its infancy. Pioneers who first landed could only be supplied initially with provisions to last them for a time which was insufficient to experiment and establish a system of husbandry capable of fulfilling their basic requirements. If the seaborne supply failed, unless they were to starve, the settlers were forced to lean on the native population, who were skilled in hunting, fishing and, to some extent, planting. The goodwill and generosity of the unpredictable American Indians could evaporate, and the attempts of the colonists to extract food supplies by force inevitably led to outright hostility and bloodshed. Instead of applying themselves to providing their own resources, the settlers were then obliged to concentrate on defence. Alternatively, to relieve the pressure on the local population and depleted natural food sources, a colony could break up into small groups, widely dispersed among the surrounding natives. Inevitably, even granted freedom from the internal strife which seemed endemic in those hot-headed days, disease, Indian attacks and accidents took their toll until the colony dwindled to extinction. All of these vicissitudes were to be suffered by the English attempting to settle at Roanoke during the last years of the sixteenth century.

The first exploratory landing took place in July 1584 when, for the second time, possession was formally taken in the name of Queen Elizabeth. Sir Francis Drake had, in 1579, performed a similar ceremony, just north of San Francisco. In June 1585 the first settlement was made, only to be abandoned the following year, just before the supply ships under the command of Richard Grenville arrived. The 15 brave men left by Grenville to guard the abandoned colony were never seen again.

In 1587 another attempt was made which included 89 men, 9 children and 17 women. Two of the latter were pregnant and gave birth to the first English children to be born in America, before the ships left for home the same year. It was the new

The *Tiger*

Loaned by Queen Elizabeth I to Sir Walter Ralegh for use on the first expedition to Virginia, the *Tiger* was described as a galeasse measuring somewhere between 150 and 200 tons. From Spanish records, she carried her main armament on two decks and, just as a thumbnail sketch on a map gave some clue to Verrazzano's *La Dauphine*, so does a surprisingly technically accurate sketch on a map help to illustrate the ship with a little more confidence.

The sketch shows a standard three-masted rig on a long hull with very little sheer from the aftercastle forward. The roundhouse forming the poop is reminiscent of the *tilt* of a galley, and the long straight beakhead is also peculiar to that of a galley where it originally served as à ram. However, the *Tiger* was neither a galley nor a galeasse in the true sense of the term. A fair general description of sixteenth-century galeasses would be as seagoing vessels with two decks capable of being rowed or sailed. The lower deck was taken up with rowing benches and the upper deck mounted most of the main armament. While Mediterranean galeasses were clearly heavy, modified galleys, those used by the English during the time of Henry VIII had more of the appearance of a sleek sailing ship. When the *Tiger* sailed for Virginia, the English had discarded the galeasse, but they had not forgotten the superior sailing qualities of its hull. Many of the Elizabethan galleons designed for speed, manoeuvrability and fighting power were built in the 'form of a galeasse' and it could be that Sir Richard Grenville's flagship was one of these.

settlers' intention to attempt to find a better location and haven on the Chesapeake, but when they called in to pick up the men left by Grenville, Fernandez claimed it was too late in the year to continue, and insisted they stay at Roanoke.

The next year was that of the Spanish Armada, and the ships sent out never arrived, preferring to chase the Spanish rather than relieve the colony. Due to lack of finance, no assistance was sent until 1590,

when the settlement was found abandoned and foul weather drove the ships from the exposed anchorage before a search could be undertaken. This was the last known attempt to reach Roanoke, although there are indications that contact was made in later years and that there was a belief that the colony continued to exist, probably on the Chesapeake. When Christopher Newport sailed in to found the Jamestown settlement in 1607, it may well be that his arrival provoked the chief, Powhatan, to wipe out the neighbouring Chesapian Indians and along with them the survivors of Ralegh's second colony.

The Virginia companies

King James, on his accession to the throne in 1603, immediately set about making peace with the Spanish and in the process made redundant the multiplicity of private warships of the privateers. It was possibly the redirected energies of the privateering owners, captains and crews, together with other factors, which inspired the fresh attempts to settle the eastern seaboard of North America during the early years of the reign of the first Stuart.

Voyages of American settlement made by Bartholomew Gosnold in 1602, during which a colony was attempted on Cuttyhunk Island in Buzzard's Bay, and Martin Pring in 1603, were sponsored by prospective investors. In 1605 a group interested in founding a colony in the region of Maine, among them Sir Thomas Arundell, who was determined on setting up a Catholic colony in America, financed another exploratory voyage. Under the command of Captain George Waymouth, the ship *Archangell* left Dartmouth on 31 March, and made landfall off Nantucket on 14 May. Shoals prevented a landing, so, short of water and firewood, Waymouth turned north, anchored off Monhegan Island and sent in a landing party. The mast trees, spring vegetation and fishing looked extremely promising, but as the anchorage was exposed, they sailed on to come to anchor behind Allen Island in a haven they named St Georges Harbour, a name which has survived. After exploring the region, making several trips up the St George River, and leaving a cross set up on Allen Island, they sailed for home on 16 June and arrived at Dartmouth on 18 July.

Arundell had left England and withdrawn from the project. In the year 1605 the Gunpowder Plot was exposed, and later attempts to found a Catholic settlement in Virginia failed to get off the ground. Nevertheless, in April 1606 two Virginia Companies were founded. The London company sought to settle in Virginia in the region of the Roanoke colonies, with a charter of rights between 34° and 41° north, and the Plymouth company was granted rights between 38° and 45° north. The overlapping territories were a quirk of King James, but were to cause no conflict as the latitude of Cape May, on the southern tip of Long Island, came to be the demarcation. The different geographical aims of the two companies reflect their hometown commercial interests. Plymouth, with interests in Newfoundland fishing, furs and train oil, wished to have an all-year-round source of these products, while the London merchants hoped to provide themselves with southern produce such as fruit, wines, dyes and sugar. At this period political troubles and piracy were interfering with trade to Spain, Portugal and the Mediterranean, and the Spanish in the West Indies were remorseless in their dealing with those who dared to intrude in their waters. Timber and iron resources were expected to be utilised in both colonies.

Another voyage to Maine was made in 1606 by Captain Thomas Hanham, with Martin Pring as master. Combined with earlier reports of precious metals in the region and the positive account of Waymouth's summer cruise, Hanham's and Pring's observations were sufficiently encouraging for the preparations to found a colony to be put in hand. Two vessels were employed, a ship, *Mary and John*, under the command of Raleigh Gilbert, a son of Sir Humphrey, and a flyboat, *Gift of God*, under the command of George Popham, nephew of Sir John Popham, the Lord Chief Justice and one of the principal investors in the company.

The ships took their departure from the Lizard on 1 June 1607. Separated on the voyage, the *Mary and John* was the first to arrive near the rendezvous at Waymouth's anchorage and was still fumbling around searching for the cross left by Waymouth when the *Gift of God* sailed straight in on 7 August. Clearly there was someone on board who had been there before. After nearly losing the *Mary and John* in a gale, the two ships anchored in the Sagadahoc on 16 August.

The settlers seem to have got off to a good start for, after the *Mary and John* had sailed for home, and before the winter had really set in, they had built several houses, a church, a fort, a storehouse, possibly completed a shallop, and set up the frame for 'a pretty Pynnace of about some thirty tonne, which they called the *Virginia*; the chief shipwright being one Digby of London'.[20]

Although in the course of the bitter Maine winter the *Virginia* was completed and a profitable trade in furs achieved with the Indians, some of the pioneers perished, among them their leader, George Popham, whereupon Captain Raleigh Gilbert took over leadership. The *Mary and John* left England in March with supplies for the colony and was able to take on a good number of furs which had been collected from around the coast by the *Virginia* during the winter. Another supply ship, which sailed from England in July, arrived with the news that Gilbert's brother had died, necessitating his return. Having found no metals, neither base nor precious, with no firm leadership, and discouraged by the severity of the previous winter, the entire colony packed up and sailed home in the supply ship and the pinnace, *Virginia*, said to be the first vessel to be built by Europeans on the north-east American seaboard. For the time being the Plymouth Company sat on its heels, content to continue to trade across the Atlantic on a seasonal basis. The company was to revive again 12 years later when another, more determined, venture was organised.

During the same year that the Popham settlers sailed, the London Virginia Company, with the patronage of such illustrious and powerful people as Sir Robert Cecil, Richard Hakluyt, Robert Rich, who was to become the Earl of Warwick, and others, set about planting their settlement in Virginia. Captain Christopher Newport, who had proudly sailed an enormous captured Portuguese carrack, *Madre de Dios*, into Plymouth in 1591, commanded the first expedition of the London Virginia Company. Two ships, the *Susan Constant* and *Godspeed*, and a pinnace, *Discovery*, with 120 settlers in addition to their crews, left the Downs on 1 January 1607. Sailing the southern route, they arrived in the Chesapeake on 16 April and laid the foundations of Jamestown on the peninsula between the James and York rivers.

Newport broke the seals of the document bearing the names of the first seven councillors, among them Bartholomew Gosnold and the most renowned of all, Captain John Smith, who, true to form, arrived in irons after creating dispute and disharmony on the voyage out. His intelligent, forthright and resourceful, if rather flamboyant, character was paramount in enabling the colony to survive during its first years. By the time Newport arrived with reinforcements in 1608, Gosnold had died and Captain John Smith had survived his adventures with Pocahontas and secured the friendship of her father, Chief Powhatan. Regardless of this achievement, on Newport's arrival Smith was languishing in the colony's lock-up under sentence of death, and also imprisoned was the elected governor, Edward Maria Wingfield. Over half of the settlers had died.

In spite of reinforcement and resupply, the infant colony was staggering under the losses caused by disease, starvation and despair. Many were soldiers brought out to defend the settlement against possible attacks by the Spanish, and took unkindly to the necessity to adapt to scratching a living and providing shelter. It was only by Smith's determined efforts, after he had been released, that the colony survived into the following year, 1609. During this year a new charter was formed, placing the control with the Virginia Company and not the Crown, and providing for much greater incentives for

emigrants. Under this charter Sir George Somers, Sir Thomas Gates and Captain Newport took command of nine ships, including the Popham colonies pinnace, *Virginia*, and 1500 settlers and sailed from England on 1 June 1609.

Arriving north of the Bahamas at the height of the hurricane season, the fleet was caught by a severe storm in which one vessel was lost and Sir George's and Sir Thomas's ship, the *Sea Adventure*, was so distressed that she had to be run ashore in the uninhabited Bermudas. Everyone got safely ashore and the party was fortunate to find an ample supply of fresh pork from pigs which had bred from the originals left there by some farsighted Portuguese navigator years before. Rescue was improbable, so all winter the marooned crew and prospective

Reputed to be the first vessel launched on the north-east American seaboard, the *Virginia* was built during the winter of 1607 and 1608 by the Popham colonists in Maine at the mouth of the Sagadahoc River from timber felled more or less on site.

She was classed as a *pinnace*, a term which was applied to a range of craft from large boats to 200-ton ships and could refer to a type of vessel or to her employment. Most pinnaces used by colonists were in the 20- to 70-ton range and the success of the colonies often depended on the pinnaces' ability to work inshore waters as well as make ocean passages. The cranky *Speedwell*, which attempted to sail with the *Mayflower*, measured about 60 tons, whereas the *Virginia* was rated at 30 tons, giving her a possible overall length of a little over 50 ft, a breadth of between 13 and 14 ft and a depth of 6 ft.

A sketch of a vessel shown on the plan of the fort which was to be built by the colonists shows a single-masted spritsail-rigged vessel which may well represent

The pinnace *Virginia* under square rig

the *Virginia*. This rig was in common use for coasting craft which had to be able to work well to windward. She also carries what today would be a fore-staysail, but what in those days was described as a foresail. When setting out on long voyages she was almost certainly re-rigged, for the heavy sprit is not a comfortable rig off the wind and in a heavy sea, or, for that matter, in a calm with an ocean swell running. Her ocean rig would quite likely be that of a form of *ketch*, a bowsprit, perhaps a small spritsail, a large square mainsail and a lateen mizzen.

As soon as she was launched, the *Virginia* was put to work collecting furs and sassafras around the Maine coastline and running errands for the colony. Unwilling to face another frigid Maine winter and disappointed in not finding metals, precious or otherwise, the settlers packed up and returned to England in the fall of 1608, sailing in one of the Plymouth Company ships, the *Gift of God,* and the *Virginia*. On the passage, the *Virginia* beat her larger companion into Plymouth by 5 days.

Subsequently, she made many transatlantic voyages, including the voyage of Gates and Somers which barely arrived in time to save the Jamestown colony from abandonment in 1610 and, at times, ran salted and dried cod from Newfoundland to Virginia. She sailed back and forth across the Atlantic for about 20 years before she was wrecked on the Irish coast bringing a cargo of Virginian tobacco to England.

settlers from the *Sea Adventure* laboured to build two pinnaces from her timbers. In May 1610 the two little ships sailed into the James River to find an appalling welcome.

During 1609, before the new settlers arrived, Captain John Smith, who had taken up the post of governor since all the other councillors had died or left, had divided the colony into three groups to live off the Indians, fishing and oysters. Unfortunately, the starving settlers lost his powerful leadership when Smith was injured by exploding gunpowder and had to sail for England with the departing 1609 fleet. Lacking strong leadership, with insufficient supplies, the new and surviving old colonists were left to make out as best they could, with the result that, from the 500 who began the winter of 1609–10, only 60 half-starved, diseased survivors remained to greet the two pinnaces from Bermuda in May 1610. That winter was to be recalled bitterly as 'the starving time', a time of terrible privation when even the dead were eaten and one man was executed for killing and eating his wife.

With only provisions for 2 weeks remaining, a decision was made to abandon Jamestown and sail for Newfoundland to get sufficient supplies from the fishermen for the voyage to England. On 7 June, leaving the little town in ruin, the colonists embarked in four pinnaces – the two built in Bermuda, the *Virginia* and one other. While these were anchored at the mouth of the James River another pinnace hove in sight and ran in to tell the departing colonists that relief was on the way, for Lord de la Warre (Delaware) was not far off with three ships sent out by the Virginia Company. Somers and Gates ordered a return to Jamestown and the crisis, when yet another attempt at settlement may have failed, was over. Lord de la Warre sent Sir George Somers and Captain Samuel Argall off to Bermuda to harvest the hogs which abounded there. Argall failed to find the islands, but Somers made his landfall, only to die there before the end of the year. The Bermudas, first known as the Somers Islands, henceforward came under the control of the Virginia Company.

By encouragement and the establishment of a firm discipline, Lord de la Warre enabled the Jamestown colony to survive and finally prosper. Hunger and troubles for the colony were by no means over, but never again was it to suffer such hardships as it had done during its first 3 years.

81

THE PILGRIMS

After 1603, the year King James succeeded to the throne of England, life for those who refused to conform to the tenets of the Anglican Church became progressively more difficult. The abortive Gunpowder Plot in 1605 created a new wave of hysteria and persecution against Catholics and, as rebels against the Anglican Church, Separatists.

One group of Puritan separatists settled in the Dutch town of Leyden in 1609 where, after initially prospering, their unwillingness to integrate with the Dutch resulted in discontent, poverty and rebellious youngsters. These irritations and an uncertain political environment spurred their leaders, William Brewster, John Robinson and John Carver, with Robert Cushman to seek another home across the Atlantic, initially in South America but finally in the new colonies in Virginia. After much negotiation and difficulty, they managed to draw up an agreement with a London merchant, Thomas Weston, and obtain a patent through the London Virginia Company. They gladly accepted the request that a number of London and other English Separatists be allowed to join them in the venture.

While the final negotiations were being completed a search for suitable vessels had produced an 180-ton ship from Harwich, and a smaller 60-ton vessel, the *Speedwell*, at Delfshaven. Short of money and inherently parsimonious, the Pilgrims, although utter tyros in the art of settlement and shipwrightry, refused to seek outside advice and help. Regardless of his experience and the fact that he had thoroughly explored a large part of the eastern American seaboard, they turned down an offer from Captain John Smith to accompany them on the voyage, and

did not even listen to his advice. Their obduracy was to cost them dearly in their choice of the *Speedwell* and their refitting of her.

Little is known of the detail of the *Speedwell*. She was understood to be about 60 tons, but this could be ambiguous for, as a Dutch vessel, she may have been measured in Dutch *lasts*, which were equivalent to about 2 English tons. If, as is likely, the 60 tons refer to the English measure, *Speedwell*'s length overall might have been in the vicinity of 60 ft, with a beam of 18 to 20 ft. A Dutch seascape including a vessel which could possibly represent the *Speedwell* shows a spritsail-rigged *jaght*, the size of which seems to more or less fit the English tonnage. The size is more in keeping with the normal dimensions of the pinnaces used in colonial activities in those days.

After her refit, the *Speedwell* was capable of embarking 66 passengers on the passage from Leyden to Southampton, and was expected to carry 30 across the Atlantic. What is certain is that she was in no fit condition to face an Atlantic voyage. The Pilgrims had purchased her without engaging the services of a surveyor, and then set about altering her so as to accommodate as many passengers as possible, almost certainly by the addition of a quarterdeck or increasing the size of the existing one. For the ocean passage it appears she was also re-rigged, maybe to the standard square main and lateen mizzen, but in doing so, the inexpert enthusiasts over-sparred her. Either she was unsound when she was purchased, or the attentions of the novice craftsmen made her so, for she was never to reach America. Reynolds, who was to captain the *Speedwell*, joined her in May, and was present when the refit was still in progress. It would have been

thought that, as an experienced seaman and one who was to chance his life in her, he would have spoken out on the vessel's faults and ill-advised modifications. Perhaps he did, but, faced with the stubborn enthusiasm of the Puritans, his protests were ignored.

In the literature of the Pilgrim Fathers there are conflicting theories concerning the debacle of the *Speedwell*. One authority places the blame squarely on the nautical inexperience of the Pilgrims, another on the cowardice of Captain Reynolds, and yet another attributes the sad outcome to a rather complicated conspiracy between Sir Ferdinando Gorges, the Earl of Warwick, and Captain Christopher Jones of the *Mayflower*, to take over, as they did, the venture for the Plymouth Company and divert the Pilgrims from northern Virginia, about Delaware Bay, to the company's allotted regions in Maine and New England.

With John Carver, Cushman and Weston completing arrangements in England, John Robinson thankfully called for a 'Day of Humiliation, to seek the Lord of his direction'[1] before his flock embarked in the *Speedwell*. Incredibly, only now did it seem to occur to them that it was impossible for the whole congregation of about 300 people to sail in the small ship. Some members were at any rate reluctant to leave, but dividing the rest into those who would go and those who would stay was a difficult and heartbreaking business. Mainly the young and fit, tradesmen and Elders were selected, 66 in all. Under the terms of a compact, those

The landfall of the *Mayflower* off Cape Cod

who remained behind under the strong leadership of Brewster, were to follow on when possible, hopefully the next year. Alternatively, should the venture fail, the pioneers were to be allowed to return unhindered.

On 22 July 1620, after emotional and heartfelt prayers, and to the accompaniment of a volley from muskets and three small cannon, the *Speedwell* sailed from her berth at Delfshaven, bound for Southampton.

After a pleasant 3-day summer passage down Channel the *Speedwell* came to anchor in Southampton, within sight of their flagship, the 180-ton *Mayflower*. Time was taken to reorganise the distribution of passengers between the ships and complete the loading. Everything the Pilgrims considered they needed had to be packed into the ships. As was customary in those days, the passengers supplied their own provisions and bedding for the voyage. Into the hold went further provisions, tools, furniture, utensils, clothing and shoes, weapons and very likely a printing press. Salt, so important for the preservation of fish, which they realised was to be their staple food for a while, had to be loaded in quantity, along with nets. The salt and fish nets came from Holland, along with two other products of that country, cheese and Dutch gin – or perhaps schnapps. All the other provisions were supplied at Southampton. The armament of the *Mayflower* belonged to the ship, so, in addition, to defend the settlement they took with them muskets, four small cannon, two 10-ft, 4-inch sakers, two 3-pounder minions and two bases firing a one-pound ball. In addition to the ship's skiff and longboat, a shallop capable of carrying 32 people and probably about 30 ft long was taken apart and stowed carefully below. No cattle or horses were taken, but probably some pigs, sheep and goats were penned on deck, and the boats contained hutches for poultry and rabbits. Dogs also were included in the small menagerie.

The loading proceeded smoothly, apart from some acrimony over accommodation when the Pilgrims from Leyden discovered the London contingent had already made themselves at home in the *Mayflower*. They would have been able to sail had not a dispute over the terms of the agreement between Adventurers and Planters flared up. And then Reynolds finally brought himself to announce that the *Speedwell* was unfit for the voyage and needed overhauling. The Pilgrims, declared Reynolds, had no one to blame but themselves, for it was they who had created most of the problems by their refusal to employ skilled labour and advice. Perhaps the captain had remonstrated before, but faced with the Pilgrims' stubborn independence, had bided his time until the faults were made apparent by the brief voyage from Holland, when he could come up with a resounding 'I told you so!'.

Attempts to improve the seaworthiness of the *Speedwell* by trimming and ballast had little effect on her crankiness. The season was drawing out and it was time the vessels were away, so trusting in God to carry the *Speedwell* over the Atlantic, the two ships sailed on Saturday 5 August. Beating down the Channel, they were somewhere off Devon when it was found the *Speedwell* was taking too much water to continue. After consulting with each other, Captain Jones and Captain Reynolds decided to put into Dartmouth. To get at the leaks, the pinnace had to be unloaded, but once this was done 'some leaks were found & mended, and now it was conceived by the workman & all, that she was sufficiente, & they might proceede without either fear or danger'[2].

On 23 August, this time with a fair wind, the ships sailed from Dartmouth. Four hundred miles into the voyage, when they were beginning to clear the Western Approaches and the steep groundswells within the hundred-fathom line, Reynolds decided that it was too risky to take the *Speedwell* any further. She was, he claimed, still leaking badly, and in addition, was inherently unseaworthy. Writers have insinuated that Captain Reynolds lacked in courage, an easy conclusion to make from an armchair. On the contrary, once he had experienced the vessel's performance at sea, he seems to have persistently warned that the *Speedwell* was unseaworthy. Doing his best for the company and the Pilgrims, he apparently made every effort to nurse what was clearly an ill-found dog of a ship as far as safety would allow, only turning back after giving her a good shakedown trial offshore. It is caution and judgment which make for good seamanship, and the captain of the *Speedwell* seems to have displayed this, for had he continued, the *Speedwell* may well have faced a long, hard slog against the westerlies, let alone storms such as the *Mayflower* was later to weather. This would have placed such stress on the doubtful timbers of the little cranky pinnace that her survival would have been very uncertain.

The *Mayflower* and *Speedwell* put back into Plymouth, where, after some hard debating, it was arranged that the *Speedwell* should return to London with 18 or 20 of the Pilgrims who had decided that the Atlantic voyage was going to be just too much of a nightmare. Twelve passengers and part of the *Speedwell*'s cargo were transferred to the *Mayflower* before the pinnace sailed for London on 2 September. While the ships were lying in Plymouth Harbour, John Carver was elected to replace Christopher Martin as leader of the Pilgrims. On 6 September the *Mayflower* began her memorable voyage to plant a colony which was to set the seal on a nation.

The voyage of the *Mayflower*

September can be a fine month in the Atlantic, but it was far too late in the year to make the westward voyage and settle a colony, even taking into account that the Pilgrims thought they were bound for northern Virginia to a region between the Dutch

New Netherlands on the Hudson and the settlements of the London Virginia Company. Initially the weather was kind, but the miseries of seasickness and confinement would not have made the sailing pleasant. Their track followed the northern transatlantic route of the Newfoundland fishermen, roughly taking a westerly course until beyond the meridian of 30° west or even as far as the Banks and the Cold Wall of the Labrador Current, before steering for the eastern seaboard of America. During autumn this route is considered preferable to the southern trade-wind passage for, apart from the greatly reduced distance, winds are more likely to be favourable, fog less frequent near the Grand Banks and off the American coast, and icebergs are less likely to be encountered.

The fine weather did not last long. During October contrary winds and gales made life miserable as the working of the ship opened the seams in her upperworks, making it virtually impossible to keep dry below. The necessity to sail close-hauled to make their westing added to discomfort as the vessel lay over, fell off waves and punched into the heavy seas. As the wind and sea rose to the extent that she could no longer fight to windward, the *Mayflower* would first lie-to under her mizzen, and then, when the violent rolling and breaking seas threatened the ship, a scrap of foresail would be set and she would be allowed to scud downwind, probably losing many a hard-won mile of westing.

It was during these October storms that one of the upper-deck beams cracked. This may not sound as desperate as it actually was, until it is realised that the heavy transverse beams were widely spaced and important structural members of the vessel. Between these main beams, smaller beams, or ledges, supported the deck but gave little additional strength to the hull. As the beam buckled downwards, a whole section of the weather deck, which was continually being swept by seas, began to crack up. Probably it was the printing press which was to save

them, for they used a heavy screw to jack up and tom the fractured beam.

Also during this stormy period, one of the seamen very nearly lost his life when he went overboard. The young man, John Howland, had gone on deck, maybe to relieve himself, and was thrown into the sea by a violent roll of the ship. Fortunately for him, the fall of the fore-topsail halliards had been washed off its knighthead just aft of the foremast shrouds and was trailing in the sea. He managed to grab this and hung on desperately until he was hauled back inboard.

The October storms passed and November brought them cold, settled weather as they steered south-west, probably not a great distance off the Nova Scotian coast. As they rolled along their number was increased by the birth of a boy, who was grandly named Oceanus Hopkins, but only a few days later, Dr Samuel's servant, William Butten, died. At dawn on 10 November land was sighted. Captain Jones knew well by the height his staff gave him that he was north of their destination. Apparently standing inshore on the port tack, the *Mayflower*, after some deliberation between the master and the Pilgrims, was put about to begin to beat to the south.

By afternoon they were fighting the rips and anxiously watching out for shoals off Monomoy Point. The diversion which now occurred lends itself to the theory that Jones was in the pay of the Plymouth Company, or even the Dutch, and deliberately sailed the ship into the race to have an excuse to put in behind Cape Cod, but the truth is probably more simple. There are not many activities more futile than trying to fight even a modern square-rigger against wind, current and tumbling overfalls. Add to this uncharted shoal water, the prospect of a long slog against the prevailing winds, and a sea-weary crew who have just made their landfall after a voyage lasting many weeks, and it is easy to decide to give it away and find a quiet anchorage. Not unopposed by some of the Pilgrims, Jones did just this; turning north, he swung around

Cape Cod and came to anchor in the sheltered lee in the harbour of present-day Provincetown.

It was Saturday 11 November. Snow already lay on the landscape and it was well past the time that they should have made themselves secure for the winter. That same day the 41 free men among the Pilgrims signed the *Mayflower contract*, binding them to '...combine our selves together into a civill body politick...'[3] for the benefit of the colony. Carver was re-elected governor and the longboat was swung out and launched. Under the command of Captain Miles Standish, not a Puritan himself, but a staunch and loyal supporter of the Pilgrims, an armed party was sent ashore to explore. The bay being shoal and the tide out, the longboat grounded well offshore, giving the men a long, cold wade to reach dry land. The resulting wet feet were blamed for subsequent nasty colds, but these were more likely the result of the poor physical condition of all the ship's complement after the long voyage.

While the carpenters set about repairing the ravages done to the shallop by nesting Pilgrims and reassembling the craft, expeditions set out to explore the region by land and in the longboat. Indians were seen, but no contact was made with them and the explorers helped themselves from stores of buried Indian corn. Game was plentiful, and water, but no suitable site could be found for settlement. Captain Jones was becoming impatient to be away and urged them that they must make haste, for the ship's stores were quickly being depleted and he must retain sufficient for the voyage home. The Pilgrims jollied along the impatient skipper, taking him along hunting on the second exploratory trip in the longboat, starting on 27 November, the same day another boy, Peregrine White, was born.

Finally the shallop was ready and, under the command of Miles Standish, set out to follow the shores of the bay south and west. On the second day they were attacked by Indians, but got away unscathed. A fast-rising gale later in the day broke the shallop's mast and damaged the rudder.

Nevertheless, they continued and at last found a bay which gave a safe anchorage for the *Mayflower* and the countryside they were seeking for their settlement. This was the site named by Captain John Smith 'Plimoth' on a chart he had made on his exploration in 1616. The shallop was sailed straight back across Cape Cod Bay to the *Mayflower* and 4 days later, on 16 December 1620, the ship came to anchor a mile out from the present location of the town of Plymouth. The voyage was over. It had been hard and very uncomfortable. Two children had been born and five had died, one at sea and four in Provincetown Harbour. Considering the mortality expected on long emigrant voyages in those days, this is a remarkably good record and speaks well for the management of the ship and the morale of all who sailed in her.

The winter was to treat them more harshly. The *Mayflower* had to continue to house the Pilgrims until shelter had been provided ashore, and Captain Jones was obliged to remain at anchor. His plight is best put by William Bradford, the only Pilgrim to leave a record of the *Mayflower*'s transatlantic voyage.

> The reason on their parts why she stayed so long, was the necessity and danger that lay upon them, for it was well towards the end of December, before she could land anything here, or they able to receive anything ashore. Afterwards, the 14th of January, the house which they had made for a general rendezvous by casualty fell afire, and some were fain to retire aboard for shelter; then the sickness began to fall sore amongst them, and the weather so bad as they could not make much sooner any dispatch. Again, the Governor and chief of them, seeing so many die and fall down sick daily, thought it no wisdom to send away the ship, their condition considered and the danger they stood in from the Indians, till they could procure some shelter; and therefore thought it better to draw some more charge upon themselves and friends than hazard all. The master and seamen likewise, though before they hasted the passengers ashore to be gone, now many of their men being dead, and of the ablest of them (as is before noted), and of the rest many lay sick and weak; the master durst not put to sea till he saw his men begin to recover, and the heart of winter over.[4]

With her canvas and topmasts sent down, the *Mayflower* lay to her anchors all that bitter winter while her crew died one by one alongside the Pilgrims. In February 1621, a month when 17 Pilgrims died, the *Mayflower* very nearly capsized, for no ballast had been taken aboard to replace her cargo. It was 22 March before the last of the colonists left the ship and the decimated crew could start preparing her for the voyage home. On 5 April the *Mayflower* weighed anchor and stood out to sea, firing a parting salute with her guns. Only half of the colonists watched her departure – the rest had perished – yet not one gave up and sailed for England.

DUTCH, SWEDISH AND FRENCH VOYAGES

So far a great deal of attention has been given in these pages to the activities of the English, but other nations, just as virile, were making their claim to the north-east American seaboard during the first half of the seventeenth century. During these years the Dutch had become the most powerful trading and seafaring nation, with interests throughout the known world: in the Caribbean, Guiana, West and East Africa, Brazil, and the Far East. It is hardly surprising that their attention should turn to the west, to the coast of North America where the French were already doing a fine trade in furs.

Henry Hudson

It was the activities of an Englishman bent on discovering a north-west or north-east passage to the East that gave the Dutch the jewel of the American seaboard, the site of New York, and possession of the mainland from Pennsylvania through Albany to New England.

Henry Hudson, like Martin Frobisher and John Davis before him, was dedicated to seeking a northern route to the Orient. Backed by the English Muscovy Company, his first two voyages in 1607 and 1608 failed. On this third voyage in 1609 he was financed by the Dutch East India Company, and in the *Half Moon* sailed north-east to seek a passage between Novaya Zemlya and the mainland but was turned back by ice and a crew of unhappy Dutchmen. Hudson suggested they try the Davis Strait or follow up a theory of Captain John Smith's that there was a passage west through the American

continent about the latitude of 40° north. The crew, doubtless fed-up with ice and cold, opted for the latter, and Hudson turned south, stopping in the Faroes in May and sailing for Newfoundland in June.

Off the Newfoundland coast the *Half Moon* lost her fore mast in a gale, but they sailed on to Maine, probably around the Kennebec River, and cut themselves a new mast. Noting the abundance of furs and fish, they continued south to the Delaware, arriving in August. No passage was found, so they turned north and sailed into New York harbour, perhaps the only Europeans to do so since Verrazzano. Their hopes were raised by the size of the inlet and they explored the Hudson as far as Albany. The very same year that Hudson reached the head of navigation at Albany, Samuel de Champlain had followed the Richelieu River into Lake Champlain, only 100 miles away.

Homeward bound to Holland, the *Half Moon* was seized by the irate English when Hudson put into Dartmouth. He was instructed that, in future, he should apply his energies for the benefit of England and not a foreign neighbour. Obeying his countrymen, he commanded an English expedition the following year, during which he discovered the large bay which now bears his name, and wintered over on its shores. When the ice cleared the next year, 1611, he attempted to resume the search westward, but his crew mutinied and Hudson, along with his son and other sick crew members, vanished forever when they were set adrift in an open boat.

Following up Hudson's discoveries, in 1610 the Dutch captains Adriaen Block and Hendrik Christiaensen made a voyage to the Hudson River. Four years later the merchants of Hoorn and

Amsterdam launched a larger expedition of five ships under the leadership of Block and Christiaensen. Somewhere near the limit of navigation on the Hudson River, Block's ship accidentally caught fire and was lost. To facilitate the exploration of the region Block built a yacht measuring 41 ft 6 ins. (12.68 m overall.) In this he sailed through Hellgat (Hell's Gate), named by him for its ferocious tides, and explored Long Island Sound. Verrazzano's Rhode Island he named Adrianbloxeyland which became abbreviated to Block Island. His survey took him around Cape Cod into Massachusetts Bay as far north as Cape Ann. Adriaen Block then took over Christiaensen's ship and returned to Holland where he supplied the information for the first detailed map of the region from the Hudson to Cape Ann.

A trading post was built on Manhattan and a fort at Albany. During the next 10 years several more trading posts were set up in the future New York State and southern New England. In 1626 the Dutch West India Company, which had received its charter in 1621, purchased Manhattan from the Indians and founded the settlement of New Amsterdam as the port for the New Netherlands Territories.

The New Sweden Company

During the 1630s a Dutchman by the name of William Usselinex pulled out of the West India Company and started to persuade King Gustavus Adolphus of Sweden that it would be in his interest to found a colony on the Delaware. His attempts to get an expedition organised failed, but other Dutchmen took his place and, in 1637, the New Sweden Company was founded. In 1638 two Swedish ships, the *Kalmar Nyckel* and the *Fogel Grip*, landed settlers on the Delaware and established the colony of Fort Christina. The Swedes settled in well and prospered but, in time, they came into conflict with the Governor of New Netherlands, Peter Stuyvesant, and the Dutch West India Company took control of the Swedish colony in 1655.

Although the New Netherlands territory stretched from Pennsylvania and Delaware through Albany to New England, it produced nothing like the wealth which was pouring into Holland from other parts of the world, and the hearts of the Dutch merchants were not set on any major effort to regain them when they fell to the English in 1664 and 1665. They did briefly hold them again in 1673, but were happy to renounce their claim in exchange for the South American colony of Surinam.

The French in Acadia and the St Lawrence

Ever since Jacques Cartier had explored the Gulf of St Lawrence, French fur traders had been active, and an important seasonal trading post had been established at Tadoussac. French fishermen had been familiar with the shores of the Gulf for over half a century when, in 1603, Captain François Pontgravé commanded the 120-ton *Bonne Renommée* and two other vessels on a voyage to 'the river of Canada'. With Pontgravé sailed Samuel de Champlain, a 36-year-old Frenchman of private means who was something of a soldier of fortune. From Tadoussac Champlain accompanied a 90-day exploratory journey which widely extended the current knowledge of the area. He noted with appreciation the possibilities of 'Kébec' as a site for a future colony, and gathered reports of other geographical features

such as Niagara Falls, the Great Lakes and Hudson Bay. Most importantly, an alliance was made with the Algonquin, Montagnais and Etchimin Indians that was to last over 150 years. Before leaving the Gulf that season, the party's interest was captured by a French fur trader, Jean Sarcel de Prévert, who had some tall tales to tell of vast amounts of copper and other metals to be found in the south, on the Acadian coast. Pontgravé and Champlain put aside their plans to further explore the St Lawrence in favour of a survey of Acadia, with a view to finding the mines.

In November of 1603, after Champlain and Pontgravé's return, Pierre du Gua de Monts, the new Vice-Admiral of France and Viceroy of New France, was granted a Royal Commission which virtually gave him a monopoly of the fur trade and, at no cost to the Crown, would establish a colony in New France. In 1604 five ships were employed, three of which were to sail for the Gulf to collect furs. Two other vessels and an 11-ton pinnace, possibly taken apart and stowed for the voyage, with 120 working-men in addition to a large number of gentlemen, a Catholic and a Protestant priest and the ships' crews, set out to explore the shores of Acadia. Although the ensuing years were rough and proved fatal to many of the French adventurers, it does seem that they were pursued by the romance of the legendary Arcadia, and it was their bucolic pace of voyaging which prevented them from fulfilling the aims of the Crown.

From 1604 to 1607, under the command of the Sieur de Monts and later Pontgravé, Champlain roamed the coasts of present-day Nova Scotia, Maine and Massachusetts, establishing a settlement firstly at Île Sainte-Croix in Maine and later resettling at Port Royal on the Bay of Fundy in Nova Scotia. The latter was abandoned in 1607 but in 1610 the settlement of Annapolis Royal was established and the French presence in Acadia was maintained.

Samuel de Champlain never returned to Acadia. His actual responsibilities on the voyages are

unknown except that he was the primary recorder of events and hydrographer. Only once, for a brief three weeks, did he assume command of an expedition. These excursions in Acadia, and an earlier voyage with the Spanish to the West Indies and Mexico, were Champlain's apprenticeship. In 1608, the year the English Popham Colony in Maine was abandoned, Champlain commanded the expedition which firmly established a colony at Quebec. He had shipped out in prefabricated form a *habitation* which was a virtual palace. For the remainder of his life Samuel de Champlain devoted himself to furthering the interests of France in Canada and widening the geographical knowledge of the continent.

Champlain is said to have made 29 voyages across the Atlantic, and in his later years wrote a *Treatise on Seamanship*. His respect for the arts of seamanship and navigation were expressed in a letter to Queen Marie de Médicis in 1613:

Madam, among all the most useful and admirable arts, that of navigation has always seemed to me to hold the first place; for the more hazardous it is and the more it is attended by innumerable dangers and shipwrecks, so much the more is it esteemed and exalted before all others, being in no way suited to those who lack courage and resolution.[1]

THE SPANISH TREASURE FLEETS

While the Spanish extended their empire in the Indies and mainland America, the initial trickle of precious metals swelled to a flood on which Spain rode precariously during the following 3 centuries. Gold and silver provided instant wealth, but undermined Spain's industries. It fed the pride of her enormously disdainful aristocracy and stunted the growth of the middle and mercantile classes. In jealous defence of the golden goose, Spain, and in particular Castile, wove a complex and impracticable web of regulation and interference that almost strangled trade with the west, impoverished or alienated her colonies and resulted in a flourishing underworld of smuggling, bribery and evasion.

It was not Spain's attempted monopoly of the New World that was shortsighted. The Dutch and English were to successfully follow similar policies, but they more often nurtured their colonies in primitive lands and milked the wealth of established nations in the East. Spain, on the other hand, bled her own colonies white by often creating scarcity and overpricing her exports to her settlers, at the same time forbidding them the recourse to external supplies. The results were predictable. As previously described, other nations began to run a lucrative but dangerous smuggling trade, frequently connived at by the authorities in the Indies.

As recounted earlier, the activities of John Hawkins in the 1560s were a typical example of this illicit trade. The only response the Crown and the Casa de Contratación seemed to be able to decide upon was to send out judges and investigating committees at an enormous charge to the poor, suffering colonists – on whom they tried to pin the blame! Where trade was thwarted, or there was a state of war, or for no reason except the chance of easy loot, others haunted the Caribbean or cruised the routes of Spain's ships rolling home deep and richly laden.

Establishment of the Spanish convoys

During the early years of colonial expansion, merchant ships bound for the Indies sailed independently, suffering more danger from the hazards of the new navigation than from the depredations of rovers. However, by the 1520s French pirates became a menace to Spanish merchantmen as they neared home. In response, King Charles of Spain provided a fleet, initially of four warships, to patrol the sailing routes in the eastern Atlantic, their cost being covered by a tax imposed on freight to and from America.

In 1526 ships were ordered to sail in convoys, but it was not until the renewal of hostilities with France in 1543 that detailed rules were laid down for the routing, timing, conduct, armament and manning of convoys sailing to and from the Indies. So effective did the Spanish system become that, in the whole history of the flotas, very few ships from the guarded convoys were lost to marauders. Most of the treasure from the Americas was transported across the Atlantic in these large fleets, but occasionally single, well armed vessels made the run, and in the eighteenth and nineteenth centuries it became more common to use very large ships, or *navios*. These often brought home the bullion from the Peruvian mines by way of Cape Horn.

The initial rules specified that no vessels under 100 tons were to accompany the convoys, and provided for two sailings each year – one in March and one in September. Once in the Caribbean, the ships separated into two fleets, one bound for the north coast of South America, or Tierra Firme as it was known, and the other for New Spain, or Mexico. A warship accompanied the convoy as far as the Caribbean and then, using Havana as a base, cruised the islands for pirates. Returning merchantmen assembled at Havana and sailed for home in convoy, while another, separate fleet sailed independently from San Domingo, which lay well to windward of Havana.

After a brief experiment in 1552, when it was proposed to arm the merchant ships sufficiently to withstand the attacks of corsairs, the convoys began to take the form they were to develop and maintain for the next century and more. By the 1560s it had become usual for the New Spain fleet to try to leave Spain about July 1, and the Tierra Firme fleet any time from March to May. Armed vessels, the *galeones*, accompanied the merchantmen bound for Tierra Firme as far as Nombre de Dios and, later, Porto Belo, and the Mexican fleet as far as Cape San Antonio. When, towards the end of the century, the silver from the mines of Potosi began to flow copiously through the port of Nombre de Dios, and French and English corsairs had developed into an even greater menace, it became customary for six to eight galleons, known as the *Armada de la Guardia*, to accompany the Tierra Firme fleet, and a couple of galleons, supported by some well-armed

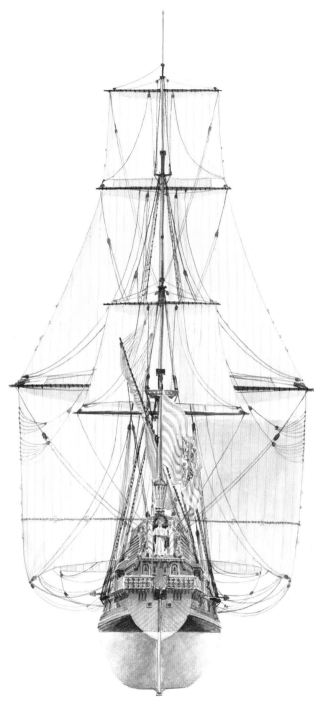

This profile of a Spanish galleon of the type employed in the Carrera de Indias has been reconstructed to the measurements provided by the studies of Carla Rahn Phillips of the University of Minnesota.

In 1625, Martin de Arana, a well-established Basque shipbuilder, was contracted by the Spanish crown to build six galleons: the *Nuestra Señora de Begona,* 541.5 toneladas; the *San Felipe,* 537.375 toneladas; the *San Juan Baptista,* 455.75 toneladas; the *Nuestra Señora de los Tres Reyes,* 455 toneladas; the *San Sebastian,* 330.25 toneladas; and the *Santiago,* 338.5 toneladas.

Strict ordinances detailing the scantlings, rig and equipment were laid down for the building of galleons for the crown. Using these specifications, Carla Rahn Phillips has calculated the proportions for a vessel of 476 toneladas, roughly an average of all six ships. The calculation of tonnage was complex and varied according to the current rules; the measurements given below provide a much better idea of the size of this ship.

Length of keel	80 ft 8 in. (24.59 m)
Rake forward	14 ft 8 in. (48.12 m)
Rake aft	7 ft 4 in. (2.23 m)
Length on lower deck	102 ft 8 in. (31.29 m)
Beam	31 ft 2 in. (9.53 m)
Depth of hold	14 ft 8 in. (4.47 m)
Mainmast	84 ft 4 in. (25.7 m)
Mainyard	70 ft 1 in. (21.37 m)

In nearly all the swashbuckling literature written about the Spanish Main and about Spanish galleons generally, the ships are portrayed as huge, lumbering, unwieldy mountains of timber. The galleon illustrated here is quite small and, although she has a 4-to-5-ft-greater beam, the length is approximately the same as that of the *Mayflower* proposed by Mr R.C. Anderson in his model built for the Pilgrim Society of Plymouth. Vessels of a greater size were used on the Indies run during the sixteenth and seventeenth centuries, including some merchantmen, such as the 900-ton hulk used by Juan de Ubilla to attack Hawkins at San Juan de Ulua, and escorting treasure galleons of around 800 tons. Although one should be careful of comparing measurements of tonnage, which might vary considerably between nations, Hawkins's *Jesus of Lübeck* measured 700 tons.

For sheer size for their time, imagine the Portuguese East Indiamen. The carrack *Madre de Dios,* captured by Sir John Burroughs and his consorts off the Azores in 1592, measured 1600 tons, was 165 ft (50.29 m) from the tip of the beakhead to the taffrail on the poop, had a beam of 46 ft 10 in. (20.73 m) and drew 31 ft (9.45 m) when she left Cochin in China. She had seven decks, which included an orlop and three 'tween-decks; her 121-ft (36.88 m) main mast had a circumference of 10 ft 7 in. (3.22 m) at the partners and the mainyard at 106 ft (32.3 m) was 6 ft (1.83 m) longer than the keel. On passage she was probably steered by whipstaff, but for manoeuvring she required 12 to 14 men on the tiller. Ships like these could only be used effectively on the long runs to the East Indies and across the Pacific. A few of the Manila galleons were reputed to have ranged up to 2000 tons.

Some comparison with an existing, if later, ship can be made if one considers the American frigate *Constitution* which has a length between perpendiculars, which is about the length of the gun-deck, of 175 ft (53.34 m), a beam of 44 ft 8 in. (13.61 m) and draws 22 ft 6 in. (6.86 m).

The seventeenth-century galleons built to guard and transport the treasure from the Indies were limited in size, not only by the orders of the Casa de Contratación de las Indias, but by reason of the depth of the Gualdaquavir bar which, as the years went by, continued to silt up. The sisters of the Atlantic galleons, the Pacific Manila galleons, were bound by similar restricting ordinances, but with no shallow bar to navigate, half a world between them and Seville, and the desire to shift the maximum load possible, the Malinenos continued to build the largest vessels they could get away with.

The rig
Several peculiarities of the rig become apparent when the galleon is drawn to scale. Firstly, the huge sail area dominated by the vast mainsail and the spritsail, which must have been quite a handful for the sailors. The massive bowsprit, steeved at 45°, measures 73 ft 4 in. (22.35 m), only 11 ft (3.35 m) shorter than the main lower mast, surely must have had more support than just the heel block and gammoning. Bobstays and bowsprit shrouds were not generally in use until the end of the seventeenth century, significantly at about the same time that staysails and jibs were being introduced. The spar shown here must have weighed tons and one can imagine the stresses imposed on it in a rolling and pitching ship.

No mizzen topsail or topmast is indicated in the specifications. These had become quite common during this period so I have departed from a strict interpretation by including the mast and sail. The mizzen topmast also provides a reasonable lead for the main topgallant braces. However, it might have been that, as the ships were designed to sail free, following the wind patterns of the Atlantic and Caribbean, a mizzen topsail was considered unnecessary and the topgallants were set flying; that is without lifts or braces. Topgallants may only have been light weather sails and, more frequently than on later ships, may have been sent down with their masts in unsettled weather, a practice which would account for the absence of the sails in many illustrations.

Painting and decoration

It seems that very little decoration was included in the contract. Black with red features, such as gunwales, rails and perhaps ports, was the pervading colour scheme. It is almost certain that carvings or depictions of the vessel's saint graced the transom of the poop and another statue was set up at the break of the poop prior to the voyage. Gilding in moderation was used here and there, such as round the quarter galleries, and a gilded and crowned lion rampant roared from the beakhead. The universal hull paint was tar and a mixture of pitch, resin, grease and oil called *alquitran*. These were used both above and below water, but as additional protection for the hull underwater, lead sheets were nailed over a layer of tarred cloth, providing a heavy and easily damaged, but effective, protection against shipworm. Ships without the protection of lead relied on tar, oil and liberal anointings of tallow.

merchantmen, the New Spain convoy.

For greater protection, selected galleons, called *galeones de la plata*, became the carriers of the treasure rather than the merchantmen and thus, although warships, they fall within the scope of this book. During the sixteenth century both fleets were termed *flotas*, which virtually means a fleet of merchantmen, and when under the protection of warships, they were known as *flota y galleones*. Later the Tierra Firme fleet became known simply as the *galeones*, while the more commercial New Spain fleet retained the designation *flota*. It is on the seventeenth-century galleons and merchantmen which sailed in these fleets, and their voyages, that this chapter focuses.

The Casa de Contratación de las Indias

Anyone today who complains about the impositions of an over-authoritarian bureaucracy might spare a thought for the merchants, captains, sailors and shipowners who engaged in trade with the West Indies and America. During the first decade of exploration and trade with the Indies, ships usually sailed from Cadiz or San Lucar de Barrameda at the mouth of the Guadalquivir River. However, when it became apparent that a whole new world lay in the west, the Spanish Crown, in 1503, founded the *Casa de Contratación de las Indias*, a house of trade which would encourage and regulate commerce with the Americas.

At this period Castile considered she had sole rights to the new discoveries and it was understandable that the populous and wealthy city of Seville, 70 miles up the Guadalquivir and deep in the heart of the kingdom, was chosen for the headquarters of the Casa de Contratación. The interests of the Seville merchants, and the need of the Crown to keep a tight control on the trade, created a bottleneck which impeded rather than assisted trade, for the Casa insisted that all ships clear and enter at Seville. This involved a slow and tortuous river passage lasting days, but worse was the danger of the bar at the mouth off San Lucar. Here heavily laden and not very weatherly ships could be forced to jog on and off for days, and sometimes weeks, waiting for the right tide, sea and wind to enter. The combined holdups at the bar and in the river could delay ships for as much time as it took to make the Atlantic crossing, and crews and passengers, under threats of dire penalties, were forbidden to disembark. Many captains, frustrated by the delay after their long voyage, or worried about the ability of their ships to keep the sea any longer, took chances with the Guadalquivir Bar, and virtually their own doorstep became their graveyard.

Captains who chose to put in elsewhere through stress of weather or enemy threats took a grave risk with the jealous guardians of the Casa. For example, in 1671, Don José Centeno, the general of that year's flota, found himself 'twixt the devil and the deep blue sea. His ship drew too much to cross the bar and he had received warnings that enemy ships were nearby. The only sensible option was to put into Cadiz and hope that his situation would be sufficient excuse for his digression. The Casa sentenced him to 6 years' imprisonment at Oran in North Africa and a fine of 6000 ducats, which would perhaps be the equivalent of $US100,000 today.

The impracticable nature of the navigation of the river, which became worse as ships became larger and the river silted up, forced the bureaucrats and merchants of Seville reluctantly to give permission for ships to load outward at San Lucar and Cadiz, but inbound ships, more often than not, were obliged to work up as close as possible to Seville to discharge. The more easily accessible port of Cadiz was put forward as an alternative and was often used as such, but Seville hung on to its monopoly until 1717, when the entire Casa de Contratación was transferred to the deepwater port.

The reason for Seville's fierce protection of its monopoly was the treasure with which the inbound ships were freighted. Gold, silver, emeralds and pearls were included in the manifests of every incoming flota, but the imports of precious metals rose to astounding proportions and often formed the greater part of the loading of many galleons. In 1594 gold and silver formed 95.62 per cent of the freight, the rest being made up from quantities of cochineal, hides, indigo and other items.

Earl J. Hamilton, in his study *American Treasure and the Price Revolution in Spain 1501 – 1650* (Harvard, 1934), has produced an analysis of the quantities and value of treasure shipped to Spain over more than 3 centuries. The figures are illuminating. Some rough estimates in modern values may indicate that initially, until 1520, $US15,000,000 of gold was imported from the West Indies. During the next decade the shipments fell to $US5,000,000 until, from 1531 to 1555, the plunder from the Incas and the development of the Peruvian and Mexican mines brought the figure back to a healthy $US78,000,000. From 1556 to 1600, thanks largely to Potosi silver, the value leaped to a remarkable $US550,000,000 and increased to $US1,400,000,000 during the last half of the seventeenth century. $US4,000,000,000, consisting of 95 per cent silver and 5 per cent gold, was imported during the eighteenth century. In total, from the year of discovery until 1820, $US8,698,000,000 of registered treasure crossed the Atlantic. In addition, it is estimated that another 20 per cent of this amount entered unregistered or smuggled, bringing the grand total to an astronomical $US10,438,000,000. Since these figures were compiled in 1934, with inflation values would now be considerably higher.

No wonder the Spanish Crown, the officials of the Casa de Contratación and the Seville merchants were close-fisted. From this wealth pouring through the city, generally one-fifth of all the precious metals was put aside for the Crown, heavy import duties were imposed and a tax, the *averias*, extracted for the maintenance of the convoys. All freight, outward and inward, had to be registered, and a mountain of paperwork, checks and counterchecks were enforced to prevent illicit trading. The harder the Casa hauled on the noose around their trade, the more cunning and resourceful became the smugglers, who could be anyone from a powerful governor to a lowly *grummete*. In spite of severe penalties should they have been caught, nearly everyone involved in the flotas brought home contraband, until, in the mid seventeenth century, the illicit trade had grown to such proportions that it almost eclipsed the registered import of gold.

A very large part of the cargo of every returning treasure galleon consisted of unregistered bullion, often exceeding the quantity shown on her register. The more organised and powerful participators might arrange to have the contraband quietly offloaded at night before crossing the bar off San Lucar. The posting of guardships and clearing all other vessels out of the area did little to frustrate an activity which nearly all condoned. Like their sisters, the Pacific Manila galleons, but not quite so obviously (the Manila galleons were known at times to have actually attempted to tow rafts of freight which could not be squeezed on board) the galeones de la plata and merchantmen were frequently overladen with the illegal private ventures of their passengers and personnel, thus compounding the risk of shipwreck or foundering of the often unweatherly and cranky ships.

The outward voyage

Weather, as was usual in the days of sailing ships, was the most significant factor in timing the voyages of the flotas. When the schedules were first established by the Casa de la Contratación, it was recommended that the Tierra Firme fleet, whose track did not normally impinge on the hurricane regions, should leave Spain in August so as to arrive at the Isthmus at the most healthy time of the year, then load and depart for Havana around February so as to rendezvous with the New Spain fleet. However, when it became customary for the merchantmen to be escorted by the Armada de la Guardia, consisting of eight or more galleons which were to carry the treasure home, the flota left sometime between early March and the middle of May. This allowed the galleons to arrive on the coast, make a quick turnaround, escort the homeward-bound merchantmen which had wintered over from the previous year, perhaps pick up the New Spain flota in Havana, clear the Bahama Channel before the onset of the hurricane season and be back in Spain in the autumn. Occasionally a fleet might leave as early as January or February, which was a fairly safe practice. However, when they arrived home, as some did, as late as December, they had run an awful risk of being swiped by a hurricane, apart from being battered by Atlantic storms.

The schedule called for the New Spain flota to leave Spain in April, which gave the fleet a chance of turning around in Vera Cruz and clearing Havana before the hurricane season set in, ideally joining the Tierra Firme fleet for the voyage home. However, dilatory organisation and a desire to miss the worst of the pestilential summer in Vera Cruz usually saw the New Spainers off about the first of July, so as to return the following year.

Outward bound, the ships assembled at San Lucar, or sometimes Cadiz, to complete their loading and take on passengers. Although it was a strict regulation of the Casa that every ship must return to Spain, many of the merchantmen were old and decrepit ships whose owners often did not want them to be able to make the return voyage, which was comparatively unprofitable as most, or all, of the registered silver was carried by the Armada de la Guardia. In the Indies rot and shipworm would finally make them unseaworthy enough to satisfy the authorities that the old hulks were unable to make the passage home and they would be sold to the colonials or broken up for their gear and ironwork.

The flotas would almost inevitably be late sailing, due to delays in the arrivals of ships, the red tape of the Casa, and the thousand-and-one details of fitting out and supply, together with the complex organisation of the large fleet. Finally a gun would thunder out a warning that the flota was to sail the following day. This was the signal to the sailors that shore leave was ended, to the passengers that they should embark, and to all that it was time to bribe and smuggle into the ships their contraband. A busy and colourful occasion it must have been, with the deep-laden ships preparing for sea. A host of small craft would be ferrying last-minute stores, cargo from foreign ships, and passengers, who could be anyone from wealthy nobility arriving in style, bound for the Indies to take up their powerful and lucrative positions, down to the lad with dreams slipping aboard to be quietly stowed away by his mates.

Anchored in the roads would have been shipping from all over Europe, bringing their commodities such as wool from England, textiles from Flanders, canvas from Brittany and glassware from the Mediterranean. All the goods and luxuries wanted by the Spanish colonies were shipped in the flota, to be exchanged for treasure from the Indies. Perhaps some ship would have included in its manifest anchors and ironwork to be hauled across Mexico to fit out a Manila galleon. In the ships of the Armada de la Guardia was loaded precious mercury destined for the silver mines where it was used to extract silver from the ore. This was carefully contained in a soft, well sewn skin and then put into a strong, watertight cask, each containing half a quintal.

One third and final inspection and inquisition by the officials of the Casa de las Indias and the fleet was ready to sail. One can sympathise with those *capitans, maestres* and other officers who had to satisfy the bureaucrats of the Casa, most of whom were probably as venal as the smugglers. The formalities and paperwork, combined with the settling of passengers, the penning of livestock and the very real need to see that the ship was ready for sea, must have driven the afterguard to distraction. But finally the officials would have been satisfied, either with the paperwork or a greasy palm, and the ships would be cleared. Even then, guards employed by the Casa remained on board until the flota was clear out to sea.

Once the entire flota had been assembled and inspected, the ships made ready to sail on the tide. With her ensigns, standards and pennants flying, anchor-a-trip, her lower yards aloft and the sails hanging in their gear, the *capitana* stood ready to lead the fleet out to sea. On being given the all-clear by the bar pilot, the fleet's ocean pilot ordered the anchor broken out and the foresail set with the following prayerful formula:

> Ease the [clew] of the foresail, in the name of the Holy Trinity, Father, and Son, and Holy Spirit, three persons and one true God only. Be with us and guard and guide and accompany us, and give us a good and safe voyage, and carry and return us safely to our homes.[1]

Once the galleon's head was boxed round, the sail sheeted and yard braced, the pilot ordered an *Ave Maria* from all on board and then handed over to the bar pilot. While the ship worked through the bar channel not a word was allowed to be spoken so that orders and responses rang out clear and true. Once clear, the ocean pilot took over again from the bar pilot, who then disembarked.

The flotas were under the overall command of the captain-general whose ship, titled the *capitana*, sailed in the van of the fleet. His second-in-command, the admiral, also had his own ship, which was known as the *almiranta*. As the flota left port, he organised the sailing order; probably several ranks arranged in a crescent, with the armed galleons up to windward. Throughout the voyage the *almiranta* formed the rearguard, chivvying the stragglers or rendering assistance if needed. Twice during the daylight hours the admiral sailed up through the flota, counting and making contact with all the ships. From the captain-general he received any instructions and passed on the next day's password, usually the name of a saint, to every ship. At night the ships were guided by the great stern lantern of the capitana. In the early days any captain or pilot who deliberately lost contact with the flota risked execution; later the penalty was a heavy fine, loss of rank and 2 years' exclusion from the Indies' trade.

During the sixteenth century it was customary for the flotas to call at the Canaries to provision, but later, to counter the activities of smugglers in the distant islands, the fleets only stopped if absolutely necessary, and no one was allowed ashore, nor was cargo permitted to be handled. From the Canaries the New Spain flota would drop down to about 16° north to pick up the trades and then sailed west to the Lesser Antilles, usually with the intention of making a landfall on Deseada, to enter the Caribbean through the clear passages north and south of Guadaloupe.

The tradewind ocean passage presented few risks to any reasonably seaworthy ship. Brisk, generally 20 to 25 knot east-to-north-east winds drove the ships comfortably along, day after day. Most of the passengers would have their sea legs by this time, and boredom, overcrowding and the inevitable shipboard squabbles would have been their worst discomfort . . . barring rats, lice, fleas and other vermin. Regarding rats, one of the many disasters which struck the homeward-bound fleet in 1622 was an infestation in one of the ships. A thousand rats were slaughtered before they left Havana, but thousands more still aboard chewed through all the food containers, ate the contents, massacred the livestock and tunnelled into the water casks, where they drowned themselves. Before reprovisioning in the Azores, the company was surviving on rainwater and, for the really hungry, the rats themselves. The crew, aided by the passengers, managed to account for 3000 of the vermin before getting home. Rats and cockroaches were always worse on the ships homeward bound from the tropics, where other little nasties such as centipedes and scorpions also hitched a ride.

A flota at sea. The nearest ship is the *almiranta*, the next in seniority to the *capitana*, in which the captain-general of the fleet sailed. The *almiranta* has clewed up her main course and lowered her mizzen topsail to reduce speed to speak to the vessel on her starboard side. One of the tasks of the *almiranta* was to sail through the fleet to communicate instructions, give aid and chivvy along stragglers.

To alleviate the boredom, the Church's multiplicity of feast days were fervently celebrated, with the waist and quarterdeck richly decorated for the Masses, which all were expected to attend. Apart from fishing, grasping on to shipboard dramas, cockfighting, mock bullfights and poetry competitions, there was little else in the way of entertainment as the ships rolled onward, rarely having to start a sheet or brace. As they approached the Indies, water would perhaps run low, the luxuries brought by individuals for the voyage would be gone, and all would be reduced to ordinary shipboard fare. Scurvy, the curse of long-distance seafarers, would rarely affect either crew or passengers; the voyage was too short.

If on schedule, the New Spain flota was off the outer Caribbean islands in August, the beginning of the hurricane season. Because of the uncertainty of their dead-reckoning navigation for longitude, it was the practice for the whole fleet to lie to at night, sometimes for days, before making their landfall. This habit is often derided by other nations and writers on the subject, but, with the responsibility for a large fleet and the chief pilot's own neck on the block should any disaster occur, it was a reasonably careful and seamanlike precaution.

Once into the Caribbean, the fleet would then cruise north-westward to leeward of the islands to the Bay of Neyba in Hispaniola or Aguada at the north-western tip of Puerto Rica, where the ships watered, and then continue as far as Cape San Antonio, the western promontory of Cuba. On this passage vessels would peel off from the convoy to make for their various destinations in Puerto Rica, San Domingo and Cuba in the islands, and Truxillo and Caballos in Honduras.

All during their voyage through the Caribbean the flota could be dogged by corsairs just waiting to snap up a straggler or cut out a ship at night. It was not uncommon to find one too many sails when a count of the flota was taken, but losses were infrequent. After passing Cape San Antonio the fleet had a choice of a summer or winter route. In winter they steered north-west past the Alcaran Reefs, then between west and south-west to the Mexican coast and finally downwind, south to Vera Cruz. The summer passage took them near the shores of Campeche, involving an approach littered with reefs and shoals. They would arrive in Vera Cruz in September after an entire voyage of about 60 days.

Vera Cruz, the only port of entry on the eastern seaboard of New Spain, was founded by Hernando Cortés in 1519. However, from November to March, the anchorage was entirely exposed to the violent northers that strike the coast, causing havoc with the shipping. It became common for vessels to shelter about 20 miles along the coast, behind the small rocky island of San Juan de Ulua, which created a tiny harbour between a quarter and half a mile wide where the freight was discharged into small craft and transported to the city. After John Hawkins's visit in 1567, the Spanish built a fort on the island, and at the foot of the inshore walls the water was of sufficient depth for the ships to make a Mediterranean moor, with their cables fast to huge bronze rings in the wall and kedges out astern. The approach to the port was encumbered with outlying reefs and, before entering, the fleet would heave to offshore to allow time for buoys to be laid to mark the channel. In 1599 the town of Vera Cruz was moved to a site opposite the island, on a barren, sandy beach surrounded by marshes and dunes. So unhealthy was the town that, like Acapulco on the Pacific coast, it only came to life with the arrival and departure of the flotas. After the ships were discharged a fair was held at Jalapa, situated at a higher and healthier site inland.

While the silver carried in the Tierra Firme galleons formed the bulk of the treasure shipped to Spain, a considerable amount was mined in Mexico. As the colony grew and became more independent of Spain, large quantities of her silver were loaded into the Manila galleons bound for the Philippines, where it was traded for oriental products such as porcelain, silk, spices and furniture, a decreasing amount of which found its way into the holds of the New Spain flota and back to the home country. Most of this oriental wealth, bought with the silver that Spain desperately needed, found a home in the palatial residences of Mexico City. Peter Earle, in his book *The Wreck of the Almiranta*, estimates that the 600-ton nao, *Nuestra Señora de la Concepción*, the almiranta of the homeward voyage in 1641, carried between 35 and 140 tons of silver in her hold, and considers that the larger figure was nearly correct. In addition, she carried a small amount of gold and jewels, and a cargo of 1200 chests and bags of cochineal and indigo. This would have been fairly representative of the cargoes shipped out of Vera Cruz at that time. The fate of the *Concepción* will be described later.

Most of the fleet would winter at Vera Cruz and sail for Havana sometime in the following May or June, avoiding the worst of the *nortes* from November to March. These ferocious northers were as dangerous as any hurricane, for on a calm, clear, sunny day, with the briefest of warnings in the form of a line of cloud on the north-eastern horizon, the wind would freshen and within half an hour could be blowing over 100 knots. Even after avoiding the danger of these winds, the voyage to Havana was difficult. The prevailing northerlies and easterlies forced the ships to make a starboard tack, often as far as the Texas or Louisiana coast, before they could make sufficient offing to come about for Cuba.

The greatest loss suffered by any flota occurred on the final part of this voyage to Havana. Hundreds of ships were lost to the navigational hazards of the sailing routes, but very few ships were ever taken by enemies from the guarded flotas. However, in 1628 the entire fleet of 15 ships from New Spain was lost to a Dutch fleet of 32 ships commanded by Admiral Piet Heyn. Piet Heyn had begun his seafaring as a corsair but was unfortunate enough to be captured by the Spanish, who condemned him to 4 years in her galleys. Once free, he continued privateering with such success he rose to the rank of admiral in the Dutch West India Company, founded in 1621 with the particular aim of harassing the Spanish and Portuguese American possessions and shipping. Home in Holland, the contents brought back from the 15 ships sold for 150,000,000 guilders and provided the happy shareholders of the West India Company an enormous dividend of 150 per cent – surely sufficient vengeance for Piet's 4 years on an oar.

With the safe arrival of the New Spain flota in Havana, it was time for the crews to live it up while they waited for the arrival of the Tierra Firme fleet. The stopover could last months or be brief, depending on the punctuality of the ships from the south, and the priorities of the flota's captain-general. The well defended and busy port was described by Vasquez de Espinosa as 'one of the best, roomiest, and deepest I know [where] ships of no matter what size are practically moored to the houses of the city'.[2]

The silver galleons

Before following the flotas on their passage back to Spain, let us trace the course of the Tierra Firme galleons from Spain to the Isthmus of Panama and then on to Havana.

Outward bound, the silver galleons, with the merchantmen tucked under their wing, followed the same track to the Indies as the New Spain flota, but when approaching the West Indies the fleet made for what became known as the Galleon's Passage between Trinidad and Tobago. There followed an easy voyage to Cartagena, during which an armed patache was sent in to collect the Crown's pearls from Margarita and, wary of attacks by corsairs along the Spanish Main, merchantmen either were escorted or detached themselves under cover of darkness to make for Caracas, Maracaibo or Santa Marta to load cochineal, leather, cocoa and gold. The

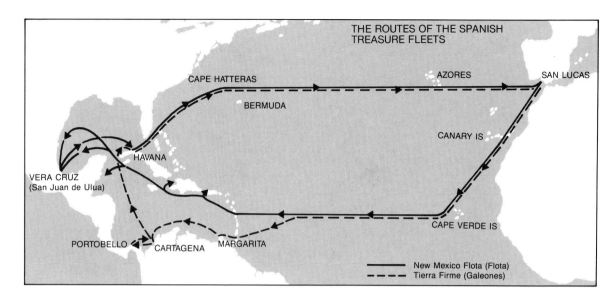

THE ROUTES OF THE SPANISH TREASURE FLEETS

CAPE HATTERAS · BERMUDA · AZORES · SAN LUCAS · CANARY IS · HAVANA · VERA CRUZ (San Juan de Ulua) · PORTOBELLO · CARTAGENA · MARGARITA · CAPE VERDE IS

——— New Mexico Flota (Flota)
– – – Tierra Firme (Galeones)

voyage from Spain to Cartagena could be expected to be completed in 30 to 40 days. From Cartagena the galleons continued on to Nombre de Dios or, after 1596, Porto Belo, to load the treasure shipped from the west coast of South America in the Pacific Plate fleet and carried by mule across the Isthmus and by rafts down the Chargres River. Warned of the imminent arrival of the galleons, sometimes by a fast patache sent ahead from the other side of the Atlantic, the bullion began to accumulate, lying '. . . like heaps of stones in the street without any fear or suspicion of being lost'[3].

Porto Belo was not a healthy place in which to linger in spite of the brouhaha of its famous fair. In the early days the fair was open for as long as 50 days but later, with the necessity for a quick turnaround of the silver galleons, only 10 to 12. Ideally, as the galleons arrived at Porto Belo, the Plate fleet would have arrived at Panama, leaving only the difficult 18-league mule track to negotiate in summer and the less difficult route by way of the Chargres River in winter.

With the fleet in, Porto Belo became expensive, overcrowded and even more of a pest hole. During 1637 the ships remained in port only 15 days, yet 500 men perished of disease. As soon as the treasure was loaded, the galleons hauled out and sailed back to Cartagena on the coastal counter-current. Cartagena was a healthier and better defended port than Porto Belo, and sufficiently to windward to enable the ships to make the Yucatan Channel on the starboard tack. At this port assembled the whole flota, mainly of ships which had arrived the previous year, traded on the coast and wintered over. At the end of the sixteenth century the number of merchantmen accompanying the galleons varied from 94 in 1587 to 32 in 1601. The number of ships became less as time passed, but the ships were larger and the aggregate tonnage was probably maintained. The flota preferably left Cartagena in time to leave Havana and clear the Bahama Channel before August, the start of the hurricane season.

The voyage from Cartagena to Havana was not without its perils. As the ships sailed on a starboard tack to make the Yucatan Channel, several isolated and dangerous shoals and reefs straddled and flanked their track. Roncador Cay and its outlying coral reefs lay only about 250 miles out, and a further 50 miles beyond Roncador was the Serrana Bank. Probably the most lethal hazard was the Serranillas, sinisterly known by the Spanish as 'Las Viboras' or 'The Vipers'. These extensive reefs were right on their course, and when seen on a clear, fine day served as a useful navigation check. In dirty weather, with the ships driving and uncertain of their position, 'The Vipers' lived up to their name when, in 1605, seven galleons and a patache sailed from Cartagena. A few days out a storm crippled all the ships and sank the patache. One of the officers of the patache later wrote to his sovereign claiming bitterly that the constable of the *San Pedro* should be '. . . hung by his testicles from the yardarm'[4] and that there was nothing in the way of tools and equipment to effect repairs or assist them in saving the ship. Three galleons limped to Jamaica, and one, the *San Cristobal*, totally dismasted, was miraculously worked back to Cartagena after narrowly avoiding being driven on to Las Viboras where the three remaining galleons seem to have perished. It is believed that their treasure lies somewhere among the reefs of Las Viboras.

On the track beyond Las Viboras a few snares remained to catch an unfortunate galleon. The San Pedro Bank, south of Jamaica, the Caymans, the Isle of Pines and the coast of Cuba itself could all tell tales of shipwrecks, but once through the Yucatan Channel and round Cape Antonio, the galleons could coast easily along to Havana on the north coast of Cuba.

If the New Mexico flota was still in Havana, the fleets then combined to sail for Seville together, the general of the Tierra Firme fleet taking over command of the navigation, unless the flota was unaccompanied by galleons. In this case the general of the flota which first arrived in Havana had precedence. Combined fleets for the final voyage

home were infrequent during the last part of the sixteenth century, but became more normal in the seventeenth century.

As the stragglers from various other ports rolled in, an enormous assembly of ships gathered and prepared for the rigorous Atlantic crossing. Although other routes were sometimes used, it was preferred to sail by way of the Florida Strait and Bahama Channel, barrelling along on the Gulf Stream, which could run at anything up to 3½ knots. To port lay the snares of the Florida Keys, to starboard the western reefs of the Bahama Bank. More ships were lost in this channel than anywhere else. The southern keys bear the grim title 'Cabezas de los Martires', and one of the reasons for the maintenance of the Spanish colony of St Augustine on the Florida coast was to rescue the victims of shipwreck in the Strait.

On the other side, in the Bahamas, lay New Providence, which was settled in the 1640s. Founded originally by 'The Company of Eleutherian Adventurers' with the aim of setting up a religiously free, hardworking utopia, they soon followed the example of their neighbours in Bermuda, who had for decades been reaping a harvest of treasure, materials, artifacts and weapons from Spanish ships which had been caught in the web of the Bermudan reefs. Most of the settlers in New Providence were themselves from Bermuda, and in their new home soon began to 'runn a coasting in shallops which is a lazie course of life.'[5] Becoming superb small-boat sailors, except for a short but exciting part of the year when they chased sperm whales, they spent their time beachcombing for ambergris and turtleshell and of course, the seemingly endless bounty of flotsam and jetsom from piled-up Spanish ships.

Provided the ships safely cleared the Strait, they were in clear water, and barring white squalls and an odd hurricane in season, jogged safely north-eastwards on the prevailing south-westerly. It was in this region that the unfortunate New Spain flota of 1641 ran into serious trouble when the General,

Juan de Campos, unwisely ordered the fleet to sail in late September at the height of the hurricane season, without waiting for the Tierra Firme fleet due later that year. The flota had reached the latitude of the settlement of St Augustine when Nemesis, in the form of a severe hurricane, scattered the ships. It is not certain how many of the 21 merchantmen were lost. Three went down with all hands, perhaps five went ashore on the Florida coast and another sank just outside Havana. The Armada de Barlevento which was accompanying the flota had every ship crippled. Juan de Campos managed to sail the capitana *Pedro y Pablo* back to Spain, only to lose her on the Guadalquivir bar. The treasure was recovered, along with a large amount not accounted for in the register. The captain-general spent the next few years trying to explain exactly how this came about.

The almiranta, *Nuestra Señora de la pura y limpia Concepción*, commanded by Don Juan de Villavicencio, was severely mauled by the storm and very nearly foundered, losing her mainmast and suffering extensive damage to the ship and provisions. When the weather eased the crew managed to reduce the water in the hold to 2 feet and a course was laid for a Spanish base in Puerto Rica. Unfortunately she struck what was to become known as the Ambrosian or Silver Bank some 33 miles north of the Hispaniola coast. Of the approximately 500 people on board, about 200 survived. Villavicencio, some crew and senior passengers reached the coast in the longboat while the remainder managed to struggle to safety on makeshift rafts.

Over the years frequent and intensive searches were made to recover the treasure from the *Concepción*. Sir William Phips in 1687 found the wreck and salvaged over 25 tons of silver, some guns and a small amount of gold, and as recently as 1979 a wreck-hunting expedition organised by Seaquest International rediscovered the wreck and recovered a substantial part of the remaining treasure.

Had all gone well with the New Spain flota of 1641, they would have sailed to about the latitude of Cape Hatteras, another dirty corner whose treacherous winds could scatter the fleet and drive a ship ashore. From that latitude, in summer, the homeward-bound flota steered to pass north of the Bermudas, whose outlying reefs seemed to have attracted the galleons like a magnet. Their next landfall lay in the Azores where a squadron of the Armada del Mar Océano anxiously waited to escort them home. Apart from the autumn storms of the eastern North Atlantic, or a lurking enemy, only one more hurdle, namely the bar at San Lucar, then lay between the ships and home. Of course, if the weary, and somewhat nerve-shattered passengers and crew thought that they would be able to step straight off the ships on to the safety and luxury of the land, they had not taken into account the officials of the Casa de la Contratación. It could be weeks before the last question was asked and the final document signed releasing them to freedom.

This brief outline of the Spanish treasure fleets has highlighted a few of the many disasters which beset the ships. In 1555 it is recorded that 15 were wrecked or lost to corsairs; the year 1563 saw 7 driven ashore at Nombre de Dios, 15 in Cadiz and 6 in the Gulf of Campeche. In 1590, 15, and in 1601, 14 were wrecked in a norther at Vera Cruz; in 1605, 4 galleons went up on the Florida Keys; in 1715 and 1733 a total of 28 ships were destroyed by hurricanes – and this list is by no means complete. On average, over the history of the flotas, seven ships were lost each year. However, although the Carrera de Indias had its risks, the large majority of the ships got through, and the courage and sacrifice of the seamen who manned the galleons kept the silver, gold, pearls and emeralds pouring into the Spanish treasury for 300 years.

Manning the flotas

As we are dealing with a fleet, and a very valuable one at that, it would be amiss not to describe the offices peculiar to the trade. Also, during the seventeenth century, there were some evolutionary changes in the duties of ranking ship's officers which are interesting.

The lord almighty of any flota was the captain-general, and should the flota be accompanied by the silver galleons of the Armada de la Guardia, this post was further elevated. Although of necessity of noble status and implicitly a soldier, the captains-general were usually no mean sailors, chosen from the best admirals, who ideally may have spent their lives at sea in various positions and were old hands on the Indies run. Often represented as a grasping lubber by writers, this was rarely the case. He was forbidden to engage in any form of trade – although some did – and was very carefully vetted and selected by the reigning monarch. On his decisions the whole economy of Spain could possibly boom or bust. The admiral of the fleet was next in command to the captain-general and could be an aspirant to that post.

The afterguard

The ranking and duties of ship's officers had changed little since the days of Columbus. The captain, whether he was a *capitan de mar* or *de mar y guerra*, was in command of the ship. It was quite likely he was less experienced than the master, particularly when joint commands became normal and preference was sometimes given to career soldiers whose nautical experience was minimal. Ideally the captain was a master of both trades and could fulfil his duties as seaman and soldier. As a seaman he directed the gunfire in battle and carried out all the duties one would expect of his rank. If he was *capitan de mar y guerra* he also had command of the company of infantry. Should he be lacking in sea experience

then added responsibility devolved upon the master or *maestre*. One can see the potential for trouble here and imagine an experienced master biting his fingernails at the inane commands of a know-it-all captain. Nevertheless, I have sailed as master under a similar arrangement and with a sensible commander found no conflict, in fact it eased the isolation of captaincy.

On Spanish merchant ships the master was sometimes the captain but it was more usual by the seventeenth century for a captain to command larger merchantmen. The master's responsibility involved the sailing and handling of the ship and he administrated the provisioning, cargo, and ship's maintenance. When it became almost universal to carry captains, the unfortunate masters were relegated more and more to merely administrative duties and lost touch with their maritime skills until, by the last quarter of the seventeenth century, the skills of an experienced mariner were no longer demanded of them, provided the ship carried two pilots. On the king's ships his position was filled by a lieutenant, who came from the ranks of the infantry but surely must have had considerable experience at sea. Logically, the lieutenant was preparing himself for the position of *capitan de mar y guerra*, a post to which a master could not hope to aspire. Although expert seamanship was still required, a similar evolution of the duties of master occurred in other navies, but the command positions went to men who were always and ever sailors and held the army, if not in contempt, then with a certain amount of forbearance.

Other fleet officers consisted of the *piloto mayor*, the chief pilot, who laid down the navigation for the whole fleet and sailed in the capitana, the *capellan mayor*, who supervised the chaplains employed in each galleon, and the *gobernador* or governor of all the companies of soldiers. Ranking only under the captain-general and the admiral, he could choose and sail in his own ship, which became the *gobierno*, and was next in line after the capitana and almiranta.

The *veedor* sailed in the capitana and was virtually the Crown's watchdog. Another watchdog, the *maestra de plata*, was responsible for registering all the silver and treasure, a position for which he had to pay a substantial bond.

The pilots on the Indies ships were a specialist breed. Most were carefully trained and examined, in fact the Spanish navigation schools were respected models on which other nations based their own institutions. Although ranking third after the captain and master, his navigational decisions could not be overruled by either. Apart from all aspects of navigation, he was responsible for ensuring that all watchkeeping duties were properly fulfilled. There was a chronic shortage of pilots, but a ship carrying a poorly trained pilot could get along following the lead of the *piloto mayor* in the capitana. A dishonest pilot who lost his ship could be executed.

Other ranks: sailors and soldiers

The *contramaestre*, immediately under the master, has been compared with the boatswain but I find a list of his duties reads exactly like those of a mate. Also, as any mate will tell you, he was the hardest-worked donkey in the ship. He was required to be literate and he was responsible for the ballasting, loading and trimming of the ship. Every aspect of the maintenance of the ship came under his eye, including careening and fitting-out. Whereas the sail-handling post of later sailing-ship mates was the fore mast and foc'stle, his was at the foot of the main mast, except probably when anchoring. He was directed in ship maintenance by the master, and in ordering the hands when ship- or sail-handling, by the pilot.

Much more aligned with a bosun was the *guardian*. He was the contramaestre's right-hand man and chosen, like most bosuns, from the leading hands among the crew. Apart from normal bosun's duties, his special charge were the apprentices, pages and the ship's boats, which were usually manned by the apprentices. His station was on the foc'stle head.

In old Spain sailors were considered of little account. The soldier, however, was honoured and relatively pampered and when employed in ships, as large contingents of 100 or more were in the silver galleons, he had a relatively easy life compared to the deprived, and in the soldier's estimation, depraved sailor.

In the early seventeenth century controversy smouldered as to whether ships could be better managed under a single captain, or *capitan de mar y guerra*, or retention of the old joint command of a *capitan de mar* or sea captain who commanded the ship and crew, and an almost independent officer in charge of the shipborne infantry. The Marquis of Montesclaros was apparently a fierce adherent of the latter and illustrates an extreme example of the contemporary attitude towards sailors when he claimed they were lazy louts, without honour, and a commander could not treat his soldiers with the 'courtesy and decency due to them'[6] while using force to drive reluctant sailors from their hiding places to do their duties – no soldier would be pleased to see himself dressed like a sailor or seated on the ground sewing sails, or stirring a cauldron of tar as sailors commonly did. His viewpoint was becoming outmoded, although there was little improvement in the lot or status of sailors. The tars, in common with those of other nations, would have probably responded with the patronising humour of sailors towards the landsmen. It is said that the tack end of the huge lateen mizzen yard was referred to as the '*matasoldados*', or 'killer of soldiers', for its propensity to slam across the deck about head height when working ship.

The mastasoldas

EIGHTEENTH-CENTURY SHIPS

By the beginning of the eighteenth century European mariners had long since worked their ships into every corner of the North Atlantic and Caribbean, and had become familiar with the ocean. Apart from the intricacies of the ice-bound waters of the far north, all had been explored, and settlements in the islands of the West Indies and on the shores of mainland America were beginning to consolidate and assume some of their present-day aspects.

Transatlantic developments

Canada was known as 'New France' and French Jesuits, explorers and voyageurs were pushing far into the interior of the continent by way of the Great Lakes and the rivers that fed these inland seas. In 1682, from the north, La Salle had followed the Mississippi from its source to the Gulf of Mexico and, by the end of the century, a permanent settlement had been established in the new territory of Louisiana. New Orleans was to be founded in 1717. France also held a firm foothold in the Caribbean, possessing the islands of Martinique, Guadaloupe, St Kitts and that part of Hispaniola now known as Haiti. The pattern of the seemingly endless intermittent wars between France and England had entered a new phase with the commencement of the second Hundred Years' War in 1689. France was shortly to lose to her rival the Canadian maritime colonies of Newfoundland and Acadia and the West Indian island of St Kitts.

Spain still tenuously held her empire, but, in the Atlantic, her monopoly of trade in the West Indies and Central America had, for some time, been undermined by the intrusions and assaults of the polyglot buccaneers and the aggressive mercantile activities of Holland, France and England. Inspired by the audacity of Henry Morgan who, in 1671, had sacked and destroyed the old city of Panama, buccaneers, privateers and merchants of these nations were already trespassing upon and looting the virtually undefended continental west coast.

Within the first decade of the century the English privateer, Woodes Rogers, was to snap up an eastward-bound Manila galleon off lower California. These ships sailed part of Spain's trade route to the wealth of the East. The galleons discharged their expensive freight at Acapulco, where much of it was sold at an annual fair. The portion designated for the Crown and goods directed on to Spain were transported overland to Vera Cruz where they were loaded into the flota for Spain. With her industries and merchants crushed out of existence by the imbalance and bureaucracy caused by dependence on vast imports of silver, gold and jewels, Spain's only real interest in her American empire was to keep the transfusion of wealth from across the Atlantic flowing into her veins. Preferably, but by no means always, the flota from New Mexico and the Silver Galleons from Tierra Firme continued to bear their precious cargos westward each year.

The transatlantic enterprises of Holland were in decline. Her vessels were mainly engaged in the slave trade and, along with every other nation, illicit trade with Spanish America, for which the Dutch used the island of Curacao as a base. Apart from applying

her resources, through the V.O.C. or East India Company, to extending her trade in the East, Holland's main endeavours during the seventeenth century had been directed towards struggling with the Portuguese in Brazil. Her infant colony of Pernambuco had succumbed to the Lusitanians 50 years before.

Together with Curacao, Holland possessed three islands in the Leewards; St Martin, St Eustatius and Saba. On the South American mainland the Dutch held Surinam, where planters were mistreating their plantation slaves abominably. On the North American seaboard, their colony of New Netherlands had fallen to the English in 1664 and the port of New Amsterdam was now New York.

During the seventeenth century other nations had tried to establish a toehold across the Atlantic. For a brief 20 years before it was overrun by the Dutch in 1655, Sweden possessed a struggling colony south of the Delaware. Only 2 years before the end of the century, Scotland had tried to establish a colony in the Gulf of Darien, with the enterprising intention of using it as a base for trade with the Pacific. However, even the hardy Scots could not cope with the pestilential climate of the region and the unwelcome attentions of the Spanish, to whom they surrendered in 1700. The failure of this venture, and the refusal of the English colonies to offer aid, is said to have paved the way for union with England.

By the year 1700, by far the most vigorous and tenacious transatlantic possessions were held by England. The Hudson Bay Company maintained thriving fur-trading posts in the north but had just lost their York factory to the French. The company was to get it back at the signing of the Treaty of Utrecht in 1713. England held the whole North American coastline, including Newfoundland, south to Florida. Her colonists were beginning to thrive and occupied themselves whenever possible by ignoring or circumventing the most recent impositions of England's Navigation Laws, which were designed to protect her trade and shipping. Fish from Newfoundland, Nova Scotian and New England waters were shipped to Europe and the West Indies. From her American colonies, naval stores were exported to England and agricultural products to the West Indies. With the profits from this trade the Americans could purchase wares from the home country and other nations. Tobacco from Virginia had made that region wealthy; in South Carolina rice had been successfully planted and, by 1700, this state had supplanted Egypt as the prime supplier of rice to Europe.

In the north, Boston was the leading port for the transatlantic trade. New Yorkers were wealthy, but interested themselves too heartily in the activities of privateers and pirates to compete in honest trade with Boston. In fact, at the turn of the century the young city was a veritable nest of pirates, among them Captain Kidd. The adventures of these freebooters took them as far afield as the Indian Ocean, from where they brought back a rich harvest of loot from plundered East Indiamen.

England's control over the Caribbean pivoted on her island possessions of Jamaica, the Leeward Islands and Barbados, which her mariners had used as windward bases to descend on the Spanish Main to plunder and to force a trade.

Barbados had established its sugar industry in the 1640s and by 1660 her fabulously wealthy planters were filling the holds of 200 English merchantmen annually. Jamaica, which had fallen to the decimated forces of the ill-conceived and planned Venables expedition against Santo Domingo in 1655, had survived her lurid buccaneering days. When Port Royal sank into the sand and sea in the earthquake

of 1692, taking with it the 4-year-old grave of Sir Henry Morgan, it signalled the end of an era. Pirates and buccaneers had by no means been driven from the Caribbean, but now Jamaica was respectable and rapidly surpassing Barbados in her sugar industry and in her strategic importance.

On the mainland coast of Honduras and on the Black River, tough, independent bands of English 'Baymen' cut and sold dyewood and refused to be dislodged by the Spanish. Straddling the northward-bound sailing routes of vessels bound for Europe and New England lay the British-held Bahamas and, out in the Atlantic, the Bermudas. England was now well on the way to the apex of her eighteenth-century maritime empire.

Sugar, molasses and that 'hott, hellish and terrible' by-product once known as rumbullion, tobacco, indigo, logwood, ginger, hides, salt from Maracaibo and hardwood such as mahogany, were the primary exports from the Caribbean.

The limits of wood and fibre

By the year 1700 the North Atlantic was a busy ocean highway with a myriad of vessels hauling the products of the Caribbean and North America, the Newfoundland fisheries, European exports and the slave trade. Numerous vessels were also bound south of the Line and beyond the Cape of Good Hope, and gradually adventurous mariners were beginning to use Drake's Passage around the Horn to the Pacific, but it was to be another half century and more before the extent of this vast ocean was fully explored. Wherever the Europeans of the eighteenth century fought, traded or explored, they needed ships – multitudes of ships, from large, well manned Indiamen and smart, fast, packets, to capacious freighters and malodorous fishermen.

The eighteenth century saw the Age of Enlightenment, when reason and pragmatic science produced great advances in technology ashore and afloat. By 1700 ships had reached a plateau in their

design and, from the first years of the eighteenth century until the Americans revolutionised ship design in the 1840s, the basic hull design of ocean-going ships changed very little. Quarterdecks and poops, already losing their prominence at the beginning of the period, gradually sank back into the hull, until, by 1800, many average-sized ships of about 300 to 400 ton were flush-decked. Even before 1600, the limit in size inherent in timber construction had been reached. The technology of the wooden ship, where timber and fibre were the predominant materials, reached a frontier which only the Industrial Revolution enabled shipbuilders to pass. The extra wooden bracing or larger scantlings which would prevent hogging or sagging beyond this limit made a vessel grossly overweight, so that, until the more universal use of iron for cross-braces, knees and more extensive fastenings, there were few ships built that even equalled in size the old Portuguese East Indiamen of the sixteenth century.

Changes aloft

It was aloft that the most obvious changes occurred, with the introduction of jibs and staysails and the gradual transformation and then extinction of the spritsail topsail and the spritsail itself. Not so obvious, but certainly welcomed by seamen, was the greatly improved standing rigging, particularly the gear supporting the bowsprit. Further improvements came with the Industrial Revolution and the greater use of iron, which replaced the superb, but less efficient, rope and wood technology of many fittings.

Very early in the eighteenth century wheel steering came into use, coppering was experimented with in the 1760s and, after a few problems with electrolysis caused between the copper and iron fastenings, this sheathing became almost universal for ships going into tropical waters, although the French continued with *mailletage* for a while. This

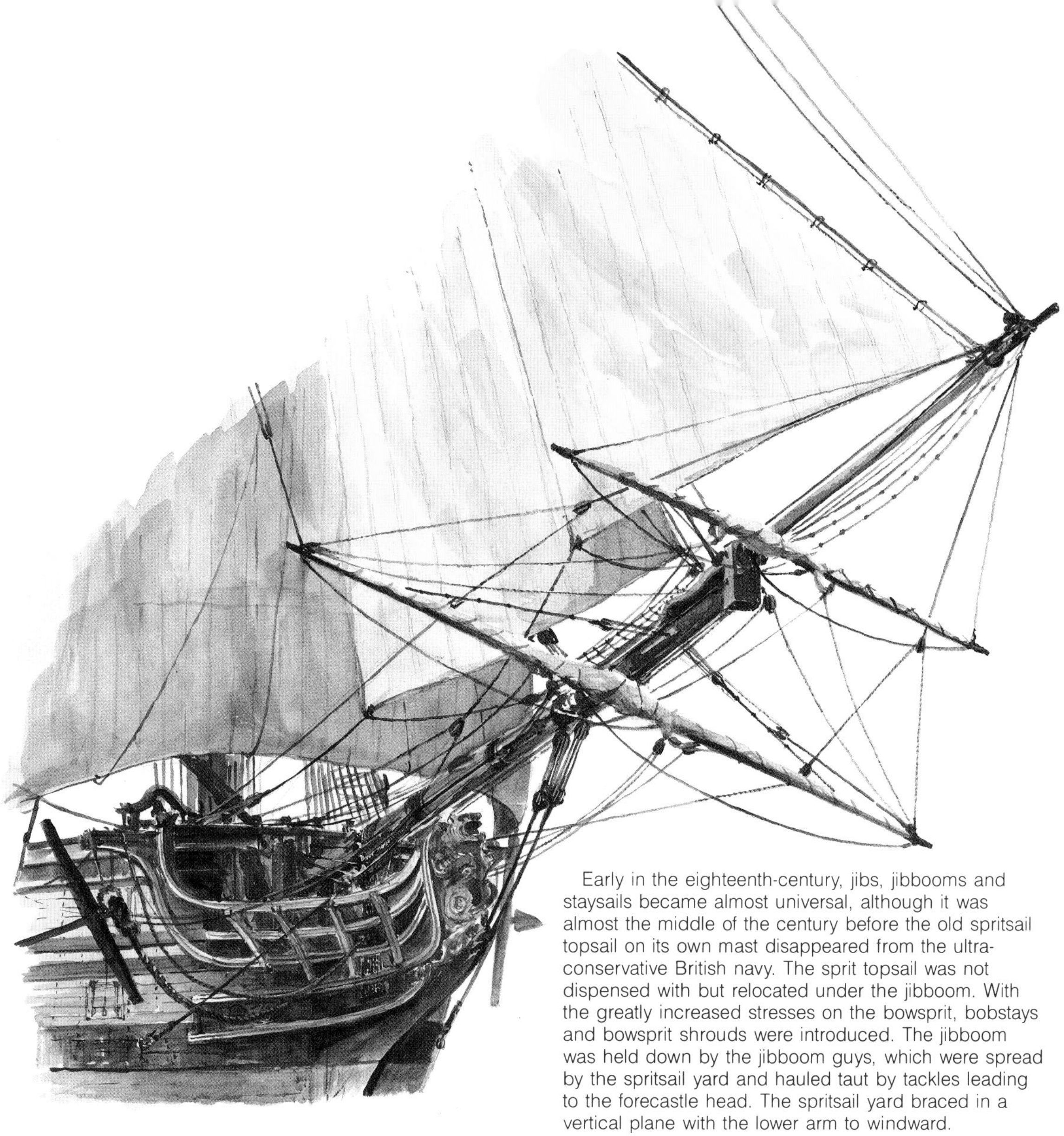

Early in the eighteenth-century, jibs, jibbooms and staysails became almost universal, although it was almost the middle of the century before the old spritsail topsail on its own mast disappeared from the ultra-conservative British navy. The sprit topsail was not dispensed with but relocated under the jibboom. With the greatly increased stresses on the bowsprit, bobstays and bowsprit shrouds were introduced. The jibboom was held down by the jibboom guys, which were spread by the spritsail yard and hauled taut by tackles leading to the forecastle head. The spritsail yard braced in a vertical plane with the lower arm to windward.

Chapman's eighteenth-century merchantmen

In 1768 a Swedish naval architect, Frederick Henry Chapman, produced a study of merchant vessels and boats. His *Architectura Navalis Mercatoria* is an authoritative insight into the vessels of the period prior to the Industrial Revolution. Not only were these years termed the Age of Enlightenment; they were also the Age of Elegance, and Chapman's ships reflect this exuberantly. Love, care and graceful adornment seem to have been lavished even on the most humble fishing smack. Chapman's drafts, as in his Plate XXXI reproduced overleaf, omit many tantalising details, particularly the nature of their accommodations and finer detail of rigging. The following illustrations attempt to depict the various classes and rigs of eighteenth-century merchantmen presented in Chapman's work.

A privateering frigate

Length between perpendiculars	160 ft (48.77 m)
Moulded breadth	46 ft 10 in. (12.45 m)
Loaded draught	21 ft 3 in. (6.48 m)
Burthen	396 heavy lasts (950 tons)
Guns	28 28-pounders on the gun deck
	12 6-pounders on the forecastle and quarterdeck
Provisions for 5 months	
Water for 2½ months	
Crew	400 including officers

These two plates from the work of Frederick Chapman depict a large, well fitted-out frigate engaged in privateering. From medieval days until its abolition in 1856, this popular maritime activity engaged the enthusiastic participation of all, from financiers, shipowners and captains down to the lowliest boy.

Until the nineteenth century there were no really significant differences between the design of

method employed iron nails with large, flat heads. These were hammered into a sheathing with their heads adjacent to each other. The rust from the nails formed a solid sheet over the hull. As it was cheaper, sacrificial wooden sheathing continued to be used on many merchant ships, particularly in cooler waters. About the same time, navigation was vastly improved for those fortunate enough to be able to afford a chronometer and finally pin down their longitudes.

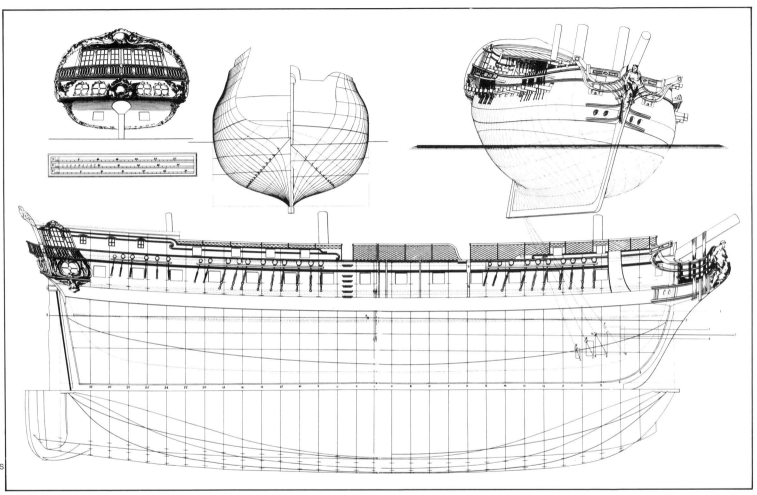

Frederick Chapman's
draught of a
privateering frigate.

warships and merchantmen. True, there were
warships which never engaged in trade, and whose
scantlings and layout were designed to carry the
maximum number of guns. Likewise there were
merchantmen which carried an absolute minimum
of armament and were designed to contain the
maximum amount of freight. Very few, if any,

vessels involved in overseas trade were totally
unarmed. Today one would have to hail from the
central Siberian steppes not to be able to tell the
difference between a container ship and a naval
frigate. In those days it needed an experienced eye
to tell the difference between an East Indiaman and
a warship, or between merchant and fighting frigate.

They carried similar rigs on similar hulls and the
armament and smartness of some merchantmen,
particularly the Indiamen, compared favourably
with naval vessels.

Monarchs were eternally short of funds for the
navies which became imperative to maintain
seapower and control of trade and overseas

Sections of the frigate opposite

possessions. Given that no great changes were needed to fit out a vessel to fight, an economical and even lucrative way for the Crown to augment its fighting forces and annoy the enemy was to authorise, by way of *Letters of Marque* or *Reprisal*, its merchant captains and private citizens to attack enemy shipping and even engage in amphibious assaults on targets ashore. These papers gave the captains authority, hopefully recognised by other nations, to engage in hostile activities against enemy shipping. Without these letters any captain who attacked a vessel of another nation could be deemed a pirate and dealt with accordingly. The letters gave a description of the ship, the amount of surety deposited against her proper behaviour and emphasised the necessity of having her prizes *condemned* and valued at an Admiralty court where the portion due to the Crown could be assessed before the sale and disposal of the ship and its contents. After this was complete, the proceeds would be shared out among the investors, owners, captain and crew.

It was rarely that any European power was without an enemy and was not either engaged in all-out war or sniping at a potential foe. Particularly across the Atlantic during the seventeenth century it was considered, regardless of the state of relations with Spain, that there was 'No peace beyond the Line' – that Vatican-backed demarcation drawn down the ocean beyond which no unauthorised, non-Spanish heretic should trespass. French, Dutch and English West-Indian-island governors always claimed to be, and often were, under the threat of attack by Spaniards. So, with no aid forthcoming from the home country, they happily issued their local craft with letters of marque and sat back to await their bonus from the prizes and loot. So it was that buccaneers found amenable employment, glory, and possible, if temporary, wealth. Henry Morgan made sure he carried his letters when he marched overland and sacked Panama.

The frigate illustrated by Chapman and the illustration of the privateering ketch which follows were in effect privately owned warships which would only take a cargo if their luck was out and it was worth their while. They would rove the seas, lurking at likely corners to pounce on shipping usually less powerful than themselves. Many of these vessels had superbly trained and loyal crews, who had signed on freely and enthusiastically, happy to sail under strict, but fair, discipline and share in the luck and prize money won by bold captains. Although they usually preyed on fat merchantmen, these rovers were quite capable of defeating naval vessels with greater armament but pressed, underfed and underpaid crews.

Privateering was not exclusively the occupation of well backed, powerful ships with large crews. Any merchant vessel could, by depositing surety and making application, obtain their letters. Around the coasts and among the islands, small craft, some no more than rowboats, often worked in teams. In the English Channel and elsewhere, luggers were popular privateering craft, being swift and weatherly. The *Truelove*, whose story is told later, was an Arctic whaler whose winter occupation was often humping wine from Portugal. She bristled with all of four small cannon. Her captain was happy to carry letters, for she could easily jump an unwary French fisherman in the Channel or Biscay and improve her profits.

Apart from the surety and some enhancement of their arms, the only expense involved in operating on the side as a privateer was the necessity of carrying sufficient crew to man a prize and sail her to the nearest port with a prize court. It was a careless or desperate privateer who sank his opponent and any hope of profit. If the prize was not worth the effort of getting her back, or the privateer had insufficient crew, the victim might be sunk, or even let go, after any valuable freight and appurtenances had been stripped from the ship.

Privateering was always a popular and favoured occupation with those with the bent for it, and the captains often won fame for themselves and carried on their business honourably, but there was a shady side. Too frequently, a privateer captain's definition of an enemy ship was rather elastic and their activities would border on outright piracy. Often, when their country was inconveniently at peace with everyone, the dedicated rover would find some other nation which had a satisfactory full-house of enemies to whom they were prepared to be hostile. This was a problem the governors of Jamaica faced when they attempted to stop issuing letters of marque to the buccaneer captains on whom the defence of the island depended. Out of employment, they offered their services, not to Spain, for that would be unthinkable, but to the governors of the French and Dutch Islands. Usually the captains continued to operate against the Spanish, but it only needed hostilities to be opened between any of the other nations to have the less patriotic of the international brethren picking off their own country's shipping.

Privateering had its abuses and sometimes atrocities, but it was generally carried on honourably by the standards of the day. The terms corsair, freebooter and rover, when applied to privateers and not piracy, has, on the whole, retained a colourful and heroic image.

A privateering ketch

Length between perpendiculars ...... 85 ft (26 m)
Moulded breadth .... 23 ft (7 m)
Loaded draught .... 10 ft 8 in. (3.28 m)
Burthen .... 54 heavy lasts (approx. 125 tons)
Guns .... 12 4-pounders on the gundeck
Oars .... 9 pairs

Manned by 90 men, with provisions for 2½ months and water for 1¼ months, this elegant ship was quite capable of scouring the breadth of the Atlantic for her prizes. This is one class of vessel which was identified by her rig, which dates back to the early seventeenth century and quite likely well before, when they were described as *catches*. Charles II had his yachts rigged as ketches and the heroic French Admiral, the Marquis Abraham Duquesne, used the long foredeck, achieved probably by taking the foremast out of a three-master, to mount a large mortar throwing a bomb weighing about 200 pounds. In 1682, the Mediterranean port of Algiers had the dubious privilege of being the first city to be bombarded by seaborne mortars from his *bomb ketches*.

The rig of the bomb ketch appears unbalanced, literally as if there is a mast missing, but it proved handy and weatherly. The unnamed privateering ketch shown here does not mount a mortar, but her rig is almost as extreme as that of a bomb ketch. She must have been very fast and from her sharp lines, flaring deadrise and gracefulness, I suspect that she is French built. It is possible, even likely, that her course had the full drop, rather than the high footed sail depicted. Her huge jib must have been a light-

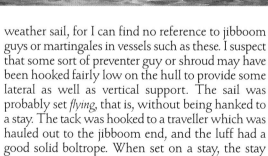

A bomb ketch

A fast privateering ketch, cleared for action

A merchant frigate

Length between perpendiculars 128 ft (39.01 m)
Moulded breadth .... 34 ft 6 in. (10.52 m)
Loaded draught .... 19 ft 3 in. (5.87 m)
Burden .... 276 heavy lasts (approx. 670 tons)

The term 'frigate' was ill defined during the seventeenth century and could refer, as in the Spanish *frigata*, to a small, fast vessel equipped with

weather sail, for I can find no reference to jibboom guys or martingales in vessels such as these. I suspect that some sort of preventer guy or shroud may have been hooked fairly low on the hull to provide some lateral as well as vertical support. The sail was probably set *flying*, that is, without being hanked to a stay. The tack was hooked to a traveller which was hauled out to the jibboom end, and the luff had a good solid boltrope. When set on a stay, the stay

was seized to the traveller on the jibboom, led through a cheek block at the topmast head and was hauled taut by a tackle from the deck. A jib set flying had to be stowed either inboard or at the end of the bowsprit, but if set on a stay, the stay could be left set up and the sail stowed on the jibboom, or, alternatively, the stay could be slackened and the sail stowed in nettings alongside the staysail. As in all vessels, the jibboom was designed to be easily run in.

A merchant frigate

A hagboat

A frigate

oars and sail, also to smaller classes of warships. In the eighteenth century the *frigate* became a definite and favoured class of vessel. Early examples were small, well armed, fast ships capable of ocean passages. Carrying from 24 to 28 guns on a single deck, they were often used as convoy escorts and privateers. Although they gradually increased in size, their use as a fighting ship continued throughout the days of sail and they were popularly described as 'the eyes of the fleet' for their service as watchdogs and messengers. British shipbuilders, confined as they were by regulation and conservatism, never could compete with the fine, fast frigates constructed by the French, and many a dashing British frigate captain considered himself in his seventh heaven if he was given command of a French prize. The Americans, during their battle for independence, found they could build large, fast frigates such as the *Constitution,* which could out-gun and outrun any ship of their size.

Chapman rates merchantmen designed on frigate lines as first-class vessels and as such they were favoured by the large operators such as the India companies. In the merchant frigate it was tried to combine speed, capacity and fighting ability to its ultimate, thus the popularity of these vessels as privateers. However, the only real apparent design difference which set them clearly apart from the vessels of the second class, which were described as 'hagboats', was the design of the tuck. Frederick Chapman even goes to the length of describing how the lines of a hagboat's buttocks can be altered to make her into a frigate. The advantage of the frigate's transom tuck is obvious. It can be pierced for two guns so as to protect the otherwise vulnerable stern, and discourage a vessel in chase. Less obvious is that it provides for more space and buoyancy aft, but requires careful and strong construction, it being a potentially weak feature.

The merchant frigate depicted here has all except her main lower stun'sails set, and from the peak of the gaff she has set a sail known as the *driver*.

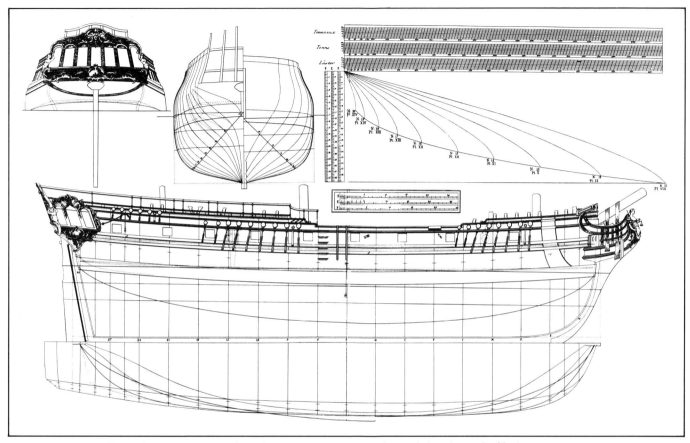

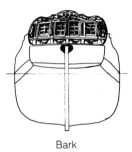

Bark

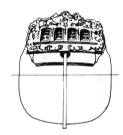

English West India trader

Chapman's hagboat. Dotted lines show how the lines of the hagboat's stern can be made into those of a frigate.

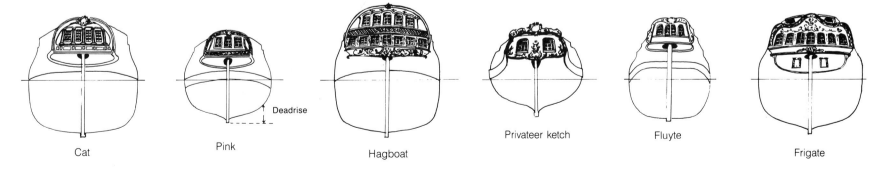

Cat

Pink

Deadrise

Hagboat

Privateer ketch

Fluyte

Frigate

109

Hagboat

Length between perpendiculars
.... 148 ft 9 in. (45.34 m)
Moulded breadth .... 37 ft 10 in. (11.53 m)
Draught .... 20 ft 4 in. (6.20 m)
Burden .... 389 heavy lasts (934 tons)

A Swedish hagboat getting under way

Relegated to the second class by the shape of her stern, the *hagboat* is basically otherwise identical to the frigate. It might be expected that the lines of frigates were more conducive to speed, but the samples of lines for hagboats do not necessarily show greater or less sharpness and deadrise than those for frigates. The ship illustrated has just weighed her anchor and, with her headsails and fore-topsail drawing, is letting her head fall off.

A pink

Usually not as large as some of the frigates and hagboats, the *pink* was defined by her stern, and also, it seems, by a large amount of deadrise. This is the amount by which the floors rise from the keel to the bilge and it was generally believed that a large deadrise gave a ship greater speed. This is a fallacy exposed in the mid-nineteenth century by the American, Captain N.B. Palmer, when he developed the lines of the prosaic, perfectly flat-floored Mississippi cotton drogher to produce the fastest sailing packets in the North Atlantic (see page 154). Compare the transverse section of the pink with that of the ketch, which was clearly designed to fly. Eighteenth-century naval architects and shipbuilders worked on the observed fact that, in their ships, large deadrise did improve speed. Blinkered as they were by a dedication to the 'cod's head, mackerel tail' philosophy, they discounted refining the ends of their ships beyond a certain point. What greater deadrise and recurve into the keel did was to force the underwater lines of their ships into a finer run fore and aft, thus sharpening the hull. Of course, it was not as simple as this. Other factors must be taken into account. Particularly in large vessels, the technology to build long, sharper ships had not been developed; most ships, even if they did not carry full batteries of guns, based their models on those that did, and this demanded a large tumblehome and fairly bluff ends. Also, at that time, there was not the all-consuming, all-American, razzmatazz demand for speed as in the next century.

Inconveniently, by endeavouring to increase the sailing qualities and speed by incorporating a large deadrise, carrying capacity was sacrificed. Thus, in

A snow-rigged pink

110

A brig-rigged pink showing a typical pink stern. Note the loading ports.

producing fast merchant ships, designers were involved in a constant search for the ideal proportions. As the pink was usually operated as purely a merchant ship, it would be expected that she would not have such an exuberant deadrise.

Timber, particularly long pieces for spars, was ever in demand. Fleets of vessels were engaged in hauling logs suitable for spars from the Baltic and, increasingly, North America, to the deforested countries of Europe. During the eighteenth century, special mast-ships transported spars from America for the British Navy, and it was quite likely that many of these vessels were pinks. Loading long pieces of timber, or logs, through the relatively small hatches in the upper and 'tween-decks of ships was difficult. A practical method was to run the pieces in through end ports, usually stern ports in those days.

The pink was one of a family of vessels which evolved from the early Dutch *fluyts*. All except one of Chapman's examples of pinks only differ from the hagboats and frigates in that they have more rounded sterns below the transom, narrower poops and more deadrise. It was the stern that really defined this class of vessel, and the archetypal pink stern is shown in the accompanying sketch. This configuration is inherited from the fluyt, and allows for loading ports to be placed high and clear. Of course, in this small ship, they displace the after accommodation forward to under the mainmast.

There are two factors which allow for a greater permissible deadrise in vessels engaged in the timber trade. Firstly, no space is lost in the deadrise as the spar timber lies fore and aft and does not require a box-shaped space for the maximum stowage, as do barrels, the universal container in those days. What is preferable is that the vessel has fairly bluff ends, and the pink has this feature. Secondly, by incorporating a large deadrise, to obtain an equivalent capacity to other classes of vessel of the same dimensions, the draught must be increased. Timber vessels do not have to work in shallow waters, for

their freight can, and was, conveniently loaded from the water at deep anchorages and dumped over the side at the destination. No working up narrow waters, or lying alongside shallow docks, or taking the ground was required of them. Larger pinks (and Chapman's largest is 435 tons) could load timber through their main hatches, could also be pierced with stern-ports, or effectively ply in general trade. Because of their swiftness and capacity, two pinks, the *Anna* and the *Industry*, were chosen as storeships to accompany George Anson's fleet to the Pacific. The commodore would not have wanted his warships held back by a couple of slow merchantmen.

Pinks, and all the other classes of merchantmen shown here, could be ship-rigged, or fitted out with any other type of rig the owner desired and which was suitable for her size.

A cat

Length between perpendiculars 134 ft (40.84 m)
Moulded breadth 34 ft (10.36 m)
Loaded draught 18 ft 6 in. (5.64 m)
Burden 326 heavy lasts (782.4 tons)

It might be noted that all the eighteenth-century vessels illustrated so far possessed a beakhead and headrails, whereas the classes of merchantmen which follow lack this feature. This is not to say that there were not exceptions where a wealthy and proud owner would grace his cat or bark with a beakhead, and there were certainly pinks without beakheads. The *Bounty* of Bligh and Christian was an ex-collier cat which possessed its beakhead before being re-rigged by the Navy for her Pacific voyage. Along with having flatter floors which would take the ground well, it was, once again, the configuration of the stern which defined the class. Like the pinks, they were another branch of evolution from the *fluyt*, having a narrow poop and transom with a full, rounded stern. Indeed, they were virtually a flatter-floored pink, and afloat and fitted with a beakhead, it would be difficult to tell the difference between some pinks and a cat.

Cats were used in all trades, including the timber trade, for which they were as well suited as the pink. However, it was in the coal trade they made their reputation and in their exploratory voyages they won glory. William Hutchinson, an eighteenth-century captain, and author of *A Treatise on Practical Seamanship*, began a long and interesting career in a small collier cat out of Newcastle-on-Tyne. Frequently he refers to, and extols, the qualities of these vessels and their seamen. Here are some samples of his observations. Firstly, while expounding the virtues of deep and narrow squaresails, he comments:

> To endeavour to make a ship sail by the wind, and turn well to windward, deserves the greatest regard, because safety, as well as many other great benefits depend upon it. The good effects of deep and narrow squaresails, can't be better recommended to answer this purpose, than by the performance of ships in the coal and timber trades to London, tho' the designed properties in building and fitting these ships, are burden at a small draft of water, to take and bear the ground well, and to sail with few hands, and little ballast, yet these ships perform so well at sea, that the government often makes choice of them for store ships, in the most distant naval expeditions; and in narrow channels among shoals, and turning to windward in narrow rivers, there are no ships of equal burthen can match them, for which I attribute a great deal, to their deep narrow squaresails, which may be perceived to trim so flat and fair, upon a wind . . .

> And they are mostly built with pink sterns,

A cat dried out alongside

rounding inwards in their upper works, that they trim the sails to stand full within five and a half points of the wind, and so little tophamper above water, to hold wind, in proportion to other ships, that when turning to windward in narrow channels, they beat ships that would beat them in the open sea, which must be owing to such reasons as have been given, and that the running ropes may run clear in making short trips, they don't coil them up, but they let them run as they were hauled.[1]

113

While admitting that the seamen of the East Indiamen, and presumably their ships, are 'the most perfect in the open seas', Hutchinson clearly deems the seamen of the collier cats the most expert at their craft in confined waters. After explaining some apparently hair-raising sailing when hundreds of ships are trying to get out of the Tyne, the manner in which the ships were rolled over the shallow bar and their method of navigating down the coast, he describes, with admiration, the way they work up the river to London. Remember, in those days the Thames was far more crowded than it is now. Large merchantmen from overseas, warships, barges, lighters, wherries, fishing boats and hundreds of large and small coasters lay at anchor or worked their way up and down the river. Many of the cats these colliermen sailed were large ships, some of them measuring up to 500 tons and more. They took a lot of stopping should a misjudgment be made:

> Their management in working these large ships to windward, up most parts of *London* river with their main-sails set is likewise remarkable, and from their great practice knowing the depth of water according to the time of tide, and how much the ship will shoot a-head in stays; they stand upon each tack to the greatest nicety close from side to side as far as possible things will admit of to keep in a fair way, and where eddies occasion the true tide to run very narrow, or ships &c. lie in the way so as not to give room to turn to windward, they very dexterously brail up mainsail and foresail, and drives to windward with the tide under their topsails by such rules as has been described, and in the Pool where there is so little room to pass through such crowds of ships, their management has afforded me the greatest pleasure, and when they get near their designed birth, to what a nicety they let go the anchor, veers out the

> cable to run freely as the occasion may require, so as to bring the ship up exactly in time in surprising little room, clear of the other ships, and lays her easily and fairly along side of the tier of ships where they moor, so that as they say they can work and lay their ships to a boats length as occasion requires.[2]

Hutchinson is describing cats which have been in some ways modified for their trade, but it is clear that, although the vessels may not have been fast, they were a very handy, capacious vessel which could take the ground well. Their qualities were recognised by Captain Cook, who chose the *Endeavour*, the *Resolution* and the *Adventure* for his voyages. All these were cats and, whereas the *Endeavour* sported no beakhead, both other ships did so.

A bark

Length between perpendiculars	131 ft (39.93 m)
Moulded breadth	33 ft (10.06 m)
Loaded draught	18 ft 6 in. (5.64 m)
Burden	335 heavy lasts (804 tons)

Although some barks displayed many of the adornments of frigates and ranged from small sloops to large ships like this one, they were nearly always less elaborate and were relegated to the fifth class of merchantmen. They could be thought of as a poor man's frigate, for their stern is formed almost identically to that of their classy sister. The remainder of the hull is similar to a cat, except that they are flatter floored and generally more boxy in their transverse section. No doubt some barks, as were cats, were fitted out with beakheads, but this did not tart them up into frigates. As in the frigate, the stern was often pierced with ports.

In earlier centuries, a bark was essentially a term for a small merchant ship, a smaller version of the naos, carracks and, later, galleons, and probably derived from the term *barge*. Gradually the term began to apply to the cheaper and more economical merchantmen which followed the design of the best ships as far as expense would allow. Discounting the fancy adornments of most frigates, the cost of building them went into the extra labour and more expensive material necessary to form their more shapely hulls. The stern of a frigate would be actually easier and cheaper to build than that of a cat or pink, so the frigate stern could be retained in building a bark. The flat bottoms and slab sides of a bark would be simple, quick and, as it required less hard-to-come-by compass pieces, less expensive in

A nineteenth-century bark

materials than frigates. They were the forerunners of vessels produced a little later which were described as 'built by the mile and cut off by the yard'.

At this time the term bark held no reference to the rig as it did in the nineteenth century. It is difficult to correctly determine how a term slides from one definition to another over time, but perhaps it happened this way. At the same time as Chapman was producing his survey of eighteenth-century ships, really classy ships began to step mizzen topgallant masts, a luxury proscribed for the thrifty barks. It was not long before any vessel which only crossed a mizzen topsail yard, and particularly the cats which sailed sans beakhead, became described as *bark-rigged*. I have read of collier cats in a slightly later period, when the typical rig had their main masts well aft and the mizzen close behind, being described as barks by their rig, although the ships were not barks by the then present or future definition.

The advantages of this rig are that, for a small loss of speed, there is an appreciable saving in gear and the manpower to handle it. Thus the bark-rig became standard for the more prosaic merchantmen of the nineteenth century when, with longer mainyards, the mizzen topsail became less efficient and was done away with. Many mightily sparred clippers ended their days cut down to barks. But, in the last days of the sailing ship, the rig came into its own. Most of the smaller, and some of the finest examples of large, iron and steel sailing ships were bark-rigged.

A Dutch fly-boat or flight

Length between perpendiculars 136 ft (41.45 m)
Moulded breadth .... 30 ft (9.14 m)
Draught .... 15 ft (4.57 m)

This well maintained, traditional Dutch vessel is hoisting in her longboat and loosing sail before weighing anchor. She is a direct descendant of the

An eighteenth-century bark hove-to

fluyt depicted on page 15 and the terms *fly-boat* or *flight* are English interpretations of her Dutch name. So successful were these vessels that little changed in their basic design over the 200 and more years they were in use. The poop has become lower and the rig is that of the eighteenth century, but little else has obviously altered. The bumkin for the fore-tack is the same, as are the hull and the configuration of the stern and poop. I suspect that the running rigging may have been a little different from other ships, for these Dutch fluyts were always renowned for their ease of handling.

A Dutch fluyt or flight hoisting out her longboat

remains to clearly differentiate the fly-boat from other vessels are the greater ratio of length to beam and draught, and the flat, but not overly broad, floors and wide rounded buttock, at least above water. They were long, fairly shallow-draught vessels, able to take the ground comfortably.

An eighteenth-century variant of the fluyt was the *bootschip*. This had a broader poop than the standard fluyt, an alteration which may have been developed in the whaling industry to enable the fluyts to carry boats on their quarters. The large tumblehome and narrow poops of the standard fluyts were not suitable.

Le Chameau

Length between perpendiculars 152 ft 6 in. (46.48 m)
Moulded breadth .... 34 ft 3 in. (10.44 m)
Draught .... 15 ft 3 in. (4.65 m)

Other vessels and rigs

All the preceding vessels, apart from the privateering ketch, have been named for features of their hull design. In each class the size can theoretically range from the smallest craft to the largest. In practice, the larger vessels were usually frigates and hagboats, but the smallest frigate presented by Chapman is a diminutive 56-ft (17 m) sloop. Names of classes of water craft can be as confusing today as in the past. Then and today, a sloop could be a small naval vessel; in the past, it would be of any rig, or be a single-masted sailing craft. A Georgian sailor, observing Chapman's little frigate cracking on down the Thames, would describe her first as a sloop by her rig, and only on a closer look would he reply, if asked, that she was frigate-built. At the same time, to add to the confusion, there were sloops which were sloops and nothing else, just as there were schooners, ketches, bilanders and luggers; all vessels which were defined largely by their rig.

The following illustrations complete a fairly comprehensive survey of the types of rig to be found

The qualities of the fluyts were appreciated by other nations. Apart from being easily handled, they were fairly fast in spite of their almost transom-like bows. They were capacious, with long holds formed by their bluff ends, ideal for carrying long timber, and they were extremely seaworthy.

Other nations built their own versions of the fly-boat, which at first glance bear no relation to their Dutch progenitor. Chapman presents the draught of a French version named *Le Chameau*, a storeship belonging to the French Navy which he claims 'sails particularly well'.[3] A glance at her lines shows why. She is very different from the Dutchman, with a run forward so sharp it would have done credit to a clipper, and the run aft has also been fined down. The stem has a similar shape, disregarding the Frenchman's beakhead, but the tuck has been greatly modified. The small accommodation right aft are common to both, but this was a normal arrangement in other classes of vessel. All that

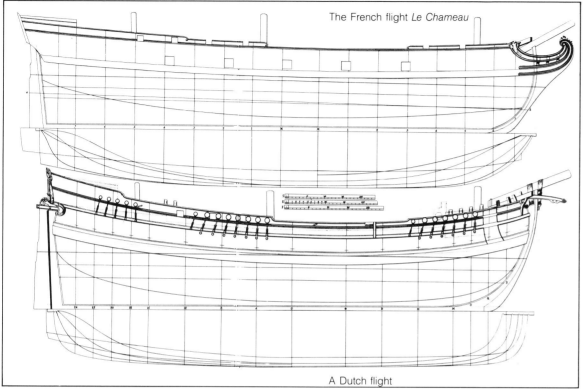

The French flight *Le Chameau*

A Dutch flight

A brig

in Atlantic waters. Although many of these were only used for small vessels, this does not exclude them from operating at times across the North Atlantic. Providing they were decked and seaworthy, the smallest sloops frequently made voyages to the Americas, and the larger fishing craft would often try their luck in Newfoundland waters.

Brig, snow, snow-brig and brigantine

The distinction of the snow rig, and what sets it apart from a brig (see illustration of the snow-rigged pink) is not only the snow-mast set up abaft the mainmast, from the deck to the maintop. At the

period in which Chapman presented his vessels there were other significant differences which can be seen if you compare the snow with the brig illustrated above. The *snow* was more of a square-rigged vessel than the brig. It set a main course (not set in the illustration) and what was to be termed a *trysail* (a relic of the old lateen mizzen) on the snow-mast or trysail mast.

On the other hand, whatever the term *brigantine* meant in the previous century, in the eighteenth it had come to indicate a rig with squaresails on the fore and all, or at least primarily, fore and aft rig on the main. The name was shortened to *brig* and, although by Chapman's period brigs were setting

main topgallants, they remained primarily fore and aft rigged on the mainmast, with a large boomed fore and aft mainsail, no sail on the mainyard, which was called the *cro'jack*, and a large trapezoid main staysail.

The then recent evolution of the snow and brig rigs were quite separate, one devolving from a vessel square-rigged on fore and main, and the other on the fore only. Not much later these styles of rig were to marry to become the popular *snow-brigs* of which Henry Dana's hard-lying *Pilgrim* is a good example. Their advantages were that the snow or trysail mast allowed the gaff to be hoisted higher than the mainyard so that a larger sail could be set from it,

117

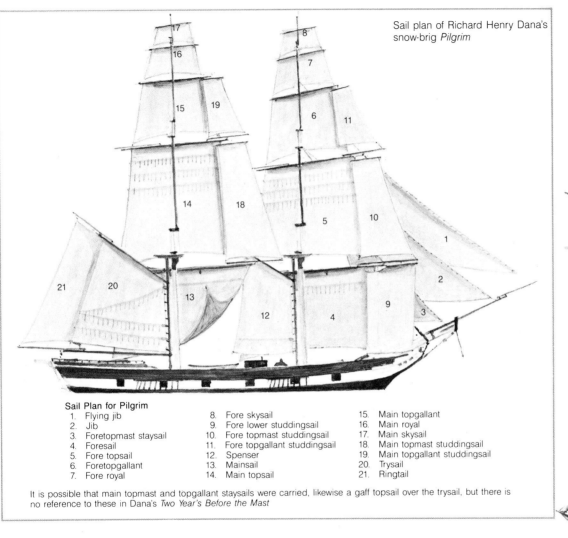

Sail Plan for Pilgrim

1.	Flying jib	8. Fore skysail	15. Main topgallant
2.	Jib	9. Fore lower studdingsail	16. Main royal
3.	Foretopmast staysail	10. Fore topmast studdingsail	17. Main skysail
4.	Foresail	11. Fore topgallant studdingsail	18. Main topmast studdingsail
5.	Fore topsail	12. Spenser	19. Main topgallant studdingsail
6.	Foretopgallant	13. Mainsail	20. Trysail
7.	Fore royal	14. Main topsail	21. Ringtail

It is possible that main topmast and topgallant staysails were carried, likewise a gaff topsail over the trysail, but there is no reference to these in Dana's *Two Year's Before the Mast*

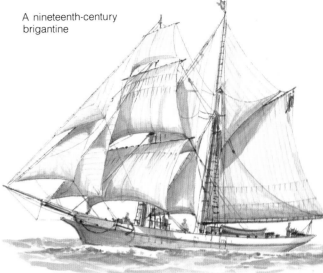

A nineteenth-century brigantine

A bilander

reduced the size of the gaff jaws, provided a spar other than the mainmast to lace or hoop the trysail to, and permitted the lower mast to be provided with *woldings*, or bands of lashings which held together built masts and prevented shakes, or splits.

The term brig left its original source, brigantine, so far behind that it became a different rig, but the term *brigantine* continued in use for a two-masted vessel, square-rigged on the fore and no squaresails on the main – the original definition of the term.

Bilander

This distinctive two-masted rig is another branch of the evolution of the brig. Originally brigantines carried a lateen or a *settee* on their mainmasts. The gaff-rigged mizzen on ships and other rigs was an eighteenth-century innovation and many large vessels, particularly warships and some Indiamen, continued to carry the full lateen spar (which, in an emergency, could be used to replace a foreyard). Whereas the brig went the whole hog with a gaff and a boom, the bilanders continued with the settee sail on the main. Give the settee a bigger drop and this sail becomes no different to a *dipping lugsail*, one of the standard boat sails of the period and the sail used by the *luggers* so popular in smuggling adventures.

The derivation of the term *bilander* is disputed but probably originally meant exactly what it said. Bilanders went 'by land', or 'near the land'; in other words, they were coasters. In the eighteenth century there were many ocean-going ships which carried this rig, but at the same time there were many bilanders, in other words, small coasters, which carried different rigs.

A schooner

Schooner

This rig has changed little; today it is still defined as a two-or-more-masted fore and aft rig, with the mainmast aft of the foremast. In the mid-eighteenth century there were few, if any, schooners with more than two masts, and possession of a squaresail or two to help her along excited no further comment. Today, this rig would be a *topsail schooner*.

The schooner rig became very much favoured on the Eastern seaboard of America, where the colonial Americans used them for general trade and developed faster versions for running contraband. The Massachusetts port of Gloucester is claimed to be the home of the classic American schooner but the really sharp, fast American schooners were not built in any numbers until during and after the Revolution.

Ketch-yacht

Yachts were not necessarily just craft for pleasure. The term actually comes from the Dutch meaning a 'swift craft' or 'hunter'. Abel Tasman's flagship was a ship-rigged yacht of some 290 tons. Thus almost any vessel built for speed could be classed as a yacht, regardless of rig. The illustration shows a yacht rigged as a ketch, one that Chapman tells us is used in the Baltic.

The ketch rig has a full set of squaresails on the main, and this one has a boomed main and mizzen with no square mizzen topsail.

Galeass

The *galeass* rig was very much used by Scandinavian countries, but was not confined to their waters. The only features which distinguish a galeass rig from a *ketch* is the single topsail and some detail in the way in which the rigging is run. The term *galeass* not only defined a type of rig which was used in many smaller vessels, but could also mean a small vessel used for carrying on lakes and rivers in northern Europe.

A Baltic ketch yacht

A galeass

A Bermuda sloop

An English cutter

Sloop

A single-masted fore and aft rig with no course. If a topgallant was carried, it was usually set flying, that is, without braces or lifts. The sketch shows this rig on a class of vessel known as a *Bermuda sloop*, a small warship developed to operate around Bermuda and the West Indies.

An English cutter

This type of single-masted rig became popular in the Revenue Service, operating against the almost universal smuggling that went on between France and England. It could be said that the cutter-rig of this period was an attempt to get as much sail as possible on one mast. A feature of cutter-rig is the method by which the jib is set. On most vessels the jib was set on its own stay as described above, or, in small craft, just set flying with the tack hauled out on a traveller. The tack of the cutter's jib was hooked on to a ring traveller which was hauled out and set at any position along the bowsprit. At each position a different sized jib was set. Note the rig requires no jibboom. This arrangement enabled the cutter to have a balanced rig under different conditions and combinations of sail.

It was the method of setting the jib which was retained and distinguished the cutters of the late nineteenth century. In the eighteenth century they could, with certain modifications, carry a full complement of squaresails. Notice that in this cutter the topmast is stepped behind the lower mast. What appears to be the topgallant, but is in fact an upper topsail, is set flying and its sheets lead to the deck and form rather poorly led topsail braces. The lower yard does not carry the course, but only serves to spread the foot of the topsail, which has an enormous roach in the foot to enable it to clear the headstay. This yard is crossed at a position on the mast where a parrel would interfere with the hoist of the mainsail, so the yard was hoisted, when required, on a jackstay on the fore side of the mast

between the hounds and the deck. The topsail sheets became the braces. The course was only a downwind sail, an eighteenth-century version of a *spinnaker*. It was set flying on its own jackyard and neatly fills the gap formed by the roach of the topsail. Not shown here, but almost certainly carried for windward work when these sparsely rigged squaresails would not set, was a staysail carried on the forestay.

A dogger or hooker

The name *dogger*, of which *hooker* may be a later variation, is of Dutch origin and meant a vessel which operated a trawl. As early as the fourteenth century doggers were voyaging as far away as Iceland and Greenland and can be classed as vessels engaged in transatlantic activities. Nobody knows what these medieval doggers looked like, but the eighteenth-century version has satisfyingly traditional lines which may have come down from those far distant times. Doggers increased in size during the seventeenth century and some were operating in Newfoundland waters. Their memorial is the rich Dogger Bank in the North Sea.

The rig is a variation of the ketch rig. Note the full lateen yard on the mizzen, a relic of when a lateen was carried during the seventeenth and early eighteenth centuries. Smaller doggers carried a lugsail on the mizzen mast.

Galiot and hoy

As with nearly all terms denoting types of rig and vessel, these are difficult to pin down to a specific meaning. Those who wish to place definitions into nice tight little compartments would be driven crazy by the slippery nomenclature of the sea. A *galiot*, as the name implies, was originally an oared craft, but in the eighteenth century it seems to have come to denote a small craft with mainly fore and aft rig, but not necessarily a ketch. Chapman adds to the utter confusion by presenting us with a 110-ft galiot

A dogger or hooker

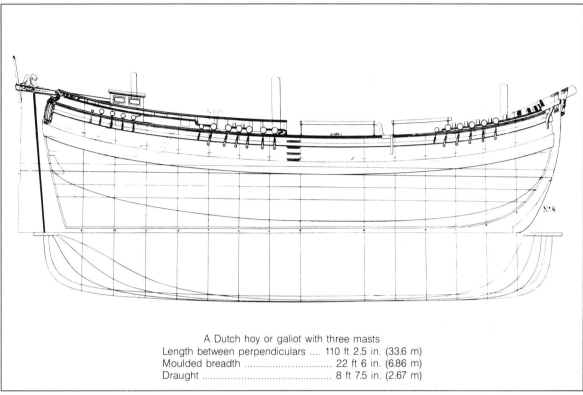

A Dutch hoy or galiot with three masts
Length between perpendiculars .... 110 ft 2.5 in. (33.6 m)
Moulded breadth .... 22 ft 6 in. (6.86 m)
Draught .... 8 ft 7.5 in. (2.67 m)

A sloop-rigged English hoy

or *hoy* with three masts. One cannot class this as a particularly small craft. To add confusion to confusion, it appears from the channels that she could have possibly been ship-rigged and looks very like a fluyt, differing only in that the tiller comes inboard over the poop deck.

The description galiot later came to describe a small Dutch fore-and-aft-rigged vessel with a single mast and leeboards, a class which operated commercially well into the twentieth century. On the other hand, the term hoy could describe any small craft of any rig. Chapman shows us a ketch-rigged Dutch hoy also termed as a galiot, and a sort of sloop-rigged English hoy and a hoy with *tjalk*

rigging, by which he means spritsail rig, which was much used for boats and was later developed to a state of perfection in Thames barges.

Most of the definitions which have been carefully put forward here can be demolished by the infuriating exceptions one would expect to find in a vigorous and versatile technology.

The lugger and chasse-marée

The lugsail is still one of the simplest and most useful of the small-boat sails, and its general use together with the spritsail for small boats, stems from medieval times. At its most basic it only

121

requires an unstayed mast, yard, halyard, tack and sheet. The sail combines the power and simplicity of a squaresail with some of the windward performance of a lateen. On short tacks the lugsail could remain on the weather side of the mast, but to get the best performance and on longer tacks it was *dipped* around the mast and the sail is still described as a *dipping lug*. In the illustration of the *chasse-marée* the mizzen is rigged slightly differently, with the tack down to the foot of the mast. This sail does not need to be dipped to perform well. When it is required to do so, it is an easy matter to flick the throat around the mast. Rigged this way, it would today be called a *standing lug*.

As mentioned before, luggers carrying all lugsails on all masts and in all positions, were favoured by smugglers, particularly around the Brittany and West Country waters. The English Revenue service favoured cutters for chasing the well handled and run-fast smuggling craft, whereas the French used the smuggler's best weapon against them and developed the chasse-marée which came into more general use as a dispatch boat during the Napoleonic Wars and not infrequently crossed the Atlantic.

A chasse-marée

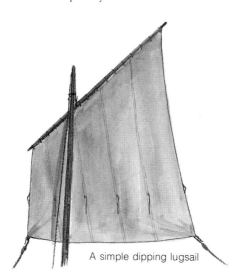

A simple dipping lugsail

Polaccas

All the types of rig and vessels illustrated so far have been developed in northern Europe. Of course there were southern and Mediterranean classes of ships and rigs which were a not uncommon sight in the Atlantic during the days of sail. One southern form of rigging set the course, topsails, sometimes topgallant, on a single mast, thus saving a lot of weight aloft. Both topsail and upper topsail yards lowered to the hounds where there was no top. No footropes were necessary as the men could stand on the yard below. The illustration, based on a painting by Antoine Roux, shows a polacca-rigged ship with upper and lower topsails backing under the mizzen topsail to dig in her anchor. The *polacca* or *polacre* method of rigging could be used in any type of vessel.

The chebeck

These particularly beautiful vessels were used, and perhaps developed, by Barbary pirates in the seventeenth century, and in the eighteenth century the Spanish and Mediterranean French found they could only catch these pestiferous pirates by using vessels of a similar design. At first they were probably all lateen-rigged, but from the middle of the eighteenth century they sailed under a variety of rigs. The illustration shows one with a polacca mainmast and a boomed, cut-down lateen mizzen. Their fine, sweet lines combined the best of the felucca and galley and they were superb sailers. It has been proposed that the chebeck was a direct descendant of, or had at least been influenced by, the caravel. Certainly they show a common

A polacca

ancestor. They were not an economical freighter but they were favoured by privateers and southern navies as well as pirates.

Rolling south on the Portuguese trades and around the Atlantic islands of the Azores, Canaries and Madeiras, ships kept a sharp lookout for distant lateen sails, possibly striped, which might signify a Barbary pirate hanging around for a prize. A captain and crew would have to work hard and run fast to outsail the chebeck and avoid having themselves and any passengers held to ransom, or sold on the block in the slave markets of Algiers or Tangiers. These pirates and their chebecks operated well into the nineteenth century, even posing a threat to the first ships outward bound for the Antipodes with emigrants.

A chebec

THE SLAVE TRADE

It is a sad comment on the history of transatlantic enterprise that, apart from the Grand Bank fisheries, the longest continuing trade was the transportation of African slaves to the New World. Apologists claim that slavery was an accepted part of life in the past and that the shipping of indentured servants and labourers from Europe to America and the West Indies in itself was little short of slavery. Another facile justification claims that the lot of those Africans hijacked across the Atlantic was better than the miserable, threatened and superstitious existence they suffered in their homelands – forgetting that these selfsame conditions in Africa were largely a result of the easy wealth and power local petty tyrants could gain by capturing and trafficking in slaves.

The trade can be said to have been initiated as far back as 1444 when the Portuguese Captain Lancarote raided a Negro village in the Bay of Arguin in modern Mauretania. They attacked the village without warning and dragged 165 men, women and children back to their ships, and another 70 were captured in later raids along the coast. These people were sold for a good profit at Lagos in the Algarve, and from that date on the traffic in Negro slaves accelerated as the demand grew and the Portuguese caravels extended their explorations beyond Cape Verde. However, the market for black slaves in Europe was not great and their subsequent lives were usually reasonably comfortable for, apart from their bondage, they were accepted as equals in the eyes of God and became assimilated into the societies into which they were sold.

After the discovery and colonisation of the Caribbean lands by the Spaniards and Brazil by the Portuguese, Negroes from Guinea began to be shipped across the Atlantic in ever-increasing numbers to replace the enslaved native populations of the New World which were decimated by their new overlords and the diseases they brought. Ironically, it was Fra la Casas, champion of the native American populations, who spurred the growth of the Atlantic slave trade when he pleaded that 12 African slaves should be imported for every colonist so that the indigenous populations could be saved. His suggestion was followed up with vigour when it was found that the Africans were better workers, and the right to import 5000 slaves annually was sold to a Genoese syndicate. Too late, the humanitarian la Casas realised the appalling commerce he had unleashed.

The first shipment of black slaves from Guinea was made from Lisbon in 1503, and soon the Portuguese began to sail their human cargoes direct from Guinea to Brazil and the Caribbean. The ivory, gold and spices which had been the mainstay of the Portuguese trade to Guinea rapidly became eclipsed by the lucrative export of cheap labour across the Atlantic. For a while the Portuguese managed to confine the trade to their own ships, but in the 1530s the Englishman William Hawkins broke into the monopoly and shipped slaves out of Guinea for Brazil, and his son, John Hawkins, made one of the first slaving voyages by an English vessel to the Caribbean in 1562. At the same time, the French, considering that they had rights in the Americas, began to combine slaving with corsairing to the Americas.

The story of a slaving voyage of John Hawkins has been told earlier. What follows is a glimpse of a late sixteenth-century venture by a Genoese merchant sailing in a Spanish ship.

A slaving voyage in 1594

Francesco Carletti was a Florentine merchant who wrote of his ultimately rather unfortunate travels around the world. With his father, who insisted on accompanying Francesco despite the fact that he had no licence to do so from Seville, the Florentine completed the first leg of his voyage from Spain to Cape Verde where the couple acquired slaves to sell at Cartagena. From Cartagena they crossed to the west coast and voyaged down to Peru in one of the specialised ships designed to sail well to windward against the prevailing southerly winds.

From Peru the Carlettis took a consignment of silver to Mexico and then voyaged to the Philippines in a Manila galleon. From Manila they sailed in a Japanese indigenous ship called a *somma* to Nagasaki and, in a similar ship, sailed to China where Francesco's father died. After sojourning in Macao for over 18 months, Francesco sailed in a Portuguese ship for Goa, calling at Malacca and Ceylon. After nearly 2 years in Goa, Francesco, with all the wealth he had accumulated by astute trading, embarked in a Portuguese Indiaman for Lisbon. Off St Helena, in the South Atlantic, the ship was taken by Dutch rovers. Lucky not to have been marooned, as was the fate of most of the Portuguese, he was taken in the prize carrack back to the Netherlands where he spent years bogged down in a mire of bureaucracy and litigation, vainly attempting to recover the fortune he had won during his 8 years of travel.

When the ship was running before the wind, the tack end of the lateen yard, sweeping over the water clear of the side of the ship, was a useful place from which to fish.

In 1594 Francesco Carletti and his father voyaged from Spain to Cartagena by way of the Cape Verde Islands where he purchased slaves to sell in the New World. Carletti described his ship as '. . . a small ship of little more than four hundred tons burden . . .', which seems a contradiction in terms for in those days 400 tons was probably above the average size for ocean-going ships, although there were many vessels much larger. The silver galleons measured from 500 to 800 tons, Hawkins's *Jesus of Lübeck* was a carrack of 700 tons, and massive Portuguese East Indiamen could range up to 2000 tons.

Francesco Carletti was a Florentine merchant and was probably familiar with the very large Mediterranean carracks besides which his 400-tonner would have appeared small. Alternatively, as he again refers to 'our little ship' on the occasion of a collision with another vessel in the flota, one wonders whether the Spanish owner who chartered Francesco the ship stretched her tonnage a little.

From other incidental remarks it can be gathered that Francesco's ship was largely lateen rigged. For instance, he described how the sailors harpooned fish from the tack end of the lateen yards. The lateen yards of a ship's mizzen and bonaventure would be too high from the water to be so used whereas the tack ends of a main

and large mizzen as shown in the sketch would be well outboard from the side of the ship when running free and not too far above the water. It is possible that she was entirely lateen rigged, but it was more common for the transatlantic ships to be square rigged on the foremast. In the collision, the lateen yard of the *levadera* was carried away. *Cebadera* was the Spanish term for the spritsail, and as for it being lateen rigged there is no problem. Later spritsails were reefed diagonally and when set were virtually a *settee* sail. Various combinations of square and lateen rig were common in southern vessels, particularly so in the caravels, which by the end of the sixteenth century, were vanishing as a class. Two hundred tons seems to have become about the upper limit of tonnage for later caravels which varied from the conventional Arabic-looking lateener to ships which were very close to galleons.

Francesco Carletti's chronicle was written for Fernando de' Medici, the Grand Duke of Tuscany, and is a fascinating personal account of how the world was in those days. His descriptions are vivid and accurate, containing a wealth of incidental detail concerning maritime activities and cultures. Unfortunately, whereas he expounds on the detail of the Japanese somma, he gives no description of the Spanish ship in which he made the slaving voyage across the Atlantic, but his account gives us a valuable insight into the early years of the Atlantic slave trade.

Most exports from Spain to her colonies in the Indies were carried in the flotas, but the African slaves, on whom the colonists came to depend, had to be shipped from the Portuguese territories in Guinea and Cape Verde. The transhipment of slaves always required fast ships which would make the passage in the minimum of time, not out of humanity, but because a dead slave was an economic loss. It was economically impracticable to ship the human cargoes to the Canaries where the flotas could have stopped, apart from the possibility of all sorts of illegal transactions which the jealous Casa de las Indias would be helpless to check. Unable to include this trade in its highly regulated fleets, the Casa licensed individual Spanish ships to engage in the slave trade.

The Carlettis set out from San Lucar on 8 January 1594, in a ship which they had chartered through a Spanish third party so as to evade the restrictions on foreigners imposed by Seville. From remarks in Francesco's account it seems that she was a galleon but lateen-rigged on all but the fore. It is interesting that he refers to this 400-ton ship as small, whereas she was in fact a respectable size for the Atlantic. Francesco was probably comparing her with the huge Mediterranean carracks and the larger galleons of the Spanish flotas.

The voyage to Cape Verde took them past the Canaries to Cape Blanco, where they '... stopped for three hours and caught at a depth of six or seven "seaman's arms" some good, fat, rose-coloured fish known as pagros by the Spaniards'[1]. A further 'nineteen days of happy navigation'[2] brought them to the Cape Verde island of Sao Tiago (Santiago), the entrepot for the Portuguese slave trade. The way in which the trade operated was by this time well established and fundamentally was to change little during the following centuries. Portuguese factors on the mainland and African slave traders from the Cape Verdes reaped the harvest of unfortunate Africans captured and sold by petty kings and despots throughout Guinea where endemic unrest was deliberately exacerbated to feed the demand for slaves. From the mainland the human cargoes were transported to Sao Tiago in small 'barks like frigates, which go both by sail and oars'[3].

Here is Francesco Carletti's account of the purchase of the slaves in Sao Tiago and the voyage across the Atlantic:

> Having gone ashore there, we rented a house and began to let it be known that we wanted to buy slaves. As a result the Portuguese, who kept them like herds of animals at their villas in the country, ordered them to be brought to the city so that we might see them. Having seen some of them and asked the prices, we discovered that we would not be in a way of making so large a profit as we had figured out with pen in hand in Spain. That occurred

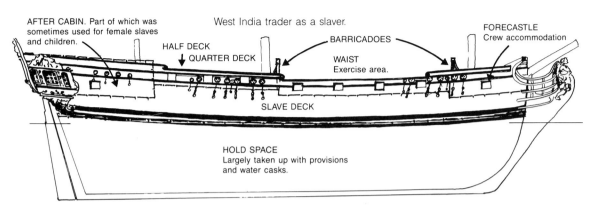

A West India trader (from Chapman)

Length between perpendiculars	102 ft (31.09 m)
Moulded breadth	27 ft 6 in. (8.38 m)
Draught	16 ft 3 in. (4.95 m)
Burden	140 heavy lasts (336 tons)

East Indiamen voyaged to the great fabulous eastern entrepots such as Goa, Madras, Batavia and Macao, where their companies had factories bulging with expensive freight for Europe. The few but commodious ports placed no restriction on a vessel's size so the ships could be large and powerful. In the West Indies trade, the requirement that the ships must be able to carry the maximum number of slaves and work the numerous small ports, lagoons and anchorages of West Africa and the Caribbean resulted in smaller vessels such as the West India trader illustrated here. She is at the smaller end of the scale of ship-rigged frigates, only differing, if one examines her closely, in the attention given to gaining the maximum amount of 'tween-deck space, even to lowering the normal height of a frigate's bulwarks.

> because many more slaves than usual were being demanded owing to the number of ships that had been arriving there, all of them wanting to take on slaves for the Indies. That caused such a rise in prices that whereas a slave ordinarily was sold for fifty scudos, or at most sixty, we had to buy them at one hundred scudos each, and then blessed those that had them to send, our provocation being the great saying, 'Either drink or drown.'
>
> At that price, we bought seventy-five, two thirds of them males and the other third females, old and young, tall and short, all mixed together – as is the custom in that country – in a herd such as that from which, in our country, we buy a bunch of swine, with all those precautions and circumstances of seeing that they are healthy and well set up and without personal defects. Then each owner makes a mark on each slave – or, to say it more accurately, marks each of them with his mark, which is made of silver and is heated in the flame of a tallow candle. The tallow is used to anoint the burned place and the mark, which is placed on the chest or on an arm or on the back so that the slave can be recognised. This thing, which I remember having done under orders from a superior, causes me some sadness and confusion of conscience because truly, Most Serene lord, it seems to me an inhuman traffic unworthy of a professed and pious Christian.[4]

Francesco here expands on his regret for being involved in the trade, hopes that he will be forgiven by God and considers that the loss of his fortune to the Dutch may have been divine retribution. He continues:

But to return to the business in slaves. I say that when we had the abovementioned seventy-five male and female Moors at the price of one hundred scudos each of first cost, some of them came, with all expenses, to cost more than one hundred and seventy scudos, this including twenty-five scudos each for the royal license, sixteen scudos each for the right to leave the Island of Cape Verde, twenty-one scudos each carrying cost from there to Cartagena of the Indies and also the cost of food and other small expenses. Further, the deaths of some of them increased the costs of this business even more. I was in charge of these slaves, and I ordered that one Moor be the head of each ten of them, selecting from among them one who seemed to be more high-spirited and intelligent, so that he might take care of what I would provide for their needs, food in particular. This was given to them twice each day, being a certain sort of fat beans that grow there, which they cook simply with water and then flavour with a little oil and salt. And thus, until such time as they should be embarked, they were kept entirely separated in two rooms, the men in one and the women in the other, naked and without clothing, they being content with the skin that nature had given them and hiding only – by means of a small piece of leather or other skin or rag or tree-leaves – that part of the body which Original Sin has made seem more shameful than the other parts . . .[5]

Francesco fell ill, either through 'fatigue or, more likely, by the different and pestiferous air of that climate'[6], and the slaves were left in charge of two Portuguese who saw to the embarkation:

The slaves were placed on the aforesaid ship hired by us, the males being accommodated on it belowdecks, packed next to one another in such a narrow space that when they wanted to turn from one side to the other they could scarcely do so. The females were in the open all over the ship, having stowed themselves as well as they could. Once each day we gave them all as much as they wanted to eat, the food being a certain millet of those countries cooked in water and flavoured with oil and salt. In the morning, for breakfast, each of them was given a handful of certain seeds resembling anise in its unripe state, but not having its flavor. Something to drink followed after they had eaten at noon. Then they drank as much as they could without having to draw a breath. And then, in the evening, if something was given to one of them, he ate it with his comrades, there being ten slaves in each group.

Thus, after having put aboard everything that we would need for such a voyage, we left the island of Sao Tiago on April 19 of that year, 1594, sailing with another ship also loaded with black slaves. We directed our prow toward the west, sailing almost always at the same height of fourteen or fifteen degrees towards the north from the Equator. We plowed through that oceanic space, three thousand miles, happily in thirty days. Then we reached Cartagena, a city of the Indies situated on the coast of what we call *terra firma*, distant from the equinoctial line by between ten and eleven degrees north. It has a most beautiful harbour. First we had seen the islands that the Spaniards call the Antilles, which occur before one reaches terra firma and are separated and spread out across that ocean by Nature in such order and quantity that they appear to be bulwarks and shelters of the incomprehensible richnesses and treasures that have been hidden from us for so many centuries in all that new world.

We had nonetheless run great peril of becoming lost, because the ship travelling with us, by inadvertence or stupidity of the sailor in charge of the helm at that hour, had struck our little ship while proceeding during the night with all sails unfurled. And, as it was much larger and heavier, it had come close to sending our ship to the bottom. But from that God saved us in His mercy, even though the shock of the collision broke in one side of our little ship's superstructure and carried away the sail and the lateen yard known as a levadera. [Lateen spritsail?] But I, who up to that time had been afflicted by the fever – which, although reduced by a fourth, never had left me – was freed of it at that hour. I believe that this was the result of the great agitation and terror over such an event, which truly was strange. For our little ship was lightly loaded and it gave way in such a manner to the force of the other ship striking it that it seemed to want to keel over on its side. But that giving way was helpful to our little ship, as otherwise it would have been sunk and everything would have been smashed.

During the rest of that voyage, as I have said, the navigation was peaceful. But it was disgusting to see one's own slaves thrown into the sea each day, it happening that many died of the flux of the blood caused by eating badly cooked or almost raw certain fish that we caught in incredible quantities throughout that voyage until we reached the islands called the Antilles.[7]

Seven of the Carlettis' slaves died on the passage, but, in spite of having an excess of licences, Francesco was thrown into prison in Cartagena, the Spanish accusing him of not having any licences at all. As Francesco put it, 'In the Spaniards' way of creating difficulties – at which, so as to extract money, they are good inventors . . .'[8].

He was released after 3 days when letters containing his authority came from Spain. Many of the slaves who were landed had been badly treated and were sick and half dead. 'We tried to restore them, not so much out of charity, it must be said, as not to lose their value and price.'[9]

We will leave the Carlettis in the fever-ridden port of Cartagena, which they left in August to sail to Nombre de Dios and make their way across the Isthmus, bemoaning the small profit they had made from their slave-trading venture.

The Middle Passage

Throughout the seventeenth century, as the Portuguese and Spanish lost their grip on Guinea and the Americas respectively, almost every other western European nation engaged in the trade, supplying labour to both Spain and their own newly established colonies. In 1713 Britain won the King of Spain's licence to supply slaves to his possessions in the Americas. This soon made her the foremost nation engaged in the slave trade, and there is a good case to be made out that it was the enormous wealth won from slaving which fuelled the Industrial Revolution and Britain's rise to power. From being by far the predominant slaving nation, Britain, after Denmark, became the initiator and champion of abolition during the nineteenth century.

The ocean crossing from West Africa to the Caribbean and the Americas, known as the Middle Passage, was the Via Doloroso of a trade more protracted, cold-blooded and inhumane than any

The *Nightingale*, with 2000 slaves on board, brought to by the ship sloop USS *Saratoga*.

Considered one of the most beautiful clippers ever built, the *Nightingale* was intended to demonstrate the superiority of American shipbuilding at the 1851 Great Exhibition in London. She was to carry American visitors across the Atlantic to the Exhibition, and then once in the Thames, her magnificent accommodation was to become a floating hotel for her passengers.

Nothing came of this plan, so she was sold and employed in the Australian, China tea and Californian trades. In 1860, after changing hands many times, she made a voyage carrying American grain to Liverpool. Her master, a notorious character, did not sail directly home but sailed for West Africa to pick up a cargo of slaves for Havana. The news that he was taking the *Nightingale* to the coast soon got around and the British

and American naval patrols were alerted. She was twice searched but found empty and released. Eluding the cruisers, Captain Bowen managed to embark 2000 slaves and get out to sea. However, only 2 days out, she was captured by the USS *Saratoga*.

The lovely ship was bought by the US Government and served as a cruiser during the Civil War. In 1865 she was sold out of the Navy to the Western Union, who employed her laying cable across the Bering Strait. Her final years, as with so many old clippers, were spent droghing timber across the North Atlantic until she was abandoned at sea in 1893.

The *Nightingale* was built at Portsmouth, New Hampshire in 1851. She measured 1066 tons, had a length of 185 ft (56.39 m) and beam of 36 ft (10.97 m). She was named for the famous singer Jenny Lind, who was beautifully represented in the ship's figurehead.

other in history. From the first modest beginnings in the early sixteenth century, through the appalling years of British supremacy in the eighteenth, to the

vicious attempts to maintain the trade in face of abolition in the nineteenth, millions of despairing black Africans were crammed into the festering

A typical American-built schooner from the second quarter of the nineteenth century. Because of their speed, many such vessels were used, or even built specifically, to engage in the illegal slave trade.

'tween-decks of the slavers and shipped to the New World, where they sweated to provide much of the wealth on which empires were built.

The Middle Passage, as its name implies, formed the middle leg of a triangular trade, each leg of which could be highly profitable to an astute merchant. In European ports ships loaded trade goods such as cloth, iron and ironware, weapons and, transhipped duty-free from the East Indiamen, cottons from India and cowrie shells from East Africa. With these products, the masters of the ships would either visit their own factors to embark a prearranged cargo of slaves, or cruise the West African shores anywhere

between Senegal and Angola, bartering for consignments of captives from African and European middlemen. Sometimes months were spent before completing their loading, and in the unhealthy climate, considerable losses could be expected among the ships' crews.

The slaves sold in the New World provided the means to purchase products such as sugar, dyewoods and tobacco, which formed the freight of homeward-bound European ships. As a gain could be made on each leg, the final profit could sometimes be several hundred per cent. When, in the eighteenth century, Americans began to engage in the trade, they developed their own version of the triangle. With the sugar purchased by the sale of their slave cargos, they produced rum which in turn was exchanged for slaves in West Africa. Rum, it was found, was more to the taste of the African slave-traders than the brandies, schnapps and gin of Europe.

In 1802 Denmark became the first country to make the slave trade illegal, but she could do little to enforce her initiative. Britain followed in 1807, and sent out ships to enforce her ban in 1808, and that same year the trade was made illegal in the United States. Until 1869, when the Cuban slave market was finally closed down and slavery abolished in the western hemispherre, slavers ran their human cargoes against ever-increasing risks as nation after nation turned their back on the trade. By far the largest contributor to the demise was the British Navy, who for the first years virtually fought on alone and had often to contend with obstruction and the sensitivities of other nations. The sloops, brigs and later steam auxilliaries of the West African station only managed to waylay a small fraction of the slave-running ships, but combined with the unremitting pressure by Britain, at that time at the height of her empire, other nations began to lend their support in other ways than rhetoric.

America declared the trade illegal as early as 1808, but powerful vested interests and the irresistible profits to be gained weakened her government's will to clamp down firmly on her freedom-conscious, recalcitrant citizens. American shipbuilders and chandlers of the north-eastern seaboard built and equipped the ships which sailed under the flags of other nations, supplying, usually through Cuba, the slaves upon which the economy of the South depended.

During the dying years of the Atlantic slave trade, when the British Navy and later other nations began to hound the slavers from the sea, the blackbirders had to be fast. Most were schooner-rigged, rakish, well armed craft along the lines of the Baltimore clippers, chosen to outrun and sometimes fight the naval patrols. As the ships were small and cargoes were becoming harder to gather, many captains appallingly overcrowded their vessels, and it was during these years that some of the worst atrocities were committed. Such were the huge profits to be made on a successful run that, after the slaves had been quietly ferried ashore in some secluded bay in Cuba, the slavers could afford to destroy the ship which had become compromised by the evidence of her cargo.

Initially only vessels found to have slaves on board could be arrested, enabling many obvious slave-runners to slip through the net and instigating the more ruthless of them to dump their load of humanity at the sight of a British cruiser. In 1822 the Dutch and English agreed that a vessel could be arrested if it could be shown that it was equipped for slaving. This provision became known as the 'equipment clause' and became universal when it was belatedly accepted by Spain in 1835 and Portugal in 1842, thus eliminating the haven of their flags for other nations.

The American Government, ultra-sensitive over the sanctity of their flag at sea, especially after the war of 1812, refused to let their ships be boarded and searched by foreigners, but were lax in maintaining their own patrols, hobbled, as they were, by powerful citizens who were making a fortune from the trade. In the years immediately following the universal acceptance of the equipment clause, American ships, and sometimes those of other nationalities, found it worthwhile to fly the American flag openly. The likelihood of being brought to by an American patrol was remote, and the captains of British cruisers found themselves in the ridiculous position of having to allow any ship flying the American flag, even if she was clearly slaving, sail on its way unmolested.

Frustrations such as these dogged the whole history of the battle to eliminate slavery. During the eighteenth century Britain had made a fortune out of the miserable trade. In the nineteenth century she presided over its destruction. Some cynics claim the change of heart was brought about by the Industrial Revolution, and that slavery and the slave trade had outlived its usefulness, but few would deny the gallant part played by the British Navy in the Atlantic.

THE ATLANTIC WHALING INDUSTRY

The whaling industry is fervently and rightly condemned today. There is no longer any need to slaughter the magnificent animals when almost all their products have alternatives which can be manufactured and are better and cheaper. It is *not* right to condemn our whaling ancestors in the light of modern thinking. Moral judgment on historical activities depends on the ethos of the period and, what to our eyes is callous cruelty, may be just and praiseworthy in its time. This applies particularly to whaling, which was a ruthless and bloody occupation at all times, but was carried out with enormous courage, endurance and sacrifice by men who were proud of their calling. Their captains were sometimes educated, skilful men who contributed a great deal to the natural sciences and geography. So, if in the following pages I should seem to be extolling the hunt of the whale, it is only as a past, and hopefully finished, occupation in which men strove mightily to master the whales, the seas and the ice.

Around the shores of the Atlantic, even back into the misty pre-historical past, whales have provided a welcome, sporadic but gargantuan supplement to the resources of the inhabitants of coastal regions. For people living on the edge of a subsistence existence, a stranded whale was akin to winning the big prize in a lottery and, human ingenuity being what it is, many communities devised ways of reducing the odds by pursuing the creature in its own element. Whoever threw that first harpoon into a large whale should rank with Jack and David among giant-killers.

Shore whaling from small boats and canoes was a common occupation by the beginning of the timespan covered by this book, but sometime, perhaps even before the fifteenth century, whaling became an industry in which whales were hunted commercially and their products sold for profit. The most likely candidates for pioneering the whaling industry were the peoples who dwelt around the shores of Biscay, particularly the Basques, who hailed from the north coast of the Iberian Peninsula. Their stormy and treacherous waters spawned fine seamen and ships, and the right whale swam at their doorstep. In pursuit of fish it is quite likely that, along with the Breton and English fishermen, they were quietly working the Grand Banks and Newfoundland coast long before these waters were officially discovered by exploratory voyages such as those of Cabot.

Apart from cod, whales abounded about the North American coasts and returning English fishermen reported seeing Basques hunting whales on the Banks. By the mid sixteenth century they were sending annual fleets to Terra Nova and the Grand Banks to fish and to the coasts of Labrador, Belle Isle and Newfoundland to service shore-whaling stations. Indications are that the Basques were at the forefront of transatlantic whaling for many years. In 1593 English whalers sailed to Cape Breton but caught no whales. However, on an island they found 800 whale fins left by a Biscay ship 3 years earlier.

The whalers of other nations

Whaling in the New World during the sixteenth century was not just the preserve of the Basques, and commercial rivalry could sometimes flare up into outright warfare, which accounts for the heavy armament carried by the Basque ships, who frequently came into conflict with the French, their main rivals. In 1578 Antony Parkhurst from Bristol claimed 'That there were generally more than a 100 sail of Spaniards taking cod and from 20 to 30 taking whales; 50 sail of Portuguese; 150 sail of French and Bretons, mostly very small, but of English only 50.'[1] This does not make it clear whether a proportion of the Portuguese, French, Breton and English ships were actually engaged in whaling, but it is clear that the Spanish, particularly the Basques, were still predominant in whaling and it is significant that when the Muskovy Company, as late as 1611, sent out two ships, the *Mary Margaret* of 150 tons and the *Elizabeth* of 50 tons, to Spitzbergen, or East Greenland as it was then known, the complement of the *Mary Margaret* included six skilled Basque harpooners from the port of St Jean de Luz who were to show the English how to kill whales.

Although it is apparent that other nations and the English did engage in whaling in the sixteenth century, it seems that, up to the time the *Mary Margaret* and *Elizabeth* sailed, they had concentrated on hunting walrus around the Arctic shores of Bear Island and Spitzbergen after these islands had been rediscovered by Barents in 1596. The first English voyage to Spitzbergen with the express intention of hunting whales took place in 1610, in the 70-ton *Amitie* and still smaller *Lionesse*. It was a virgin hunting ground, the unwary whales were easy to catch and Jonas Poole and Thomas Edge, the respective masters of the ships, had no trouble in filling the ships with blubber.

For the next 100 years the Arctic seas around Spitzbergen were fished by all European nations, with the Dutch becoming by far the greatest

A late eighteenth-century Dutch *bootschip* engaged in whaling. The bootschip was a late development of the fluyt, the main feature being the wide poop allowing for better stowage for boats.

participants. Rivalry between the Dutch and English in the early years frequently resulted in bloodshed, and the London-based Muskovy Company monopoly was challenged by their own countrymen from York and Hull, who were not beneath vandalising each other's property left at Spitzbergen. These vicissitudes and a lack of enthusiasm in hunting whales outside of the bays of Spitzbergen, combined with the phenomenal rise in Dutch maritime activity and power during the first half of the seventeenth century, almost entirely eclipsed the English in the Arctic. In fact, after 1630 the British sent out very few ships. In 1622 the Dutch built the blubber town Smeerenberg on Spitzbergen and virtually monopolised the industry. The internecine bellicosity of the English compares dismally with the peaceful cooperation of the Dutch towards each other.

By the 1640s whales were becoming hard to find around the shores of Spitzbergen and the ships had to hunt in the open sea and along the edge of the ice. The Germans began to send out ships in 1640. Both Dutch and German ships had iron plating around the bows and internal strengthening to navigate in the ice, a practice which became more common early in the eighteenth century as the whales were driven from the open waters.

It was only when whalers began to extend their search for whales to the south on long voyages through warmer climates that the blubber was tried-out on board. In Arctic waters this was unnecessary as the blubber would keep well until it could be got to try-works ashore, either at places such as Smeerenberg or all the way to the whaler's home port. Once the whales were killed, they were flensed alongside the ship or towed to the shore try-works if it was handy. Flensing at sea became more common as the hunt took the ships farther away from their bases, but retention of the shore bases was economical as the processed oil took up far less space in the ships than raw blubber and the whalers could remain on the grounds the whole season.

I have briefly outlined the history of Arctic whaling, although the regions in which the whaling took place lay in the Greenland and Barent's seas and not the Atlantic as defined by the scope of this book. However, in 1719 the Dutch made the first whaling voyage to the Davis Straits and from this time onward the whole region of the summer ice edge, from Novaya Zembla to Labrador, including the Barent's and Greenland seas, the far north-western Atlantic and the Davis Strait, was annually hunted for whale, and we can fairly consider that the ships involved in the hunt were truly Atlantic ships.

In 1725 the British took the first halting steps at reviving their whaling industry when the South Sea Company built 12 ships. They were extravagantly run and poorly fished and the venture petered out after 7 years, having made a thumping loss of £177,782 3s. However, the year following their demise, 1733, saw the first bounty of 20s. per ton instituted by the British Government, and from this time onward, and more particularly from 1750, when the bounty was increased to 40s., the British whaling industry began to revive and finally dominate Arctic whaling.

Before we follow the fortunes of British whaling and the story of one particular ship, we should glance at the awakening interest of the New England colonies in whaling activities. Since the first exploration and settlement of the American east coast it had been noted that whales were plentiful not far off shore, and beached whales were quite a common occurrence. During the seventeenth century and the early eighteenth century it was not necessary for American whalers to search far afield, although in the Massachusetts archives there has been found a record of a sperm-whaling voyage proposed as early as 1688. In that year the captain of the brigantine *Happy Return* requested

License and Permission, with one Equipage Consisting in twelve marines, twelve whalemen and six Divers – from this Port, upon a fishing design about the Bohames Islands, and Cap florida, for sperma Coeti [sperm] whales and Racks [wrecks]: and so return to this Port.[2]

By the early 1700s whaling was a well established industry and whale oil an important export to the Home Country and the European

Sixteenth-century Basque whaling ships in Red Bay, Labrador

A tentative reconstruction of the Basque whaling ship, the *San Juan*.

Approximate burthen .... 250 tons
Length on weather deck .... 72 ft (22 m)
Breadth .... 24 ft 6 in (7.5 m)
Length of keel .... 48 ft (14.75 m)
Approximate draught .... 10 to 11½ ft (3 to 3.5 m)

the Cape Verdes and the coast of Brazil. In these voyages the experience was gained which enabled the Americans to follow the whale to all corners of the globe and dominate the sperm-whaling industry in the late eighteenth and nineteenth centuries.

With the institution of the 40s.-per-ton bounty in 1750, British whaling activity steadily increased until, in 1756, 67 English and 16 Scottish ships were engaged in whaling throughout the summer and trading during the winter months. For the remainder of the century British whaling in the Arctic flourished, although there were poor seasons and conflict with the French interfered with the industry. During the Seven Years War, which started in 1756, French privateers lurked off British ports in the North Sea, the whalers were harassed by naval press-gangs from whom they were supposedly immune, and their ships were commandeered for transports. In the sixties American sperm whaling in the South Atlantic offered severe competition – for instance, in 1766 Nantucket sent out 118 ships which brought home 11, 969 barrels. The Dutch continued to send out the most ships, but their numbers started to decline in 1770, although they still averaged about 180 ships a year until 1778. In 1770 there were 59 British ships in the Arctic. In the 1780s British Arctic whaling boomed until, in 1787, 250 ships were engaged. It was during this decade, in 1784, that the Hull whaler *Truelove* made her first whaling voyage to the Arctic.

The Basque whaler *San Juan*

The first vessels sent out by the Basques to the New World to engage in whaling were probably naos or carracks similar to those of Cabot and Columbus. By the mid fifteenth century galleon-type ships seem to have been favoured, probably because of their handier and better sea-keeping qualities. The codfishing fleets to Terranova employed ships of

continent. Small sloops and schooners were making whaling voyages to the southward and out east of the Grand Banks, and in the 1730s American ships were operating in the Davis Strait. Later, in the 1760s, British regulation and interference in the operation of American whalers in the north drove them even farther afield and they began sailing to the Azores,

The model constructed by Marcel Gringas of Parks Canada, each piece of which faithfully reproduces the fragments recovered from Red Bay, Labrador.

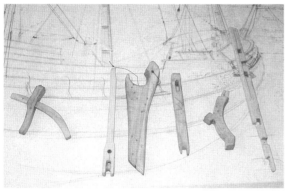

Structure of stern and rudder

Some left over pieces of the vessel. *From left to right:* Part of a large dismountable cleat; perhaps part of a davit; part of the hawse; this looks like an anchor cat but appears a little small; perhaps the forward end of the forecastle; this is probably part of a capping rail, pierced by the timber-heads.

were recovered and cast in latex for study, eliminating the lengthy and complex preservation techniques which would have been necessary with the original timbers.

Marcel Gringas, a model-maker, was employed to scale down and exactly reproduce each fragment of the ship and attempt to assemble the pieces. The lower parts of the ship such as the keel, keelson, floors and first futtocks were reasonably straight-forward, as these had to a large extent retained their integrity to each other. Nail, bolt and trenail holes, markings and shape, all carefully and faithfully reproduced in the model, were clues to find a home for more uncertain and vagrant pieces, until, after years of patient work, all the disparate but identified parts were assembled. There, on the table, stood the graceful model of most of the underwater hull, including the transom stern and rudder, of a mid-sixteenth-century Basque ship. Above this, supported in space, hung other identified parts, such as the capstan, an anchor hawse, a main channel and so on.

Left over were dozens of mystery pieces, one perhaps the riding beam, another maybe the carved, curved post of the forward end of the forecastle deck. An intriguing jigsaw, for each of these miniature fragments, which you can hold in your hand and contemplate, had a home and a purpose in the original ship. Even some of the identifiable parts contain mysteries. How, for instance, did the heavy timbers and odd shape of the structure of the hawse fit into the configuration of the ship? Why were there two sets of holes where apparently the main brace led inboard, and exactly how were the pintles and gudgeons of the rudder arranged? Regarding the latter, most rudders then, and later, were hung so that they could be easily lifted either to protect them when aground or for maintenance. In the base of the *San Juan*'s rudder there is a groove to take a strop under the pintles for the rudder to lift off. Unfortunately, very little of the upper hull and superstructure has been recovered. Perhaps this was destroyed in the salvage, or broken up later, but it

generally less than 200 tons but the whalers were larger and could range up to 600 tons, which was a fair-sized vessel. The find of the remains of one of these Basque-built ships, and its recovery by the Underwater Archaeological Department of Parks Canada, has brought to light some fascinating detail concerning the shipbuilding practices of the Basques.

During 1565, shortly before she was to sail home for Spain with a cargo of whale oil, the 250-ton Basque ship *San Juan* dragged her anchors and drove

aground on Saddle Island in Red Bay on the Labrador shore of the Strait of Belle Isle. The ship apparently was not a total loss and much of her gear, cargo and perhaps reusable timbers seem to have been salvaged. What remained of what may have been the *San Juan* was rediscovered in 1978 by Bruce Bennett, a wreck-finder employed by the Underwater Archaeology Department of Parks Canada. During the following years, under the direction of Robert Grenier, the chief of the Department, most of the remains of the ship leaves a major and perhaps unsolvable problem as to the form of the upper parts of the bow and forecastle.

The *San Juan* was not a whaler in the sense of being employed to hunt whales. She was a freighter which, each spring, put out with personnel, supplies and quantities of barrel staves and hoop irons for the shore-whaling stations on the coast of Labrador. All through the summer months, while the whalemen chased and killed the Greenland whale and northern right whales in boats very similar to the craft of later years, the ship lay to her anchors, while casks of whale oil, tried-out ashore, gradually filled her holds. In the autumn, with her hold hopefully crammed to capacity, she would take on board the whaling men, coopers and cooks and leave the bleak shores of Labrador for the milder winter of northern Spain.

The only other ship recovered from about this period, but predating the *San Juan* by some 40 to 50 years, is the *Mary Rose*, a royal vessel and a warship, far grander than the humble *San Juan*. It is immediately obvious that the lines of the two ships are similar. They are much finer than those of later vessels, which had to carry heavy ordinance, and the graceful arc of the stem and hollow forefoot are also common to both ships. However, there are some features of the construction of the *San Juan* which are quite startling.

The short beechwood keel is distinctive and, incidentally, different from other keels recovered at Red Bay, which have the conventional squared timber running the whole length from sternpost to stem scarph. The keel of the *San Juan* is carved to include the garboards, T-sectioned in the centre but sweeping up to a Y at each extremity. The after-end is extended by an elegantly carved knee, which includes the base of a short rudder shoe. The raked rudder-post is scarphed to this knee, and the whole assembly is held together by another massive knee which forms what deadwood there is. No half timbers are used, but each rising floor is carved entire

from grown, suitably grained wood. This arrangement is also found in the old cogs, so conforms to an ancient tradition.

The floors, other than those notched to the deadwood knee, are shaped and fastened flush to the top of the keel, with a limber hole on the centreline, and the oak keelson is notched and set over the floors. These notches in the keelson show that, for some incomprehensible reason, the floor timbers cross the keel at a slight angle, rather than at right angles. Fourteen of the midship frames are formed by the futtocks scarphed together, and fastened directly to the floor, indicating they were assembled before being set up. The remainder of the futtocks and frames hang free, secured by trenails to the planking and clamps. Fastenings are a combination of trenails, iron nails and bolts.

The *San Juan*'s capacious hold was designed to accommodate the maximum number of *barricas*, which were barrels with a capacity of 225 litres. The depth of hold, distance between decks and even the dimensions of the pump well were arranged so as to leave no waste space nor interfere with the stow. Hold pillars, which would have seriously inhibited the overlapping stowage of barrels set on their bilges, were not employed. The ship was laid out conventionally, with a continuous upper or weather deck on to which the hawse entered under the conjectural forecastle, with the main capstan located aft, under the quarterdeck.

A 'tween-deck with about 5½ ft (1.7 m) headroom ran clear from forward aft to the transom just below the counter of the after superstructure. A heavy board, forming the lower part of the counter, was pierced with the tiller port and two hawse. The deck appears to have been laid on ledges secured at their outboard ends to the beam-shelf and inboard to carlines laid over the beams, one on each side of the centreline, allowing the space between them for hatchways. A set of hold beams also ran below the 'tween-deck, and on these a deck, or partial deck, was also laid. The transom was pierced

on the starboard side at this level with a large port, which almost certainly served as a loading port for timber. It is very close to the waterline and would have been of necessity firmly secured and caulked before putting to sea. No doubt, these ships were not laid up idle during the winter months, but traded, perhaps as far afield as the Baltic and Mediterranean.

The transom

So little of the upper parts of the vessel has been found that any reconstruction must be conjecture based on a few clues. The quarterdeck bulwarks were pierced with low, semicircular gunports and a long main channel, and parts of the shrouding indicate there was a gang of seven shrouds, with hearts instead of dead-eyes, either side of the mainmast. What has been found seems to show that the foremast was only supported by three shrouds on each side, and, if this was the case, it must have been a very small mast, perhaps without a top and topmast.

An interesting find was a board which was roughly engraved with a depiction of a ship which may represent the *San Juan*. In my attempt to illustrate the Basque ship I had to come to conclusions on some basis which would fit what has been found and what is understood of the practices of the period. The crude engraving on the board shows a ship with the raised, carrack-type foredeck, six shrouds on the main and four on the foremast. I have followed the ancient artist's concept – after all, he was there – and given the *San Juan* a similar forecastle and four shrouds on the foremast. Quite honestly, I am uncomfortable with the idea of that mast, with even the small foretopsail, which most ships carried in that period, being supported by only three shrouds each side.

Pieces of vertical fenders located from the vicinity of the forecastle appear to indicate that the sides tumbled well inboard, forming almost a whaleback on which sat the triangular forecastle deck. A curved and carved piece fits neatly to the fore end if this is correct, with the tenon in the beakhead knee and perhaps a carved head in the mortice on top. The absence of nail holes on the lower part may indicate that the lower bulwark strake was either absent or discontinued, to allow an outlicker to pass outboard for the fore tack. However, the *San Juan* was built at a time of transition, when the old nao or carrack type of ship was being superseded by the galleon, and it is because of this that, given so few clues, my reconstruction of the forward part of the vessel could be totally in error. Apart from the inscribed board, it is quite possible – indeed, some clues indicate – that she could have had a forward configuration the same as that of the vessel shown in my first chapter *(Illus. 16)*.

The puzzle of the two sets of leads where the mainbrace standing and running part comes inboard at the aft end of the quarterdeck I have tentatively solved by leading the maintopsail sheets to the spare set. This was the practice before the lead was changed so that the sheets ran in along the mainyard and down to the deck.

The illustration shows a deep vessel whose profile rather belies the kindly lines of the hull. These are rather spoiled by the deeply submerged transom which must have inevitably caused considerable drag. The pieces from which the model is constructed, because they reproduce all the damage and wear of the centuries, make the shipwrightry appear crude and rough. This was not so; the *San Juan* was superbly built and demonstrates immense care in the selection of timber and the painstaking reinforcement of potentially weak areas. Just take, for example, the carved keel and garboards, and particularly the strakes which land on the lower part of the square tuck. What modern boatbuilder would take the trouble to seek out curved or compass pieces and adze them to include the three lowermost short diagonals of the transom?

The *Truelove*

All whaling was hard work and often perilous, but whereas the southern whaler cruised his leisurely way around the world on voyages lasting years, visiting the various whaling grounds in their season, the Arctic whaler put out each year to the Greenland Sea or Davis Strait, thrusting his ship far into the ice and risking crew and ship in pursuit of whales. Masters of these vessels became the world's greatest experts, not only at handling their sailing ships in ice, but on the Arctic generally. The most noted of these men must be the Scoresbys. William Scoresby published the two-volume definitive work, *Arctic Regions*, in 1820, and his father, William Scoresby Senior, invented the crow's-nest. Their ships were as remarkable as their masters, many of them surviving decades of punishing work, thumping through ice and being periodically squeezed clear out of the water in the pack, as well as regularly weathering the rigorous Atlantic crossings. They were paragons of strength and durability. Remarkable, but not entirely alone in her longevity, was the *Truelove* of Hull.

The three lower strakes of the transom

A sixteenth-century sailor's graffiti

Built in Philadelphia in 1764, the *Truelove* was captured by the British in the American War of Independence and sold to a shipowner from Hull who put her into the wine trade between her home port and Oporto. Armed with 12 guns and capable of 9½ knots, she survived the attentions of hostile French cruisers. In 1784 she was strengthened, and with a crew of 40 under Captain R. Clarke, sailed for the Arctic whaling grounds. Every year until 1795 the *Truelove* earned her living amongst the ice of the Davis Strait and Greenland Sea, returning to take up her trade as a merchantman during the autumn and winter, surviving not only the ice but French frigates and privateers. After 2 years sailing as a transport, she was back whaling in 1797.

This method of breaking ice, known as milldolling, was not good for the boat which was slung under the bowsprit and lowered onto the ice. The boy would then rock the boat to break the ice, but if it was too thick the boat was repeatedly hoisted and dropped.

The Hull whaler *Truelove* working through the ice of the Davis Strait. Built in Philadelphia in 1764, she sailed the Atlantic for over 120 years, most of them in the rigorous Arctic whaling industry.

138

All through the war years, the brief peace in 1802 and 1803, and the resumption of hostilities with France in May 1803, the little *Truelove* survived the summer ice of the Arctic whaling and the winter storms as an ordinary trader. In the autumn of 1802, with the threat of invasion hanging over Britain, she sailed for Oporto for wine and, hoping for a bit on the side, she bore the letters of marque of a privateer. In 1806 she made her first voyage to the Davis Strait. With peace in 1816, whaling boomed, but the natural hazards were increased by the discovery of large numbers of Greenland whales on the west side of Baffin Bay, a region difficult and dangerous to reach and impossible in bad seasons.

From 1821 to 1831, under new ownership, she was engaged in trading to Oporto and the Baltic, and avoided the disastrous year of 1830, when out of 91 ships that sailed for the Davis Strait, 19 were lost, 21 returned empty, while hardly a ship was not damaged. On her return to whaling the *Truelove* sailed each year for the Strait and survived the years 1835 and 1836 when bad ice conditions and weather beset the ships and whaling was poor.

Most whaling fleets, apart from that of Peterhead, were in decline by 1840, but the *Truelove* soldiered on, being only one of two ships that sailed from Hull in that and the following year. In 1847 Captain Parker of *Truelove* brought home to Hull an Eskimo man and wife, aged 17 and 15 years. They were exhibited in Hull during the winter and aroused keen interest.

In 1849, the *Truelove*, now a venerable 85 years old and still under the experienced Captain Parker, and the *Advice* of Dundee took on board relief stores for the missing Franklin expedition, with the intention of landing them as far up Lancaster Sound as possible. After a difficult passage through the ice to Melville Bay, in the course of which four whalers were crushed in the ice and lost, they fought through to the North Water. Off Ponds Bay Captain Parker managed to catch 11 whales and, as the *Advice* was also well fished, the two ships sailed on their mission

up Lancaster Sound. They found their passage blocked by ice and landed their stores and dispatches on Cape Haye, where they set up a signal pole. Barely had they completed their work when the wind increased to a strong gale, but, by superb handling, the two little ships managed to weather the ice, and when the gale eased they headed south, back to the whaling fleet.

There were more adventures for the *Truelove* the following year. She was very nearly wrecked in Melville Bay by being squeezed in the ice, and at one time every ship in the ice was caught and had to be temporarily abandoned, their crews taking to the boats and ice with clothes and provisions.

In 1852 the *Truelove*, still under the command of Captain Parker, fished every bay down the south-west shore of the Strait; on board she carried Christopher B. Chapel, the master of the *MacLellan*, an American whaler. The previous year, as an experiment, Chapel had left 13 men in Cumberland Gulf to winter over and take advantage of the spring run of whales. In her search for the Americans the *Truelove* went as far as Kemisuack, farther than any whaler had been before.

During the season of 1853, although the *Truelove* was one of the best fished ships, Captain Parker was not happy. He had lost 10 large whales, one of which took down her harpoon gunboat 120 fathoms and dragged it in the mud before the harpoon drew and the boat was recovered. Another went away with 10,800 (3292 m) of line and, when the end was belayed to the ice, the harpoon drew, and a third whale went under a flow, took out 24 lines and the harpoon broke. Using the ship's capstan, it took 15 hours to recover the more than 3½ miles of line. To cap off the captain's woes, one midnight, while wearing ship off Cape Dyer, the *Truelove* rammed a large piece of ice which stove in the bow and broke twelve timbers. As it was blowing hard the old ship was in great danger but the damage was shored up and they kept her afloat until daylight. A harpooner named McKenzie went over the bow to inspect the

damage, lost his grip and fell. Regardless of the high seas running, a boat was got away but failed to find the man. The ship put into the Danish settlement of Holstienberg and, fortunately, the next day the Franklin search ship *Phoenix*, under Captain Inglefield R.N., came in and with the help of his carpenters the *Truelove* was repaired.

The next year, 1854, Captain William Wells took over the *Truelove* and had a good season, the catch including several bears, two of which were brought back alive. The captain's method of capturing the fierce animals was simply to lasso them from a boat . . . manned by a very smart crew! The secret was to pass the line through the ringbolt outboard on the boat's stem so that the angry bear could be hauled up to the bow and held secure. Failure to pass the line through the ringbolt on one occasion resulted in the bear climbing aboard while the crew took to the freezing ocean.

The year 1858 saw the beginning of experiments with iron screw-propelled whalers when the *Innuit* sailed from Peterhead. Having had some success in sealing, the *Empress of India* was built and sent out, equipped with reinforced bows 12 ft thick, 110 men and 11 boats. The first ice she struck holed and sank the steamer, and her crew were ignominiously rescued by the sailing whalers. The *Innuit* also went to the bottom. However, wooden bark-rigged screw-steamers proved ideal and remained the best type of vessel for working in ice.

The *Truelove* had three near-disasters in 1861, a bad year all round. Under her new master, Captain William Barron, she was south of Cape Farewell in a gale on a pitch-black night with thick sleet falling. The sea was so high that the watch lashed themselves to stop being washed overboard while the *Truelove* lay to under a close-reefed maintopsail and balance-reefed main trysail, with the reefed main-stay sail ready to run up in an emergency. Suddenly an iceberg loomed right under the lee bow, the worst position for a ship lying to, just head reaching and drifting to leeward. Captain Barron had the staysail smartly run up and this just gave her sufficient way to weather the 'berg, but even so, the ship passed so close that the backwash flooded her decks.

Later, in the Strait, the *Truelove* had another near miss with a 'berg when a strong northerly gale brought down the ice and beset the fleet. Her next escape was in the vicinity of Anka Padluk, where huge glaciers come down to the sea. The ship was moored to an iceberg when the nearby glaciers calved and the huge, newborn icebergs created such a swell that *Truelove's* mooring lines carried away. Captain Barron was obliged to get out in spite of the blinding snow. Icebergs were on the move all around them and the water was so shallow that rocks could be seen passing under the ship. What happened next reads like a re-enactment of 'Jason and the Clashing Rocks'. Right ahead of the *Truelove* loomed up two large 'bergs, hardly a ship's length apart. Taking a calculated risk, Barron bravely stood through the narrow channel and was just clear when the icebergs crashed together. Huge pieces of ice cracked off their sides and fell into the water right under the whaler's stern.

Until 1868, when *Truelove* made her last voyage, during which she took 760 seals, the old whaler worked Arctic waters every year. In 1862, with a tremendous crash, she fell over on to her bilge while in drydock. It would have been imagined that the ancient vessel would have been severely damaged; but when she was refloated, replaced on the blocks and the dock emptied, it was found she was completely unharmed. When Captain Wells left her in 1867, he claimed that *Truelove* was '. . . still handy as a cutter, safe as a lifeboat, tight as a bottle, and ready now, as of old, to do her duty faithfully.'[2]

The following is Captain Barron's description of the *Truelove*:

In shape, the barque is very much like the one in which William Penn arrived the time he made the treaty with the Indians. The sides batter inwards towards the top of the gunwales, and this makes the vessel much broader at the water line than the deck. In nautical language, the sides are known as 'tumbling home', because they fall in above the bends . . .

. . . she formerly carried a bust of a man for a figurehead, but it was taken off on the account of the ice accumulating on it. Her bulwark was called pig-sty bulwark, i.e., every other plank out to allow the water to run freely off the deck. It was filled up in 1854, which made the deck much warmer. Her speed was as high as 9½ knots, but her usual speed is 8 knots per hour.[3]

After retiring from whaling and sealing *Truelove* continued to work, mainly to Norway in the ice and timber trade. In 1873 she was sailed to Greenland under the command of Captain Thomas Weatherill, where she loaded kryolite ore for the Pennsylvanian Salt Manufacturing Company. She was warmly welcomed home in Philadelphia, for she had been built there 109 years before, and arrived to a brass band and cheering crowds. Captain Weatherill was presented with a magnificent silk Stars and Stripes, 20 ft long and inscribed 'The "Truelove", built in Philadelphia, 1764'. She sailed from Philadelphia for Hull with a cargo of petroleum, resin and turpentine.

In 1877 the *Truelove* was owned by Dhal and Sadler of London and under her master, Thomas Kidman, she left Shields for Tarragona with coal. Working down the channel, the crew, considering her unseaworthy, refused to sail further and she put into Brixham, where she was inspected by a surveyor who wrote:

On my arrival on board, I found her trimmed by the head, in order to repair the stern. On examination of the topsides, I found them sheathed over with wood; several shifts of the wash strake were off. The caulking in her upper works, I found in many places slack, the topsail yards had been sent down on deck; three of them in a defective condition, the other will require repairs [She must have been converted to double topsails at some time in the then recent past]; also the rigging appears to want a general overhaul. The vessel being loaded with coals and sheathed over with wood sheathing, I am unable to ascertain the condition of the hull and fastenings. During my stay on board, she made very little water.[4]

The surveyor considered her unfit to continue, but she was repaired and refitted and later completed her voyage to Spain.

She was still registered with Lloyd's in 1887-8 and owned by J.S. Ward of London, but seems to have been broken up shortly after, then being over 120 years old. The *Truelove* was a credit to her builders. She survived the American War of Independence and the long wars with France, once taking an active part as a privateer. More dangerous to her were the storms of the Atlantic and the ice of the Arctic, but these she weathered, with only two brief respites, for 84 years. She was constructed at a time when the British considered that American ships were built of inferior timber and when, particularly during the Napoleonic Wars, the life of many British warships barely exceeded their launching. She was not kept like some precious old yacht, occasionally taken out for a sedate sail; she sailed in all weathers, working the toughest occupation in which any ship could be employed in, often being squeezed out of the ice to sit on top, a valuable attribute which saved her many times. She was also considered the luckiest vessel ever in the Hull whaling fleet. Truly a remarkable ship.

THE GRAND BANKS

From a misty past, perhaps even before the days of Cabot, up until the present century, the maritime history of the North Atlantic is interwoven with the prolific fisheries around the coast of Newfoundland and particularly over the vast Grand Banks projecting hundreds of miles to the south-east. For these regions, over a period of nearly 5 centuries, large fleets of sailing vessels set out annually from the ports of France, Britain, the Lowlands, Spain and Portugal to gather the harvest of codfish which provided one of the staple foods of Europe.

While Portugal, and later Spain, were probing farther afield in the south, French and Portuguese fishermen were pioneering the codfishing around Newfoundland and Cape Breton. It is even possible that the grounds were being quietly worked prior to their official discovery by John Cabot in 1497. Joao Vaz Corte-Real and Alvaro Martins Homem are reputed to have discovered the *Terras de Bacalhau* in 1472 and, by 1502, the first Guild of Codfishing Shipowners was formed by fishermen from ports in Portugal and the Azores. As has been stressed before, the evidence for pre-Cabotian discovery and exploitation of the Newfoundland fisheries is dubious and mainly circumstantial, but it is certain that, at the dawn of the sixteenth century, an ever-increasing number of small sailing ships were crossing the Western Ocean in pursuit of cod off the shores of Newfoundland. During the first half of the century all the necessary techniques of fishing and processing had been developed and were to change little over the following years.

The first record of a Norman vessel fishing the Banks is in 1504, and as early as 1506 both France and Portugal had established inshore fisheries around Newfoundland. The French used small ships of about 100 tons, with a crew of under 20 men. These ships could be quickly filled on the prolific Banks and there is evidence that two voyages were made annually. The first began at the end of January, fought westward in the bitter and contrary weather, fished until full and returned. The second voyage began in April or May to return before September. Their catches were salted on board and dried ashore at their home port. Any doubt about the seaworthiness of their ships and ability of the seamen in those early years of ocean voyaging must be laid to rest by the endeavours of these French fishermen who, each year, faced part of a winter in the North Atlantic to sail to the Banks and return without touching land.

Alternatively to making out-and-back voyages and returning with wet fish, vessels of most nations fishing inshore around Newfoundland and on the Banks would fish until full or nearly full, and put into bases in the harbours and coves of Newfoundland and Cape Breton. They sailed from their home ports in the spring, supplied with provisions for 6 months. Arriving at their bases, their first task was to catch bait and reclaim and repair the *flakes* or drying platforms built along the shore. As the sixteenth century wore on, the best harbours of Newfoundland, such as St John's, where sites for flakes were claimed on a first-come, first-served basis, became so crowded that shoreline space was scarce. Inevitably squabbles and outright battles were fought among competing fishermen for the best sites, so that 'fishing admirals' were chosen to settle disputes and organise defence against the piratical activities of rovers who preferred to earn their living in other ways than by hanging a hook and line over the side.

Apart from fine ships and seamen, the French and Portuguese had three other factors which spurred their fishermen to make the long voyage across the North Atlantic. In both countries agriculture was poorly developed, both possessed large Catholic populations with their multiplicity of fast and fish days, and both were blessed with large resources of solar salt, huge quantities of which were imperative in the processing of cod caught off Newfoundland. Portugal also found in the Newfoundland cod a solution to the problem of supplying her East Indiamen with protein, for meat products were limited in supply and in techniques of preservation. By the time an exhausted and sea-weary complement of an Indiaman thankfully stepped ashore at Goa they would have been heartily sick of Newfoundland salt cod.

English and Spanish vessels also occasionally fished Newfoundland waters, but, until the mid sixteenth century, the English continued to rely mainly on Icelandic cod, and the Spanish sent their ships to fish off the coast of Ireland. By the end of the sixteenth century, English fishermen, by numbers or by bloodymindedness, had become predominant in Newfoundland waters, occupying the eastern coast and the Avalon Peninsula. The French continued to use the south and west, fronting on to the Gulf of St Lawrence. When attempts to settle Newfoundland began in 1610, they confronted immediate and continuing hostility from the English fishermen who, by 1615, numbered around 5000, sailing in 250 ships of about 60 tons. Within the next 20 years these figures, both men and tonnage, had doubled.

During the following centuries the intrepid, skilful and unsung fishermen from most of the Atlantic maritime countries of Europe brought home their valuable catches, while the navies, privateers and pirates of every nation preyed on them for their provisions, their seasoned and skilled seamen and sometimes their ships. The outbreak of any minor war in Europe saw navies and corsairs hot-footing across the Atlantic to warn and protect their own fleets and pillage the enemy fishermen. The hundreds of small ships, and some not so small, became almost an annual international community afloat, to an extent that vessels set out to provide the service industries specifically required by the inshore fishermen and Grand Bankers. Storeships, dispatch craft and vessels freighted with clothing, provisions and hardware – veritable floating shops – cruised the grounds selling to whoever would buy.

Bulk carriers, or *sacks*, plied back and forth across the ocean, either relieving their own fishermen of their catches to make room for more, or buying to sell anywhere between South America, Europe and the farthest reaches of the Mediterranean. From the earliest years, the cosmopolitan gathering of fishing and other vessels in Newfoundland and on the Banks provided a perfect opportunity to circumvent expensive duties and navigation laws, and engage in a little free trade, far from the prying eyes of authority.

In the eighteenth and nineteenth centuries vessels from the eastern seaboard of America began to work the Banks and revolutionised the design of ships with their fast Gloucestermen and bluenose schooners, and in the 1850s or thereabouts New England fishermen introduced the *dory* to the industry. Still launching their one-man dories into the bleak waters of the Banks and Davis Strait, the Portuguese persisted with their large and beautiful auxiliary schooners until very recent times. Thus the Portuguese were among the first, and were the last, to work the Grand Banks in sailing ships.

Stockfish, as it was produced in Norway and Iceland for the European market, is simply sun-dried and no salt is used. Newfoundland cod, after splitting, is too large to turn into stockfish, so it is first salted. Inshore fishermen, as they can get their fish to their bases quickly, only lightly salt the cod, but ships fishing the Banks would heavily salt their catch before landing it for drying. Before the dory came into use (and after, when the weather kicked up too rough for the boats), fishing was carried out with handlines over the side, and a good day's catch for one man could amount to 350–400 large cod. At the end of a day's fishing the fish was headed, gutted and split before being passed below for salting. The process hardly changed from the first half of the sixteenth century to the last half of the twentieth. Jean Pierre from Renaissance St Malo could have taken over from Jacinto Martins from twentieth-century Ponta Delgada, and hardly caused a hitch in the team. In the fish holds the cod are very carefully salted before stacking in bins formed by adjustable boards. The pressure of the stacks and the movement of the ship causes the excess moisture to be squeezed from the fish, and the resulting pickle had to be pumped out and the compartments restowed as the contents settled.

The Portuguese measured their catch in *quintals*, which was the equivalent of 60 kilograms of salted and dried fish or *bacalhau*. As bacalhau is less than one-third the weight of wet fish, when the First Fisher of the *Argus* caught 500 quintals of cod in a season, he had actually hooked a hundred tons or more. An average catch would be about 150 quintals for the fishermen of the *Argus*, but considerably less for earlier, smaller and less well equipped vessels.

Most fish caught during the latter half of this century was preserved with ice but there is still a market for both stockfish and bacalhau. In the past there was a keen demand for byproducts of the cod. The tongues were salted in barrels and considered a delicacy, air bladders were preserved for the manufacture of a gelatin used in jellies, glues,

cooking and brewers' finings, and, in the sixteenth century, livers began to be saved for that horrible product, cod-liver oil. Renaissance children were spared the trauma of having to swallow spoonfuls of the stuff, for its medicinal properties had not been recognised. The oil, known as *train oil*, was produced by rotting the livers and used for tanning and lamps. Modern fishing vessels are equipped with liver boilers, an evil-smelling apparatus guaranteed to send any green hand rushing for the rail.

The depth of water on the Grand Banks is small enough to allow fishing vessels to anchor while fishing, but weather conditions might be such that it was preferable to drift, using sail to make the vessel lie beam-on to the wind. French eighteenth-century engravings show vessels lying with a square mizzen set to counteract the tendency of the vessel's head to fall off downwind. The fishermen fished from positions along the weather rail so that their lines ran clear of each other. It would be imagined that an anchored vessel would have to put a spring on the cable or use sail to enable her to lie partly across the current. Facing the weather and standing for hour after hour on the wet and slippery decks was too much even for those rugged eighteenth-century fishermen, so that each man was provided with a barrel to stand in and an apron which shed water outside the barrel. Also, some form of wind-break was erected to protect him from the wind.

It was the Americans, with their new-found fire and independence during the nineteenth century, who brought the most significant changes to the fishing. Not operating on a transatlantic basis, the beautiful Gloucester and bluenose schooners do not come into the scope of this book, but some note of the contributions made by their fishermen cannot be avoided. It was the fishing which attracted the Pilgrim Fathers to New England, and the development of this industry was the key to colonial prosperity. As recounted earlier, the New Englanders developed their own version of the triangular trades, shipping good quality fish across the Atlantic and

the poorer, unmarketable fish to the West Indies to feed the plantation slaves. Molasses was purchased and bought back to New England and distilled to rum, which was used to procure slaves in Africa. The wealth and power of many of the leading New England families was based on this trade and its several variations.

These eighteenth-century drawings show the arrangements for fishing, splitting and stowing on a French vessel.

A large eighteenth-century fishing vessel from Normandy. She is lying-to under a squaresail bent to the crojack yard, effectively preventing the ship's head paying off and providing the minimum amount of way. The men fish from the weather side, their lines dragging clear as the vessel drifts to leeward. Canvas shields protect the men from the wind, apparently a method peculiar to ships from Normandy. Fishermen from Brittany used curved spars to spread a canvas dodger along the windward side. Forward and aft of the men fishing a hand is stationed with a net to try to pick up fish which have fallen off the hooks.

After Independence, and particularly after the war of 1812, New England fishermen applied their experience and knowhow to exploiting the Grand Banks, the only source of fish in quantities sufficient to keep the now independent fisheries and New England states prospering. Prohibited from drying fish in Newfoundland, the catch had to be salted and brought wet to Nova Scotia or further south. Fishing from vessels rarely over 65 ft in length, it paid to have fast sailers to minimise the time spent running the catch back to port as soon as they were filled. Those special American creations, the schooner and Baltimore clipper, had, for sheer survival, been built to out-run the ships of other nations who were always ready to use any excuse to pounce on unprotected American ships. The lessons learned in their construction were used in the design of American offshore fishing schooners in the early nineteenth century, but it was during the forties and fifties, when the maniacal craze for speed spread to the fishermen and Andrew Story of Essex built his famous schooner *Romp*, that the fishing schooners showed radical changes, firstly to very sharp lines, then to shoal, flat-floored *clipper* schooners and finally, in the 1890s, to the *Indian headed*, or round-stemmed schooners, epitomised by the Gloucesterman *Elsie* and the Nova Scotian *Bluenose*.

Dories of one type or another had been in use for inshore fishing long before their adaptation into the *bank dory*. Perhaps a variation of the flat-bottomed *bateau* of the St Lawrence, a type of dory was used in New England as early as 1726. First used on the Banks during the 1850s, the dory quickly became popular and was the first American boat to be built on a large-scale production line. By 1870 there were 5 standard lengths, ranging from 12 to 16 ft inclusive. The flat-bottomed, flared sides of the dory do not present a particularly stable craft when empty, but, ballasted by bait, gear and fish, they become remarkably stable and seaworthy. Their shape allows them to be easily stacked on deck after the removal of the thwarts.

The advantages of being able to fish clear of the mother ship were numerous but, most importantly, it enabled the men to spread their endeavours over a wider stretch of ocean and also got them clear of the bones and offal littering the bottom around the anchored ship; a mess which was considered offensive to the cod. Working from boats, each fisherman could set his own *bultow*, or longline, and continue handlining while the obliging fish hung themselves on the hundreds of hooks strung along his gear. There were dangers. Fog and sudden gales took a grim toll of the dorymen, and, as would be expected in such a perilous occupation, there were dramatic tales of survival.

The magnificent Portuguese auxiliary schooners were the last Grand Bankers to fish under sail, and in 1950 the author and shipmaster Alan Villiers sailed in the four-masted schooner *Argus* to experience a season's fishing on the Grand Banks and in Davis Strait. Coming from the pen of a twentieth-century man, no better insight into the rigours of this type of fishing can be given. Each year fleets of these schooners put out from Lisbon,

The Portuguese Grand Bank schooner *Creoula* launching her dories. Slightly smaller than the *Argus* at 665 tons, the *Creoula* was built at Lisbon in 1937.

Oporto, Aveiro and Figueria da Foz, to sail first to the Azores to pick up the rest of their crews and then on, either to the Banks or, as in 1950 when sardines had been unobtainable in Portugal, to St Johns to purchase bait. It was here, a few years later, when I was apprentice on the Liverpool, St Johns, Halifax and Boston run, that I remember being very impressed by the colourful and workmanlike

The Portuguese Grand Bank schooner *Argus* (696 tons) built in Holland in 1938. Although fitted out with an efficient auxiliary diesel, generators and other modern equipment, her passages across the Atlantic and about the fishing grounds were made under sail.

Portuguese schooners rafted up around the harbour, waiting for their bait.

At the time I thought that the seemingly old ships were the end of an old tradition, kept going by the installation of diesels and the lack of finance to invest in new ships. I was wrong, at least in part. As in any other industry, Portuguese Grand Bank fishing had its bust and boom years. In the early 1930s a new and reforming government sought to restore the fortunes of the Bankers, which had reached a particularly low ebb, by establishing the *Gremio*, a guild of cod-fishing shipowners. The Gremio had the power to force all owners, merchants and fishermen to submit to a regulated and organised

system, with the aim of providing a living for the fishermen and cheap fish to the Portuguese people. Not only did the Gremio regulate the industry, but it assisted in the formation of a modern fleet, established schools, and improved the techniques and working conditions of the fishermen and their families. In 1936, 57 vessels were working on the Banks; all were sailing ships, of which only 22 had auxiliary power. In 1950, when Captain Villiers sailed in the *Argus*, 62 vessels were engaged, including 18 trawlers ranging from 1200 to 1500 tons and 13 motorships designed for fishing from dories. The rest were sailing vessels, all except two equipped with auxiliaries. The sailing fleet included 14 four-masted schooners, 16 three-masters and one barquentine, the *Gazela Primerio*, which had been built in 1883 and continued fishing until 1969. She still sails today under the care of the Philadelphia Ship Preservation Guild.

The only other really elderly vessel was the 271-ton three-masted schooner *Ana Maria*. All the other vessels had been built after World War I, and included four steel ships, one of which was the *Argus*, built in Holland in 1938. All the ships were well found, equipped with radio and had vastly improved conditions from the years prior to the Gremio. However, the traditions of the fishermen still survived, and not many occupations in western countries demanded so much courage and endurance from its participants.

Below Captain Villiers describes the work of a doryman:

I remember a day on the Grand Banks when, after mid-morning radio consultations with a dozen ships, our captains and the others decided to launch dories in a stiff nor'wester which looked like easing, only to find the wind rising to alarming force within the hour, and the sea with it. The North Atlantic can be a treacherous ocean. It was dangerous

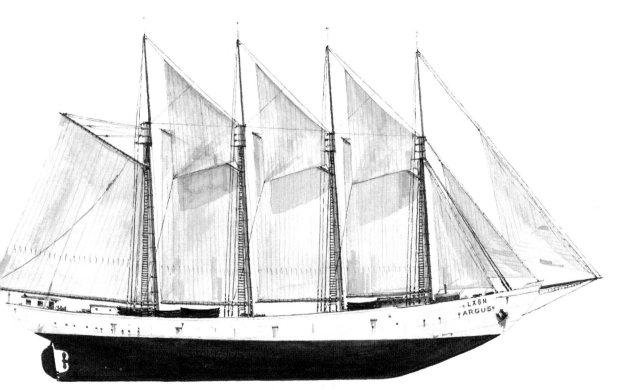

work, getting the dories back. The ship was rolling and plunging, with few people aboard until the dorymen returned. The dorymen had to be most circumspect in the manner they approached, lest they be stove or swamped – swamped by the rush of waters or the breaking sea, or the water gushing from the washports as the schooner rolled. Frequently her rail went right under, scooping up the sea, and all this water gushed through the washports again, imperilling any dory unfortunate enough to get in its way. There were many washports, some near the pounds. The dories must approach them.

When each dory had been emptied of fish, its occupant leapt nimbly over the rail. The dory must then be nested down. The thwarts and bulkheads were rapidly rigged down once it was inboard, the tub of line hoisted out, with its bait; then the mast and sails were removed, and the oars stowed snugly in the bottom with the fishing gear, so that the next dory could fit in, like a cup on a stack. All this took time and meanwhile the wind had risen steadily. The best dorymen came last, at the time of the greatest danger, and the captain always waited for them anxiously. Francisco Batista, the First Fisher; João de Oliveira, the Second Fisher; Francisco Martins, the First Fisher of the Azores, and his compatriots Paul Pereira and Manuel dos Santos Rafael; and a dozen more including old Manual de Sousa from Fuzeta and his son, and Antonio Rodrigues, from Fuzeta – veteran of forty-two campaigns – for these he waited, day after day, and watched them as they came, always with their dories full, and the First Fisher's fullest of all. Sometimes I could not see how that man dared imagine he could keep his dory afloat, though he took every possible precaution. He would sail back for miles, one split and cold-furrowed hand grasping his steering oar and the other the mainsheet, his lips split, his hands like red ploughed fields, torn with the constant handling of his lines, raw with the cold, sodden with sea-water, his fierce and fearless eyes always on the sea, his immense skill sailing the dory which under any other man would have sunk long ago.

'He has never sunk a dory,' Captain Adolfo said, watching him carefully lest the record be broken. 'Not yet!'

This was an unusual record. Most of the good fishermen had had to swim at least once, when over-filled dories sank beneath them or overturned in the sea. Captain Adolfo never knew when the First Fisher's record might not be lost, and his life with it. Yet day after day he came back, the sea lapping at the gunwales and every breaking wave within millimeters of coming over his stern. Sometimes he gave his lines and some of his fish to relatives who fished near him, or to the green fisher Manuel Lopes da Silva, who was his protégé and whom he always brought back in the thicker fogs. When he knew a full dory would be in more danger than usual, he had a nephew, or cousin, or young da Silva in close company, not to save him – he did not think of that – but to save his fish. Frequently he would stop, bail furiously, gauge the danger of the rising sea, and discard more fish to the friends in company, or carry on. Back alongside, I often saw that Captain Adolfo was more worried about the First Fisher's safety than that remarkable man was himself. He would go on gaffing up his fish, his dory alongside and still in the gravest danger, working with savage speed and indomitable energy while the broken water swept into his dory. As long as he could get more weight of fish out than weight of sea washed in, he was safe. Yet often it was a near thing. Other dorymen, back earlier, had made quite a business of gaffing up their fewer fish. Not he! He just got on with it, all his energy directed to the job in hand, his fierce eyes upon the sea as if he could quieten it by his own inflexible determination. Day after day he came, his relatives bringing his lines and gear, and, in his dory, only his fish and himself; sailing and bailing, pitching out gallons of water and cods' blood as his overladen dory wallowed in the sea, staggering on. Day after day he came, he and the other good dorymen, jumping in the tumult, thrown up on the crests of seas all round the bows, for they always worked to wind'ard, coming to the ship well ahead of her so that they were not drifted past and into greater danger; each waiting his turn and his chance to get alongside. Often it rained, a hard, merciless rain, as the sea rose, and the little red dories leaping in the spray looked like overladen ants toiling in a surf. Yet one by one, skilfully handled, they slipped in under the bows, while the ship rolled heavily and the seas swept across her decks and the wind howled in the rigging. The *Argus* tugged at her anchor, plunging and jumping like a big dory herself, pitching violently until her forefoot was right out of the water; but slowly and steadily the nests of the recovered dories mounted, while the dorymen and the deckboys, the mates and the engineers and the cooks, toiled at the tackles.

'Hoist away bow! Hoist away stern!'

'Easy all!'

No other shouts. One by one, the sodden dorymen, watching their chance, leapt to the rail and climbed inboard, as their dories

SAILING SHIPS FROM 1800

emptied and were hooked for lifting. Up they came as she rolled, with speed but with infinite care. I saw the First Fisher come over the rail after bringing back his thirtieth full dory – he often filled twice in a day, or even in half a day – bailing for his life; his dory even when empty still in great danger, for the sea was so high that sometimes the frail red box hung for a perilous moment above the schooner's rolled-down side. I saw the First Fisher come over the rail and, with a foot on the swifter, gave a last fierce look at the tempestuous and deceitful sea which for so long had been his enemy and would be again on the morrow.

For a second, he hung there in silence, looking; but his fierce eyes seemed to be saying, 'Defeated again, you implacable wet hell! Defeated again!'

Yet for how long?[1]

The *Argus* that year, 1950, returned to Lisbon on 30 September with a full load of between 900 and 950 tons of cod in salt bulk. During the 6-month voyage she had called at Ponta Delgada in the Azores both outward and homeward bound, had called and been delayed at St John's for 18 days and had later put into North Sydney near Cape Breton for 9 days to replenish her bait. Most of the 6-month voyage she spent fishing the waters of the Grand Banks and Davis Strait.

Nowadays the white schooners are gone from the Banks, but an occasional relic may still be seen, I understand, fishing in rocky places where trawlers dare not go and using launches instead of dories. Gone also are their masts and sails, apart from perhaps a steadying sail. Their auxiliary diesels, once a standby to be used only when absolutely necessary, have now usurped the power of the schooners' sails.

While ships were small, commerce needed large numbers to keep the freight moving. In the 1820s it was estimated that Britain and her empire alone possessed 27,859 merchant ships. Add to this total all other vessels employed by America and other European nations and the figure becomes truly enormous. However, the average capacity of all these vessels would not be much above 100 tons, and very few ships would be over 1000 tons. I have read somewhere that during the mid nineteenth century a vessel sailing across the Atlantic was rarely out of sight of another ship, and when the wind was foul for the Channel, hundreds of ships would anchor in the Downs, off the Kentish shore, to wait for a change.

Early in the nineteenth century there were signs that the maritime world was changing. The Americans were proving themselves able to design and build swifter and more radical craft than the French, whose ships had long been held as the finest in the world. Smoke from steam-engines was just beginning to soot the sails of some small vessels, and, in 1819, the auxiliary paddle wheeler *Savannah* crossed the Atlantic from Savannah in Georgia to Liverpool.

During the 1840s the sailing ship took a gigantic leap in design when the American extreme clippers graced the oceans for a brief few years. From the experience of their design followed the more practical medium clippers, both the wooden American ships and the British composite ships such as the *Cutty Sark*. Then, from the 1870s, iron produced the most rugged and enduring sailing ships ever built. The peak of large sailing-ship technology was reached in the magnificent steel German ships and

barques such as the *Pruessen* and the *Passat*. However, by the time the first iron sailing ships were being built, steam had driven sail from the more worthwhile and lucrative North Atlantic runs. Apart from a few small vessels which had found themselves a niche, and the occasional transatlantic cargo for the larger ships, only the old strained sailing ships found regular employment in the Atlantic, hauling lumber from Quebec and perhaps logwood from the south. Nevertheless, even after World War II there was the odd barque or schooner, enduring a poverty-stricken old age, scraping a living in Atlantic waters. Only the Portuguese, fishing the Grand Banks and Davis Strait, continued to employ sailing vessels on a regular basis, and nearly all of these were powered by auxiliary diesels.

From the time that steam ruled the North Atlantic, most sailing ships found their employment round the capes, to Australia for wool and grain, and South America for phosphate. On these long runs, using the powerful winds of the Southern Ocean, and the familiar sailing routes of the North and South Atlantic, the large sailing ships remained economically viable for many years. When the *Pamir* tragically foundered in 1957 and her sister, the *Passat*, was withdrawn from service, it signalled the end of the large commercial sailing ship. Fortunately, since that nadir, there were people who were not prepared to let the skills and tradition die. Nowadays there is an ever-increasing number of traditionally rigged sailing vessels, many of them square-rigged, gracing the oceans, finding work in providing a challenge for young – and older – people and often presenting a proud symbol of the tradition of the community from which they operate.

THE POST-OFFICE PACKETS

During the sixteenth and seventeenth centuries, as Europeans were acquiring trade and possessions far away from their homelands, their lines of communication became ever more extended and dependent on the sailing ship. Initially, the task of the English Royal Mail Service was the delivery of diplomatic correspondence, but in the seventeenth century private mail began to be carried on the payment of postage. However, in Europe, where packets of mail could be *posted* overland, unrest and wars interfered with the delivery to such an extent that sea routes might be preferred, even to destinations on the Continent. In 1688-9 the first three *packet ships* initiated a service between Falmouth in south-west Cornwall and Corunna in Spain, from where the mail went overland.

Falmouth, with its large harbour and safe roads, easy to work in and out in most winds, was ideal for this purpose. The mail, light and easily handled, could be posted down from the capital and other locations in England, avoiding the pirates and privateers which always infested the Channel in those days, and likewise avoiding delays which foul winds could cause in the restricted waters. Once out of Falmouth, a westerly wind, which could have caused weeks of delay in the Channel, became a favourable 'soldiers' wind' for Spain.

When war with Spain prevented Corunna being used as the continental destination, the packets sailed to Lisbon, and it was not until the middle of the eighteenth century that transatlantic services were established, with sailings to American east-coast ports and the West Indies. Particularly after the American Independence, Halifax and Bermuda became important way ports for the Post-Office packets, which would continue from these ports to the United States. Early in the nineteenth century, the packets also ran important services to South America.

Until near the end of the eighteenth century, when a more efficient inland network was set up, all mail was collected and sorted in London, where it was bundled into packets for various destinations. Post-boys, under threat of a period in a 'house of correction' if they dawdled at less than 6 miles an hour, relayed the mail to Falmouth in about 6 days. At Falmouth the agent and his staff sealed the packets into weighted leather bags, which would be dumped over the side if the packet ship was likely to be captured by an enemy. With the packets' ability to out-run, and in many cases, out-fight, predators, passengers often preferred to travel in their limited and pokey accommodation, and bullion was frequently included in their freight.

Whereas the Falmouth packets were a recognised, scheduled operation, they were not the only means of sending mail overseas. 'Ship-letters' could be sent in any vessel whose captain was prepared to accept them on payment of the postage, and it was the later competition with the New York sailing packets, and finally steam, which put the Falmouth Post-Office packets out of business by 1850, after 160 years of service.

Most of the Falmouth packets were small ships and brigs ranging from 150 to 200 tons, designed for speed. Their capacity for freight was limited and, in peacetime, they were lightly armed and manned. In time of war they were capable of carrying, and were supplied with, extra armament and crew but, in view of the losses that occurred, this did not prevent merchants from complaining that they were too lightly armed and manned, both in peace and war. Every packet was provided with a limited number of cabins for passengers and their fares were pocketed by captains and owners. In the ships about the end of the eighteenth century there were generally six cabins, each measuring about 6 by 4 ft.

Usually the packets were owned privately, with the captains as part-owners, many of whom became influential and wealthy members of West-Country society. As the ships could be very profitable, shares in the ships were also often acquired by Post Office officials in Falmouth and London. The captains were commissioned by the Admiralty to operate the service. A contract was then drawn up with the Post Office, which paid the crews' wages, insurance, all maintenance costs, and supplied all victuals.

The service was popular with seamen who appreciated the regular runs and leave in their home port. They also received the blessing of protection from impressment, a fate which threatened nearly all seamen, particularly in ships bound inward. Until the practice was firmly put down during the Napoleonic Wars, sailors could, in addition to their pay, make enough money from private, illegal ventures to enable them to buy or build houses and become comfortably off.

The little packet ships, if unable to show a clean pair of heels, were not always an easy prize for an attacker. Two French privateers, *L'Atalante* in 1793 and *Le Jeune Richard* in 1807, were captured by packets, both against heavy odds; the latter privateer was boarded and defeated by the captain and only six men of the packet *Windsor Castle*. On 24 June 1803,

The Post office Packet *Duke of Marlborough* pursued by HMS *Primrose*

Newfoundland. For their bravery and discipline, Captain Fellowes and the crew were later awarded £200.

One of the most bizarre and embarrassing incidents occurred in 1814 when a Post-Office packet and one of His Majesty's sloops failed to identify each other and blazed away for hours before their mistake became apparent. On 12 March at 2.30 pm the packet brig *Duke of Marlborough*, with nine passengers, including women, and a crew of about 28, was off Cape Finisterre, bound from Falmouth to Lisbon, when a strange brig hove in sight and gave chase. Captain John Bull of the *Duke of Marlborough*, complying with his standing orders, made sail and ran while flying her private signals and a small blue ensign. When the stranger hoisted its colours, those in the *Marlborough* thought them to be American and continued to run until nightfall, when it was apparent that her pursuer was closing fast. At 6.30 pm Captain Bull made private night signals, but still got no response. By this time the strange brig had opened fire and when, about an hour later, the distance between the ships had closed, an all-out battle ensued until about 10 pm. By this time the *Marlborough* was badly damaged. She had fired over 160 rounds from her 12 guns, had 1 passenger, an army lieutenant, killed, 3 seamen badly wounded and 8 others slightly injured. During a pause in the gunfire it was learned that her attacker was the British sloop HMS *Primrose*.

By this time 3 men from the sloop had been killed and the master and 11 others wounded. If the 'butcher's bill' of the *Primrose* is a measure of the fighting calibre of the officers and crew of the *Marlborough*, then it does them credit, although it would have been better directed at their nation's enemies.

only 2 days out from Halifax and bound for England, the packet *Lady Hobart*, Captain William Fellowes, was engaged by a French privateering schooner, *l'Aimable*. The Frenchman was defeated and sent back into Halifax with a prize crew while the *Lady Hobart* continued her voyage. Her good fortune did not hold as, 4 days later, she hit a very large iceberg and was badly damaged. Everything was done to try to stop the leaks and to lighten the ship, including jettisoning the guns and anchors, but she was soon awash and foundering. Before she sank, her passengers, including three women, and her crew, in all 29 people, got safely away in two boats. After 6 days of fog and freezing conditions, with only 45 pounds of provisions and 5 gallons of water, they managed to make the 350 miles to the coast of

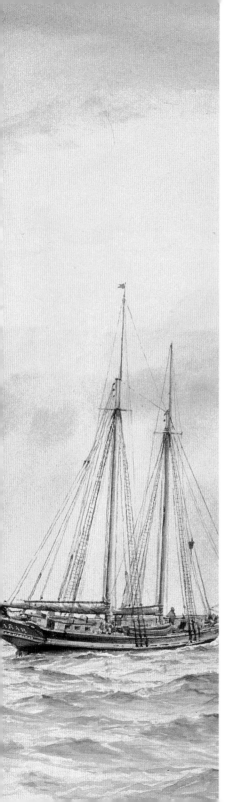

AMERICAN TRANSATLANTIC PACKETS

With the coming of peace in 1815, young America was on the threshold of initiating a further revolution which would challenge and transform the concepts of centuries of slow, conservative but steady advancement in ship design. Within a few decades the exuberant Yankees were to astonish the world with the largest, finest and swiftest wooden sailing ships ever built.

Americans were no novices at building fast ships for, even before the Revolution, the colony had been so hamstrung by the navigation laws and tariffs of the Mother Country, which skimmed the cream and most of the milk off the lucrative trades, that most self-respecting and aspiring merchants in the New World had run their ships on illegal ventures where speed was an essential insurance. For Americans, fast ships became even more of an imperative for survival at sea during the turbulent years of the Revolution, the Napoleonic Wars and the war of 1812. In those confusing times the American merchant ship was given an uncertain reception by European navies and privateers. It was wiser to duck and run from a well armed stranger.

When the smoke of the war years cleared and nations began to resume relatively peaceful trading voyages, increasing wealth and settlement in America created a demand for better, and preferably faster, merchant ships. Most American vessels were small, very few being over 400 tons, and these larger vessels were of a design virtually unchanged since the eighteenth century. Shipowners paid dues and other fees on the measured tonnage of their vessels. Careful of their pockets, they were not inclined to change the design of the blunt-ended, wall-sided, flat-floored freighters while the system of measurement by which tonnage was calculated remained unchanged. The formula had been introduced in 1773 and, as it was based only on the parameters of length and breadth, it penalised hull forms which strayed too far from an uninspired box with excessive depth. For one of these ships to make an average speed of 5 knots on an ocean passage was considered flying. Most voyages probably averaged between 2 and 4 knots, and I know from the experience of sailing the replica of Bligh's collier, *Bounty*, about the Pacific, that we estimated passage times on an average of 4 knots – and that was motor-sailing when the wind was foul.

The fast ships that America possessed were small and developed for wartime conditions where comfort, capacity, and in many cases, caution, had been sacrificed for speed. These found peacetime employment in luxury trades where high freight rates were of no consequence and, as we have seen, in providing the illegal slave trade with fast ships. By 1818 transatlantic mail had for long been carried in ships described as *packets*. The American ships were better than their continental sisters, which were smaller and called at Bermuda or Halifax, considerably lengthening the voyage, but none, European or American, sailed to any regular schedule. Other merchant ships, also described as

A Blackball packet crossing the Grand Banks

packets as they were on a regular run and sometimes carried mail, boosted their income by accommodating passengers, but these sailed at the shippers' convenience when the vessel's loading was complete, thus passengers were often left hanging about for weeks while a delayed consignment of corn from upcountry found its belated way to the port, or even while their ship awaited a fair wind to clear the coast.

On 24 October 1817, an advertisement appeared in the New York *Commercial Advertiser* declaring that, in January 1818, a line of packet ships would initiate regular sailings between New York and Liverpool. This line was later to become officially known as the Black Ball Line, and was founded by the New Yorkers Isaac Wright & Son, Francis Thompson, Jeremiah Thompson and Benjamin Marshall, all Quakers and related by marriage. They launched their venture with four ships, the 384-ton *Pacific*, the *Amity* and *Courier*, both about the same size as the *Pacific*, and the larger 424-ton *James Monroe*. All launched in New York, these ships were not built especially for the task but selected from the available packets for their comparatively large size and speed. The *Pacific*, for instance, owned by Isaac Wright and Francis Thompson, had been built in 1807. She had been running between New York and Liverpool from before 1811 and it has been remarked that she had a turn of speed which would not disgrace her among the later clippers. She finished her working years as a whaler, sailing until she was 75 years old.

The first of the 'Blackballers' to sail was the *Courier*, which had been scheduled from Liverpool on 1 January 1818 but in fact did not get away until the fourth. A day later, on a snowy winter morning, sharp at the advertised hour of 10 am, Captain James Watkinson sailed the *James Monroe* clear of her berth alongside the Steamboat Wharf in New York and stood down harbour. On board she had seven passengers, a low-value cargo mainly of apples, and a small bag of mail. As her fore-topsail was hoisted, there came into view, below the lower reef band,

the large black ball which to become renown in the Western Ocean for the next 60 years.

With its ships sailing, come hell or high water, on the first of the month, the Black Ball Line contradicted all the 'informed' opinions and head-shakers. In spite of a slump in shipping during the next 2 years, the line prospered, competing successfully with non-scheduled rivals, and acquiring a name for reliability and, for the cabin passengers at least, comfort. The company's first large ship, the 481-ton *Nestor*, was purchased in 1820.

In late 1821 the Blackballers had their first scheduled rival when Byrnes, Trimble & Company founded what was to become the Red Star Line with the ships *Manhattan, Hercules, Panther* and *Meteor*, timed to sail on the twenty-fourth of the month. The following year seems to have witnessed a scramble for a place in the Atlantic packet trade. In February 1822 the Black Ball Line responded to the challenge of the Red Star Line by instituting an additional sailing on the sixteenth of the month and reducing the fare for a cabin passenger to 35 guineas. Another company, the Blue Swallow Tail Line, operated by Messrs Fish, Grinnell & Company, entered the arena, timing their ships to sail on the eighth of the month, with the first sailing in September, thus completing a weekly scheduled transatlantic service. Griswold & Coates launched the Black X Line to London, but did not really get it off the ground until 1824, when Fish Grinnell cooperated with their Red Swallow Tail Line, and together the two companies virtually operated as one. Also in 1822, a company known as the Old Line under Francis Depau, Isaac Bell and Miles Burke began regular sailings between New York and Le Havre. Shipping was indeed booming.

Boston and Philadelphia leapt on the band-waggon with less success. The Cope Line of Philadelphia survived, but the Boston & Liverpool Packet Company (or 'Jewel Line', for their ships were named *Emerald, Topaz, Amethyst* and *Sapphire*) foundered for want of outward freight. They were

scuppered in part by the completion of the Erie Canal, which had been begun in 1817. The middle section had been opened in 1820, and the entire canal was completed in 1825. The magnificent waterway channelled all the produce of the west to New York, and the holds of the New York vessels and Boston ships often had to sail south to pick up an outward freight of cotton. Others tried in later years to establish a scheduled Boston line, but without success until 1844, when Enoch Train founded his White Diamond Line.

Many other companies later ran packets in the Atlantic; companies such as those of Robert Kermit, the Black Star Line and the George Cross (or 'Red Cross') Line, owners of the famous *Dreadnought*. One further important company remains to be mentioned. E.K. Collins, later the founder of the Collins Line of steamships, owned, among other vessels, an 827-ton ship, the *Shakespeare*. In 1836 and 1837 he had built the 895-ton sisters *Garrick, Sheridan* and *Siddons*. With these he founded the Dramatic Line, the naming of which needs no further explanation. In 1839 the largest American merchantman of her day, the 1009-ton *Roscius*, was added to the fleet.

The continuing success of the New York packets until their decline and extinction in competition with steam, was owed not only to the enormously increased emigration and transatlantic travel during the middle decades of the century, but to the practical economics of managing the ships. A non-scheduled regular trader would generally make two round-trip Atlantic voyages throughout the year, sailing when her freight was complete. The owners of a scheduled packet line ran the risk of their ships sailing only partly laden, but by using four ships and sailing on time, 'full or not full', they delighted the shippers and passengers and attracted the fine freights of high value and little bulk. In addition, the ships could make three complete voyages during the course of a year, thus increasing the earning capacity of the vessels by 50 per cent. However, the third voyage

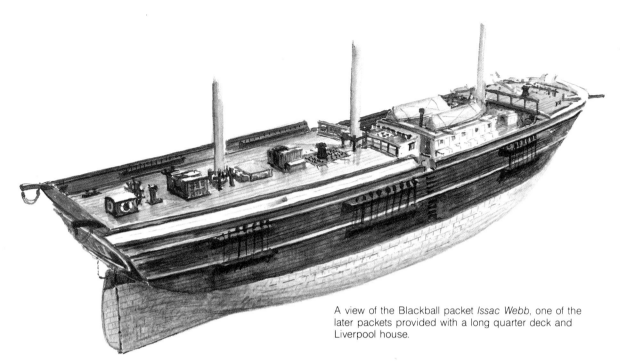

A view of the Blackball packet *Issac Webb*, one of the later packets provided with a long quarter deck and Liverpool house.

was made during the winter months when passengers and freight were less available and the North Atlantic was at its worst. Driving the ships westward against the bitter winter gales severely strained both ships and men and was considered unfavourably with a winter rounding of the Horn.

Forcing the sailing ships to maintain a strict schedule of departures created a rugged challenge to the ships and particularly to the men who sailed them. During the first years the packets were not purpose-built ships but regular traders put on the run. It was left to the captains to crack on, to carry sail to the limit of prudence and beyond. No snugging down to lie out a contrary gale. With a reluctant reef or two in the topsails, the ship was driven to windward, smashing through the steep Atlantic gale-spawned seas, masts cracking and backstays thrumming under the enormous stresses of wind and violent motion. Gear was always maintained in first-class order – it had to be.

Gradually a special breed of ships and men evolved, peculiar to the packets. The ships, powerfully built and rigged, somewhat squarer in sail plan than their sisters in other trades, increased in size and improved in design and speed. Hull design, until the clippers of the late forties and fifties created a revolution, retained the 'codfish' aspects of all ships since Matthew Baker, with the maximum beam forward of amidships. During the thirties it was found necessary to provide the greatest possible deck space for the thousands of emigrants travelling west, in addition to increasing the cargo capacity. The fine run aft of the earlier ships, influenced by the success of the Baltimore clippers, filled out to sharp ends with little run and less deadrise. The resulting fuller run and the moving of the point of maximum beam further aft now permitted the fore mast to be stepped further aft. Viewed from above, the straight sides and bluff ends almost formed a rectangle. Even after the clippers had demonstrated the efficiency of their design, most Western Ocean packets retained full and buoyant bows above the waterline for the very practical reason that the packets had to claw to windward thousands of miles westward against the prevailing winds. No doubt the sharp and lofty clippers could, in reasonable weather, out-run and out-point even a first-class packet, but they would be miserably wet and, when the westerlies began to huff and puff, could not carry sail as did the packets on their square, lower and more powerful spars.

The early ships were usually flush-decked, with a roundhouse aft. Passenger accommodation was provided below in the 'tween-deck spaces and the deck was relatively clear, having only the usual barnyard consisting of a house for the cow and pens for other animals provided for the passengers' table. The boats, stowed over the main hatch, were likewise made to serve as accommodation for the menagerie. The Blackballers during the early years were, in common with many other ships, painted black with varnished bands running the length of the hull. Inside the bulwarks, the boats and deckhouses were all light green. Later these colours were to change to the almost universal Indiaman colours, signifying all the ethos of empire, power and security of the period, with painted ports on a white band, white bulwarks, boats and deckhouses, and white and black spars.

The later and larger packets featured a quarterdeck under which the cabin passengers were accommodated. This greatly improved the comfort of the travellers but was cursed by the sailors who reckoned it got in their way.

Nothing was spared to fit out the passenger accommodation in the most lavish manner. The taste and workmanship that graced the cabins and saloons is almost a lost art today. Nathaniel Hawthorne, who was American consul in Liverpool during the 1850s, wrote, rather sourly, of the later packets:

There is no such finery on land, as in the cabin of one of these ships in the Liverpool trade, finished off with a complete panelling of rosewood, mahogany and bird's eye maple, polished and varnished, and gilded along the cornices and the edges of the panels. It is all a piece of elaborate cabinet-work; and one does not altogether see why it should be given to the gales, and the salt sea atmosphere, to be tossed on the waves, and occupied by a rude shipmaster, in his dreadnought clothes, when the finest lady in the land has no such boudoir.[1]

Changes in design of the packets during the thirties have already been noted, but the second half of the decade saw the beginning of a revolution in marine architecture which was to result in the magnificent clippers of the forties and fifties. As discussed earlier it was considered that an element of design which greatly contributed to speed was the *deadrise*, or the V of the bottom. Within practical limits, the more deadrise that could be built into a ship, the greater was her potential for speed. The ideal Baltimore clipper had a large deadrise, her maximum beam forward of amidships, rounded, but sharper bows below the water than earlier ships, a long fine run aft, and a considerable drag, or increase in draft towards the stern. Already, by the mid thirties, the packets had gradually modified most of these characteristics, with little loss in speed provided the ships were driven as hard as they were designed to be. But deadrise was still considered absolutely essential – except by two, later famous, men; Captain N.B. Palmer and the shipowner E.K. Collins who, impressed by the performance of the Mississippi cotton droghers, introduced perfectly flat floors. The result utterly confounded the critics by considerably reducing passage times.

Collins's Dramatic Line schedules conflicted with those of other lines and the packets now found themselves sailing on the same days, resulting in the inevitable trans-ocean races in which the skippers did their damndest to out-sail one another. The Dramatic captains were probably exemplified by Nat

Palmer, who really proved the worth of the flatbottoms when, as master of the *Siddons*, he decisively out-ran the fastest U.S. Navy frigate *United States*, a larger vessel with a full Navy crew. What cracking on there must have been during these voyages.

The lessons learned from the packets, particularly those of the Dramatic Line, of which the *Roscius* was the swiftest, profoundly influenced the design of the extreme clippers and resulted in the development of the later clipper packets. Extra incentive in the search for speed and efficiency under sail was given in the year before the *Roscius* was launched, when, on the same day, the *Sirius* and *Great Western* steamed into New York, the former 17 days from Cork and the latter 15 days from Bristol.

During the 1840s the packets increased in size and where amenable to their particular employment as Atlantic, passenger-carrying vessels, incorporated features which were appearing in the China clippers. Trade and shipbuilding were booming and these years produced the first flowers of a new type of vessel from designers such as John Willis Griffith whose fine, hollow-bowed *Rainbow*, designed especially for the China trade, was launched in 1845, and Donald McKay, whose 1404-ton packet *New World* caused a sensation in New York and Liverpool. Sailing for Messrs Grinnell, Minturn & Company, she was then, in 1846, the largest American merchant ship, and sharp for a packet. Many of these large packets now boasted two continuous 'tween-decks with substantial headroom and were capable of packing in hundreds of steerage passengers. As the forties drew to a close, these decks were ever more packed with the poor and destitute Irish, fleeing the horrifying potato famines of 1845 to 1849.

But it was not only the New York shipowners who McKay impressed. Enoch Train, a Boston owner intent on establishing a Boston line of scheduled packets, had heard the praises sung of the young shipbuilder then working in partnership at Newburyport. Train visited McKay at his yard and

immediately awarded him the contract to build the *Joshua Bates* (620 tons), the first ship of the Boston White Diamond Line.

The White Diamond Line was inaugurated in 1843 and got off to a shaky start, suffering from the perennial lack of outward freight and fierce competition for mails from the New York packets. In spite of these and other tribulations, Enoch Train's hard-headed determination, coupled with the fine McKay ships, finally persuaded the Liverpool merchants to cooperate. With the encouragement and assistance of Enoch Train, McKay established a shipyard in Boston and, among a host of famous ships, went on to build five more vessels for the White Diamond Line. The 751-ton *Washington Irving* was launched in 1844 and featured the long quarter-deck, deep waist and topgallant forecastle, along with a large 'Liverpool house', between the foremast and the main hatch. In 1846 the 894-ton *Anglo Saxon* came off the ways. With the aim of the passenger and immigrant trade, she was made particularly attractive with lavish decoration and accommodation. No longer was the waist dominated by the barnyard and the main hatch was left clear as the longboat was now stowed on the house. Additional boats were carried on quarter and stern davits.

Now began the decade of the true extreme clippers, built to compete with anything afloat in the China trade or in supplying the demands of the California gold rush. Late in 1850, McKay launched the *Staghound*, one of the first extreme clippers. At 1534 tons she was the largest merchant ship ever built up to that time and was constructed for speed and the California trade. With lessons learned from these big ships, the size of the Atlantic packets took what might be called a quantum leap. Only 7 months after the *Staghound* took to the water, McKay launched the 1851-ton *Staffordshire*, which was to earn the title of 'Queen Clipper Packet of the Atlantic'. Even larger vessels were to follow when, in 1853, both the *Star of Empire* and, perhaps McKay's favourite ship, the *Chariot of Fame*, were built. The sisters were designed to combine the ability to carry large freights with speeds which could compete with, if not show a clean pair of heels to, the challenge of the steamers.

During these years packet lines other than Train's were meeting competition from steam by employing larger and faster sailing ships. The Red Cross Line's 1400-ton *Dreadnought* began her legendary career in 1853 and *Ocean Monarch* was launched from the East River yards in 1856. She appears to have been the largest sailing packet ever built, measuring 2145 tons. The first half of the decade saw the American merchant marine achieve the zenith in prosperity and in the production of superb sailing ships. However, the transatlantic steamers were now well on the way to proving their reliability and safety and were beginning to wrest the more lucrative contracts and freight from the packets. The sailing ships began to rely on more general cargoes and their steerage capacity, milking the flood of emigrants who, in some ships, suffered appallingly from the ruthless, hard-fisted Yankee officers, packed and filthy accommodation and food which barely enabled them to survive.

Depression followed by the Civil War did irreparable damage to American merchant shipping and, even before that tragic conflict, the prosperous days of the Atlantic sailing packets were well and truly over. By providing cheaper freight and fares and mainly unscheduled service, some survived until the eighties. According to Basil Lubbock, the last passage of the last sailing packet was made in 1883 by the aptly named *Ne Plus Ultra* (1300 tons) of the Black X Line.

The masters and men of the Western Ocean packets

The brief era of the Atlantic sailing packets not only evolved a rugged, tough sailing ship but bred captains whose names still resound, and seamen who, for sheer toughness, if not always expertise, were probably unequalled at any time. As one version of the popular shanty, *New York Gals*, warned:

> *My flash man, he's a Packet Rat,*
> *An he sails in the Blackball Line,*
> *An' he'd be a saucy son-of-a-bitch,*
> *That'd tackle that man o' mine.*[2]

The American packet *Queen of the West* leaving New York in the 1850s. She was built by Brown and Bell at New York in 1843 and measuring 1168 tons she was large for her time. First sailing under the flag of Woodhull and Minturn, she was taken over, along with the firm, by the Swallowtail Line. The illustration shows her leaving the East River with the Battery and Garden Island in the background.

If captains were hard on their crew, they were no less hard on their mates, particularly if the watch officer's nerve collapsed and he ordered a reef in a topsail one moment before the Old Man thought it was necessary. There are apocryphal stories about padlocked sheets and halyards and the master who locked the mate in the chicken coop for a few days – and clucked at the culprit whenever he passed by.

The only way a packet captain could meet the constant challenge of maintaining his schedule and attracting shippers was to mercilessly drive his ships and crew, always setting every stitch of canvas the ship could carry while steering and trimming to take advantage of every slant of wind. His aim at all times was to make a fast passage and to do this humanity was more often than not a luxury he could ill afford. Packet captains, apart from usually being hard citizens, were often also shrewd businessmen, well educated and paragons of society. Their names and the names of their 'flash packets' were bywords, and a successful captain was a rich man, at the zenith of the era often earning as much as $5000 a year, a fortune in those days. Apart from either owning shares in the ship or receiving a small fixed salary, the bulk of his earnings was derived from various percentage rake-offs from the gross takings on freight, cabin passengers and steerage. In addition, he kept the whole of the mail money. The packet captain earned every penny and these incentives were necessary to attract steel-nerved masters with the skills, drive, ambition and business skills which made them the finest captains afloat.

A gentleman he may have been ashore – and to his cabin passengers – but the packet captain was all too often a veritable Jekyll and Hyde, particularly as competition from steam, and rivals, became fiercer during the late 1840s and '50s. Once on his quarterdeck, he could become a brutal, merciless tyrant, backed by three savage mates armed with iron fists, belaying pins and knuckle-dusters, mates who took a pride in their ability to 'knock down and drag out' the toughest crowd of packet rats. Of

The Lightning

This clipper ship does not rightly belong in these pages for she was designed for and sailed in the Australian emigrant trade. Nevertheless, one of her many claims to fame was possibly the fastest day's run by any sailing ship, and this was achieved on her maiden voyage from Boston to Liverpool.

She was one of four ships built by Donald McKay for James Baines's Australian Blackball Line operating out of Liverpool, and was an extreme example of hollow, or flared, bow among the clippers. Not including her stun'sails, ring-tails, Jamie Green, watersails and every other kite which could be hung on her, she spread 13,000 yards of canvas, which included a moonsail above the main skysail. She was registered at 1468 tons, had a length of 244 ft, a beam of 44 ft and a long 92-ft poop.

On her maiden voyage, commanded by the famous hard-driving Captain 'Bully' Forbes, the *Lightning* dropped her pilot at the Boston Light at 3 pm on 18 February 1854. On 1 March her log recorded:

Wind S, — strong gales, bore away for North Channel, carried away the foretopsail and lost jib; hove the log several times, and found the ship going through the water at the rate of 18 to 18½ knots per hour; lee rail under water, and rigging slack; saw the Irish land at 9.30 p.m. Distance run in the 24 hours 436 miles.

The observation that the last recorded fix was the previous noon, 28 February, has made some critics doubt this record, but it was accepted at the time. In her early years on the Australian run she made some fine passages, and, apart from a voyage carrying troops to India, continued in the trade until 31 October 1869, when she caught fire at Geelong and was scuttled.

course, not all Western Ocean packets were so ruthlessly commanded and officered, but the practice was all too common and the ships got a reputation as 'blood-boats'. They were considered the hardest school in any merchant service afloat.

From this school of hard knocks there emerged a character known as a 'packet rat'. The Americans produced first-class seamen but the packet rat was a breed of his own. He shipped for the voyage, was usually paid in advance so that he was working out what was termed a 'dead horse' most of the voyage, and he took more pride in his toughness than his seamanship – he 'wa'nt skeered of no bucko mate'. He came aboard drunk and 'flying light', with only the rags he wore – no spare gear, oilies or 'donkey's breakfast'. These he could rob from the 'raynecks' (green hands), or steerage, and if he did not succeed, he was enured to working aloft, half naked, even in the teeth of a mid-winter North Atlantic gale. He scorned the men who sailed in other trades and detested foreigners. He came back for voyage after voyage, fighting, cursing and often thieving until age or accident caught up with him.

From the 1850s onward, the better seaman turned to easier employment, leaving only the roughest and most villainous rats to man the packets. These were the years when one could almost sympathise with a bucko mate. Extreme, but representative of the packets in these years were the troubles of Captain Samuel Samuels of the clipper-packet *Dreadnought*.

The *Dreadnought* and her captain

Now the Dreadnought's *a-sailin' the Atlantic so wide,*
Where the high roarin' seas roll along her black side;
With her topsails set taught for the Red Cross to show,
Bound away to the west'ard – O Lord let her go!

Then a health to the Dreadnought *and all her brave crew,*
To bold Cap'n Samuels an' his officers too;
Talk about yer flash packets Swallow-tail and Blackball
Now the Dreadnought's *the bloodboat that outsails them all!*[3]

Captain Samuel Samuels had been at sea since the age of 11 and had attained command of his first ship by the time he was 21. He soon proved himself so successful that he was considered worthy enough by the owners of the Red Cross Line to have a ship built especially for him. The *Dreadnought* measured 1400 tons, with a length of 200 ft, beam of 40 ft 3 in. and, to match Samuel's reputation, was designed to carry sail in high winds. She was launched in October 1853 and began a career under Captain Samuels that has become legendary. She possessed all the sail-carrying attributes that her captain and designer could hope for. When other ships lay to, their crews would later tell Samuels they could see the *Dreadnought*'s keel as she jumped from sea to sea under every rag she could carry, earning the title 'The Wild Boat of the Atlantic'. The *Dreadnought* was not a flier. She broke no records, but she made good times and, vital in the packet service, maintained her schedule over years with more reliability than any other sailing liner. This was the result of a happy combination of a powerful ship and a determined, skilful master who was so confident of his own and his ship's performance that, from her second voyage, he guaranteed to deliver on time or refund the freight charges.

Samuels was a hard man even in the hard school of packet captains. He spared neither himself nor his men, driving his ship all day and harder at night while he catnapped on a short shelf he had built in the aft companionway. Just how resourceful this man could be is illustrated by the way he subdued a gang of tough packet rats who signed on to settle a few old scores.

On the 11 July 1859, even before the *Dreadnought* left Waterloo Dock in Liverpool, Samuels had been warned that he had on board 30 out of a gang known as 'The Bloody Forty', and he was advised to dismiss them or expect trouble.

Even before they made their departure from the south coast of Ireland, trouble began, escalating to an outright and violent mutiny. During the follow-

ing days, while the ship battled westward, under-manned and in a state of seige, Captain Samuels, with the aid of one ancient revolver, his dog and the second mate, stood off the mutinous packet rats, finally subduing them with the help of some Dutch passengers. If it can be believed, those hardened thugs were as meek as lambs thenceforward, even attending divine service which ended with a prayer which brought tears to their eyes. When the *Dreadnought* docked, news of the mutiny had leaked ashore, alerting the police who sent down a squad to the dock. They arrived just as that savage crew were farewelling their captain with three hearty cheers.

That tough old skipper was indestructible. Three years after the mutiny, the *Dreadnought* was boarded by a huge sea. By the time things were sorted out, the rudder had gone and Samuels lay on the soggy cabin sole with a compound fracture of his leg and a gashed head. Dissuading tough old Samuels from amputating his own leg, the officers, with much pulling and heaving, managed to get the bone at least joined, if not exactly straight.

For 3 days the captain lay on deck directing an ultimately unsuccessful attempt to rig a jury rudder. While work continued on a second, attempts were made to get the ship under sail, but she would not make the desired course for the Azores. Samuels solved the problem by sailing the ship backwards 280 miles, taking them close to Fayal, when, with the second makeshift rudder shipped, they safely made port. Samuels had the leg indifferently set during the 52 days it took to repair the ship. He then sailed the *Dreadnought* back to New York where he had to give up his command.

The *Dreadnought* ended her career in 1869 when she drifted ashore in a calm on the Tierra del Fuegan coast on a passage to San Francisco. Her crew were picked up some 3 weeks later.

Under this rig, and after losing her rudder, Capatin Samuels, suffering from a compound fracture in his leg, managed to sail the packet *Dreadnought* 280 miles towards the Azores . . . backwards.

The Red Cross packet *Dreadnought* was known as the *Wild Boat of the Atlantic* for the way in which she could be, and was, driven by Captain Samuel Samuels. In the illustration, the fore and main skysail yards are being sent down in expectation of worsening weather. The fore and main sails are reefed, the crojack and topgallants furled, and the topsails have their first reef in. Reefed topgallants are set over the topsails. This is a handy method of carrying sail when rising winds or squalls may require a quick response. The topgallants can quickly be lowered and the course got in, leaving the ship comfortably under reefed topsails.

The *Dreadnought* was built on the Merrimac at Newburyport in 1853. She measured 1400 tons and had a length of 200 ft (61 m).

THE EMIGRANT SHIPS

Inscription on a monument in an emigrant cemetery, Grosse Isle, Quebec

Hand in hand with the revolution in technology, the nineteenth century was a century of social revolution. People, dissatisfied with their prospects in the old countries, were on the move. The poor, made homeless by enclosures and other agricultural inflictions, craftsmen unable to compete with industrial production, educated middle-class citizens who could see the injustices of a society managed by an aristocracy – all sought a happier life across the Atlantic. From the cessation of hostilities in 1815, the flow became a torrent. Approximately 5,400,000 emigrants arrived in the United States ports during the 40 years following 1819, and this figure excludes those who shipped out to Canada, or British North America as it was then known. The transport of these people became a major industry, often poorly regulated and open to the most horrifying abuses. There were many conscientious agents, masters and owners who cared for their steerage passengers, but the dark side of human nature too often won through, with the result that the poor emigrant suffered appallingly. Hunger, exposure, disease, abuse, robbery and shipwreck were only too often his, or her, lot, particularly during the late 1840s and '50s when famine in Ireland spurred the impetus to emigrate.

North-American emigrants

The goal of most emigrants was to find sanctuary in the United States. The Irish, in particular, having suffered enough under the English, had no wish to continue under Great Britain's rule in Canada and, if they had the money, they shipped out directly for New York. The Americans, anxious to discourage a huge influx of poor, dispossessed and starving people, enforced a stricter Passenger Act than the British, and from the late 1830s exacted a $1000 bond on the 'lunatic, idiot, maimed, aged or infirm'[2], and a tax of $2 a head on landing. Even more severe acts were passed in 1847, pushing the fare to New York up to £7. The American ships were safer, better managed and more expensive. At about £2 or £3 a head, the fare to Canada in British ships was much less costly, and, once ashore, if the emigrant was reasonably fit and healthy, he could walk to the United States. Unfortunately, the chance of arriving safely in a British vessel was considerably reduced. A bad year was 1834, when 17 ships were lost in the St Lawrence and 731 emigrants perished. As will be seen, 1847 was to be infinitely worse.

Emigration was grasped by the authorities as the only solution which would relieve Britain of her poor and dispossessed, a solution which was seen as even more imperative after absentee landlords, misrule, and evictions had driven the poor Irish to become dependent on the potato, a crop repeatedly subject to failure. The first warnings of blight appeared in 1845 and the harvest of 1846 was a total failure. Not only in Ireland but all over Europe both potatoes and rye failed utterly and other crops were scanty. It was hard for the poorer citizens of other nations, but for the Irish it was a unmitigated disaster.

The 1847 holocaust

In addition to the famine, 1847 was the year of the plague. Typhus and relapsing fever caused by lice, already at epidemic proportions in 1846, broke out into a dreadful plague in 1847. Both diseases were considered as one and described as 'famine fever', and typhus, with its revolting symptoms, was variously described as 'gaol' or 'ship fever'. That other sinister companion of famine and distress, dysentery, more often than not afflicted the victims of fever. That year the St Lawrence did not open until May, and on the seventeenth the first ship, the *Syria*, anchored off Grosse Isle, the quarantine station 30 miles below Quebec. On board were 241 emigrants, 84 of whom had fever. These, with those who were already showing signs of sickening, were brought ashore to the quarantine hospital which could, at a stretch, accommodate up to 200. Within 4 days, 8 more ships arrived with 430 cases. The hospital facilities were already swamped.

By 31 May, anchored in a line stretching 2 miles below Grosse Isle, 40 ships were waiting to disembark over 1000 sick and dying. Ashore, 1000 emigrants lay in sheds, the hospital and the church. Over 45,000 more emigrants were expected. The summer was a nightmare. The line of anchored ships grew to several miles and the fever-stricken emigrants totally exhausted the resources of Grosse Isle. Uninfected passengers were permitted to undergo quarantine in the ships, but delays in clearing the sick from the vessels resulted in further

1847 was the year of the Great Famine in Ireland. Over 100,000 emigrants left the United Kingdom in that year; 17,000 died crossing the Atlantic and 20,000 died in Canada. At Grosse Isle, the quarantine station 30 miles below Quebec, the authorities and doctors were quite unable to cope. Boats brought the sick and dying from the multitude of ships anchored for miles below the island, and dumped them on the muddy beach to crawl ashore. From the holds of the ships rose 'foul air . . . as dense and palpable as seen on a foggy day from a dung heap.'

infection. The *Agnes* arrived with 427 emigrants, but, after lying at anchor under quarantine for 15 days, only 150 remained alive. All that could be done was to allow the healthy, after a cursory inspection, to go upriver to Quebec and Montreal, where they

spread the disease ashore. Beseiged by the sick and dying, Montreal, which received most of the emigrants, suffered the worst from the epidemics.

Meanwhile, Grosse Isle, the anchored ships and the river about them had become a hell. From the ships' holds rose streams of 'foul air . . . as dense and as palpable as seen on a foggy day from a dung heap'[3]. Ships arrived with no water or provisions, most of the Irish having relied on the insufficient 7lb a week the ship provided, and even the uninfected were described by a doctor as 'ghastly, yellow looking spectres, unshaven and hollow cheeked . . .'[4] Fresh water was unobtainable, for the river was 'a floating mass of filthy straw, refuse of foul beds, barrels containing the vilest matter, old rags, tattered clothes'[5] dumped from vessels cleaning

their holds. From the ships to the beach at Grosse Isle, a procession of boats brought the sick and dead to be dumped on the beach. Those who were alive were left to crawl ashore through the mud as best they could. The year 1847 was truly a holocaust in Ireland and Canada. Canadian charity was generous, but quite unable to cope with the heartbreaking torrent of people starved from their own land to face the frigid winter after surviving the dreadful passage. It has been estimated that from the 100,000 emigrants that left the United Kingdom in 1847, 20,000 died in Canada. As grim are the figures for those who succumbed in the ships; 17,000 died crossing the Western Ocean.

European ships in the passenger trade

In 1807 the Treaty of Tilsit between France and Russia had curtailed the supply of Baltic timber to Britain. An alternative source was provided by her provinces in America where the trade proved so profitable that, by 1845, 2000 ships were employed hauling timber from British North America. Westbound freights for the thinly populated colonies were hard to find and if the ships could not get a load of coal or salt for the Newfoundland fisheries, they were forced to sail west in ballast. Depression following the wars, increasing population and decreasing living standards, inspired people to emigrate, and the means to do so was provided in the empty 'tween-decks of the timber ships. By 1845 the *passenger trade* had become more profitable than the carriage of any commodity.

The timber ships engaged in trade to British North America at this time were usually small ships and brigs of 200 to 400 tons, many of which were old and ill found. Smaller ships, ketches and schooners were not uncommon, and when the famine struck Great Britain, these vessels, which in no way could fulfil even the meagre Passenger Act of the time, found employment lifting cargoes of misery from the small ports and coves of Ireland.

Little was needed to prepare the ship for her steerage passengers. Six-foot-square berths were constructed in the 'tween-decks and into each of these berths, no more than a section of a platform running each side the length of the 'tween-deck, four passengers were crammed, men and women indiscriminately. Not until 1852 were single men berthed separately. Down between the berths, if they were lucky, an alley might be graced with rough tables and benches. Water closets, if there were any, were on deck, and there was never more than one for each 100 passengers. Of course these were inaccessible in foul weather and most used pots, cans and buckets in the 'tween-deck . . . if they were not too sick to reach them.

Cooking was done on deck on 'a large wooden case lined with bricks about the shape and size of a settee, the coals were confined by two or three iron bars in front'[6]. It was kept going all daylight hours while the weather permitted, and was surrounded by squabbling emigrants who rarely managed to more than half-cook the little food they had, consequently diarrhoea further fouled the steerage. Single women had a hard time to get near the galley and frequently were forced to eat their food raw or go without. The provision of some extra boats, a few medicines, water, often from poor and tainted casks, 7lb a week of food per head and sufficient fuel to keep the galley going completed most of the requirements of the Passenger Act, which entitled any vessel of sufficient height in the 'tween-decks to take part in the passenger trade.

The British Passenger Act of 1842, as did all previous acts, carefully avoided any stipulations which would unnecessarily raise the cost of the voyage. Although it required that the height of the 'tween-deck should not be less than 6 ft and there should be no accommodation deck below the waterline, little was provided for the passengers' comfort. Each passenger was to be issued 7lb of provisions weekly, 3 quarts of water daily, and fuel for cooking was provided by the ship. Medicines

were to be carried, but a doctor was not necessary. It also became compulsory to carry lifeboats, but it was rare if a ship carried more than four – totally insufficient for the number of souls on board.

During the years of the exodus from Ireland, and to a lesser extent, England and Europe, it was impossible to enforce the Act at the dozens of minor ports where the emigrants embarked. Ships fit only for breaking up were put into service, knocked-up

The captains of American transatlantic packets loading at Liverpool would not permit passengers to embark until all cargo had been loaded. Understandably, it would be impossible to work cargo while hundreds of steerage passangers milled around in the 'tween decks. Once the cargo was complete, many ships left the dockside immediately so as to catch a tide or save time and berthage. Consequently, the only opportunity for the passengers to board was at the dock gates or, if this was missed, out in the river. The confusion and panic as frantic emigrants struggled to get aboard was appalling.

gimcrack berths were installed in ill-ventilated 'tween-decks. Sharp 'passage brokers' conned naive and desperate refugees to part with the last of their money for a passage in these 'coffin ships', while landlords, to clear their lands of starving paupers, offered free passages and then overloaded the vessels with the utterly destitute and often half-naked and diseased victims of the famine. The emigrant ships usually sailed between April and October to avoid the winter in the North Atlantic, but by the onset of the winter of 1846, the most severe in memory, the demand for passages was so great that, for the first time, the trade continued through the winter. Most managed to raise the fare to enable them to embark for America.

In 1847 the agents of Lord Palmerston (one likes to think without his knowledge of the human suffering involved) cleared 2000 tenants from his property in Sligo. Nine vessels were employed to ship out these destitute people from their own land to arrive in Canada in an appalling condition, the later ones quite unfit and unprepared to face the icy winter. The *Eliza Liddell* landed in St John, New Brunswick, only widows, children, the aged and destitute. The *Lord Ashburton*, arriving at Quebec on 30 October, just before the ice closed the river, brought 477 emigrants, 107 having died on passage. Of those landed, 60 were ill, 177 were almost naked, and 87 had to be given clothes from charity for the sake of decency. On 2 November, after the St Lawrence was closed by ice, the *Aeolus*, another of Lord Palmerston's ships, came into St John. Of her 240 passengers, 99 per cent became an immediate charge on the town, being without clothing, and their numbers made up of old people, widows and young children, all in poor health. This was at the onset of the frigid Canadian winter and the citizens of St John were quite unable to provide food and shelter. In desperation they offered free passages and a supply of food if the emigrants would return to Ireland.

The greatest losses and misery were generally to be found in the ships sailing from the smaller ports, particularly in Ireland. Here there were no inspectors to enforce the Act. Cecil Woodham Smith, in his book *The Great Hunger*, describes a typical example of a coffin ship:

> . . . the barque *Elizabeth and Sarah*, which sailed from the small harbour of Killala, County Mayo, in July, 1846, arriving in Quebec in September. She had been built in 1762 and was of 330 tons burthen. Her list of passengers, as certified by the officer at Killala, showed 212 names, whereas in fact she carried 276 persons. She should have carried 12,532 gallons of water, but had only 8,700 gallons in leaky casks. The Passenger Act of 1842 required 7lb of provisions to be given out weekly to each passenger, but no distribution was ever made in the *Elizabeth and Sarah*. Berths numbered only 36, of which 4 were taken by the crew: the remaining 32 were shared between 276 passengers, who otherwise slept on the floor. No sanitary convenience of any kind was provided, and the state of the vessel was 'horrible and disgusting beyond the power of language to describe'. The passage from Killala, largely through the incompetence of the captain, took eight weeks: the passengers starved and were tortured by thirst, and 42 persons died during the voyage. Finally the ship broke down and was towed into the St Lawrence by a steamer sent by Alexander Carlisle Buchanan at his own expense, since the government did not permit such an expenditure. The voyage of the *Elizabeth and Sarah* was a local speculation, and passages had been sold in districts round Killala by means of circulars which were incorrect in almost every particular.[7]

Stories such as the above were not uncommon at any time during the height of the immigration period, but during the famine years reports and tales of lost and foundered ships, mismanagement due to greed, starving, sick and shivering emigrant humanity, were all too familiar. Not every emigrant to North America suffered the deprivations and dangers described above. Dutch and German immigrants, in particular, arrived in fine fettle and contrasted vividly with the Irish. The 247-ton Bideford barque *Civility* normally made two voyages to British North America each year. In the journal of a William Fulford it is recorded that her passengers on the first voyage in 1848 suffered only the periodical gales, cold and foul drinking water which could be expected. The worst accident was the loss of the passenger's galley and a broken jibboom. As soon as the weather cleared, the galley was rebuilt, a new jibboom made, and a hatchway ladder built, all by craftsmen from among the passengers.

In this West-Country ship it seems to have been expected that all should pull together, a tradition inspired by an earlier illustrious sailor from their counties. When in fog or near ice, and in crossing the Grand Banks, emigrants helped by keeping lookout and one gets the impression from the journal that there was an active interest taken in the working and navigation of the ship. On the Banks, opportunity was taken to fish, and not only with their own lines. A boat was put over to swipe 30 fat cod from the longline of a French fisherman, and one wonders how common this pilfering was, for Fulford, a fervent evangelist, makes no protest.

The captain of this ship was friendly, considerate and caring of his steerage passengers. When the weather permitted, all bedding was ordered up to air and the 'tween-decks cleaned, and when they came to quarantine at Grosse Isle the ship passed through with ease, Fulford claiming that the doctor declared they were 'the most decent and healthy'[8] passengers he had ever examined.

The American emigrant ships

In the early years of the emigration period, prospective migrants would find their way to a port and arrange their passage with the captain. This lack of organisation was not to last; firms such as W. & J.T. Tapscott of New York, and Caleb Grimshaw & Co. of Liverpool, were not shipowners but chartered the whole 'tween-deck spaces of west-bound ships and filled them with migrants. It is interesting to note that the latter firm, Caleb Grimshaw & Co., had been a leading firm of Liverpool slavers, and were no doubt experts at packing the maximum number of people into a ship. Not until the 1840s did the regular packets, faced with growing competition from steam, and enormous demand, turn to shipping steerage passengers on a regular basis.

In the late 1840s more than twice the number of emigrants to the United States sailed in American ships, which were larger, faster and better manned than most ships of other nations, although they had a grim reputation for brutality. As more of the packets, both scheduled and otherwise, turned to the emigrant trade, good seamen, sickened by the conditions and filth, found employment in pleasanter trades, such as that around Cape Horn. Their places were filled with a tougher breed but a poorer sailor, the 'packet rats'. To handle these crews, the afterguard had to be brutal, and their brutality all too often extended to the poor emigrants. With the thugs that often made up a large part of the crew of the later period, violence was normal and unaccompanied girls and women were lucky if they arrived in New York unmolested. In 1860 an act was passed in Congress to protect female passengers by inflicting large fines or imprisonment if the offender did not marry the girl. It was not sympathy for the women that inspired this act, but the huge number of illegitimate children cast on the charity of New York.

Even before an emigrant saw the silt of the Mersey change to the green of the Irish Sea, he had suffered abominably. Liverpool was rife with villainous runners, thieves, touts and dishonest boarding-house keepers who squeezed every last penny they could from the migrants waiting to embark. So well organised were some gangs that all the details of a likely mark were sent on to kindred gangs in New York, which had a society equally adept at fleecing the newcomers.

After a farce of a medical inspection, usually no more than a glance at their tongue, the migrants were allowed to board their ship. No provision for safety or convenience seems to have been provided. No captain could embark steerage passengers until the last of the cargo had been loaded and, once this was complete, his only concern was to get out as fast as possible if the tide served. The passengers were left to board as best they could as the ship was warped or towed from her berth to the lock at the entrance of the dock. Here the majority would manage to scramble over the bulwarks, but often leaving behind a few of the more feeble, late or less agile people, who would then be forced to hire a boat to get out to the ship in the Mersey. Getting on board could be the most dangerous part of the whole passage, and drownings were not infrequent. In the river, before the pilot left the ship, the passengers and crew were mustered and a roll was called, the passengers coming forward and showing their ticket as their names were sung out in a rhyming chant:

> Paddy Bile [Boyle] Come here awhile
> Joseph Brown Come down.
> William Jones Show your bones. [9]

While this was going on the ship was searched for stowaways and liquor, for American ships were dry. It was not unusual for the search to reveal several stowaways who, if they could not pay their passage, were put over before the ship cleared the river. Many a hopeful stowaway chose a barrel for his, or her hiding place, hoping that the searchers would be unlikely to break open every one in a tier. The searchers soon had him yelling to be let out by turning the suspected barrels upside-down. Those who escaped this initial inspection and were later discovered at sea, were tarred and feathered before being put to work.

What a voyage as an emigrant was like on one of the more brutally run Yankee packets is best described by the letters of Vere Foster, a philanthropist who took a late-season passage in the steerage of the emigrant ship *Washington* so as to experience for himself the trials undergone by Irish migrants on the voyage to New York. He was a relative of Lord Hobart, a member of the Board of Trade in London, and with the insight gained from the voyage he hoped to be able to mitigate the hard conditions and abuse of the poorer emigrants. The *Washington* was a large and well-found ship of 1655 tons and at times carried as many as 1000 steerage passengers. Just how rough the Yankee officers could be to their charges, Foster was to find out.

What follows are short extracts gleaned from a letter from Vere Foster to Lord Hobart. It was written in the form of a diary and too lengthy to include in its entirety. These snippets are representative of the whole content of the letter.

> The serving of the water was twice capriciously stopped by the mates of the ship, who, during the whole time, without any provocation, cursed and abused, and cuffed and kicked the passengers and their tin cans, . . . [While writing a letter of protest to the captain] . . . the first mate, Mr Williams, knocked me down flat on the deck with a blow in the face . . . he also made use of the most blasphemous and abusive language.
>
> I presented the letter to Captain Page. He asked me the purport of it, and bade me read

it. Having read out about one-third of it, he said that was enough, and that he knew what I was; I was a damned pirate, a damned rascal, and that he would put me in irons and on bread and water throughout the rest of the voyage. The first mate then came up and abused me foully and blasphemously, and pushed me down, bidding me to get out of that, as I was a damned b --. He was found by one of the passengers soon afterwards, heating a thick bar of iron at the kitchen fire; the cook said, 'What is he doing that for?' and the mate said, 'There is a damned b -- on board, to who I intend giving a singeing before he leaves the ship.'

[Provisions were not issued to the steerage passengers until one week out, and then the quantities were short.] Whenever provisions are served out, a sailor stands by with a rope's end and lays about him, with or without the slightest provocation. The captain never appears to trouble himself in the slightest degree about the passengers, nor even visit the part of the ship occupied by them. The first and second mates, the surgeon and the man specially appointed to look after the passengers, and the cooks – all these seldom open their lips without prefacing what they may have to say, with 'God damn your soul to hell, you damned b --,' or, 'by Jesus Christ I'll rope's end you,' or some other expression from the same category.

A delicate old man . . . had just come on deck, and after washing, was wringing a pair of stockings, when the first mate gave him such a severe kick with his knee on his backside as he was stooping down, that he threw him down upon the deck, since which he has been obliged to go to the water closet three or four times a day, passing blood every time.

The doctor this evening heaved overboard a great many chamber-pots belonging to the female passengers, saying that henceforward he would allow no women to do their business below, but that they should come to the filthy privies on deck. I heard him say, 'There are a hundred cases of dysentery in the ship, which will all turn to cholera, and I swear to God that I will not go amongst them; if they want medicines they must come to me'. This morning the first mate took it into his head to play the hose upon the passengers in occupation of the water closets, drenching them from head to foot; the fourth mate did the same a few mornings ago.

Another child, making about 12 in all, died of dysentery from want of proper nourishing food. . . as there was no regular service, the man appointed to attend to the passengers seized the opportunity, when the sailors pulling at a rope raised the usual song of -- *Haul in the bowling, the Black Star bowling, Haul in the bowling, the bowling haul* – to throw the child overboard at the sound of the last word of the song, making use of it as a funeral dirge.

To attend to the 900 and odd passengers on board the 'Washington', only one man was appointed, and he a brute.

Fortunately, although the ill treatment experienced by Vere Foster was not uncommon, it was by no means the rule. There were humanely managed and kindly run ships, but a passage in the steerage of the best ships bound across the Western Ocean could be distressing enough without the callous treatment by officers such as those of the *Washington*.

THE BRITISH SCHOONERS

The Newfoundland Trade

The inshore cod-fishing industries of Newfoundland and Labrador provided employment for small transatlantic sailing vessels well into the present century. At all times there was a demand for vessels to deliver salt and supplies and load the salted and dried cod, a trade in which vessels from London and England's West-Country ports such as Barnstaple and Bideford were particularly active. With the coming of peace in 1815, the fishing industry prospered and grew, particularly along the coast of Labrador. The fishing, salting and drying was carried out by independent fishermen and their families living in the isolated and deep coves of Labrador and Newfoundland. It needed small vessels to work into these inlets and pick up the individual produce of the fishermen, at the same time exchanging salt and supplies.

Topsail schooners were found to be eminently suitable for this trade. They could work well to windward against the westerlies, beat into narrow guts which would baffle a square-rigger, and they were economical to run. Hundreds of these schooners, and some ketches, mainly from Wales, Scotland and the West Country, came to be employed in the trade.

Until about 1870 the schooners sailed from Britain with general cargo, loaded salt at the Portuguese ports of Setubal or Trepani for Newfoundland, from where they sailed to Labrador to load fish for the Mediterranean, arriving just at the right time to pick up a cargo of fruit for home.

The *M.A. James*, one of the Portmadoc-built topgallant schooners known as the Western Ocean Yachts. At 124 tons she measured 89 ft 7 in. (27.31 m) on deck. She was built in 1900 and was specially designed to work in the small, shallow creeks of Labrador. As late as 1950 she was still afloat as a hulk at Appledore.

After 1870, when the fruit trade was lost to steam ships, other cargoes were found. During the winter months the little vessels sought employment in the home trade.

Dried and salted fish was also stockpiled at the larger ports of Newfoundland and Labrador, from where it could be collected, either by the schooners, or by larger vessels bound for South America.

Fast passages were often made, but always eastbound. The fastest of all was probably in 1855 by a brigantine named *Belle*, which, it is claimed, flew from Harbour Grace to Lisbon in precisely 1 week. Getting west, even from Newfoundland to Labrador, could be a battle and more than one vessel, sailing coastwise, was driven right across the Atlantic. In 1890 the schooner *Rescue* loaded a cargo of coal at Sydney in Nova Scotia for Harbour Grace in Labrador. She almost literally fulfilled the 'coals to Newcastle' adage by delivering her cargo to the coal port of Swansea in Wales. Another schooner, sailing from Newfoundland to Labrador in 1929, fetched up after 48 days in Tobermory Bay, Scotland.

The use of British schooners in this and other trades in the Atlantic reached its height between

The *Madeira Pet* in Chicago

1890 and 1910 and led to the development of some of the finest small ocean-going vessels of the time. Those designed at Porthmadog in Wales were particularly notable, and their grace and speed earned them the praise of sailors, who named them the 'Western Ocean yachts'. Many of the small vessels engaged in the Newfoundland trade were lost during World War I and the British schooner trade never recovered. The last schooner, the *Lady St Johns*, sailed in 1930. The industry was taken up mainly by the Danes, Canadians and Portuguese. The Canadian schooners were primarily built of softwood in Nova Scotia and were larger than both the British and Danish vessels. The latter were of typically full Scandinavian lines of the Baltic schooners and were very successful both in performance and safety, and some were still working in the Newfoundland trade well after the end of World War II.

The topsail schooner *Madeira Pet*

During July of 1857, the citizens of Chicago, which had become a city of 60,000 inhabitants, were stirred when they heard that a small British schooner had

arrived at the North Pier. The Erie Canal had been opened over 30 years before and other canals had been formed to bypass Niagara and make the Detroit River navigable, but the Erie Canal was too shallow for deep-draught ocean-going vessels. The British schooner *Madeira Pet* had come by way of the St Lawrence, where the Lachine and Williamsburg canals had been completed during the 1840s. The locks in these canals were 200 ft long and 9 ft deep, quite sufficient for the 97-ft *Madeira Pet*, the first overseas ship to navigate the St Lawrence canals and the Great Lakes. She was not, however, the first to run a cargo from Chicago for, the year before, a barque named the *Dean Richmond* had made a voyage to Liverpool.

The *Madeira Pet* was towed to a berth at the foot of La Salle Street to discharge, and on the day following her arrival was officially celebrated with a 100-gun salute from the Chicago Light Infantry and two brass bands. Hundreds of visitors came down to see the schooner, and the entertainment went on until midnight.

After discharging her cargo of 240 tons of cutlery, earthen and glass ware, china and paint, she loaded hides and one barrel of whitefish for Queen Victoria. The schooner was towed out, once more to the accompaniment of a band, on 5 August.

By the Great Lakes sailors she was not considered suitable for the inland seas, but they liked her appearance and when the wind blew fresh she gave the Lakes schooners a run for their money. Apparently possessing finer lines than most of her English sisters, the *Madeira Pet* had been built at Rye in Sussex in 1850 by Hessell & Holmes Co., for G.F. Carrington of Guernsey. She was intended for the Azores orange trade and was launched by Don Miguel, the Pretender to the Portuguese throne. Her measurements were:

Length	97 ft (29.6 m)
Breadth	18 ft (5.5 m)
Tonnage	83 tons

THE TIMBER DROGHERS

Until the middle of the nineteenth century, wood was the mainstay of all construction work and provided the material for a vast array of items which today would be produced in metal or plastic. By far the hungriest consumers of the forests of Europe were her ships – a single first-rate vessel would swallow several square miles of oak, elm and ash. North America's forests provided an alternative source, but here shipbuilding and the export of lumber was not to reach its peak until the nineteenth century.

In Quebec the French had begun to build seagoing ships as far back as 1663. After 1731, at the instigation of their minister of marine, M. de Maurepas, the French launched an increasing number of transports, merchant vessels, corvettes and frigates until the British conquest in 1759. However, in the Old World enthusiasm for these ships was not keen; the woods such as red and white oak, spruce, elm and birch were considered inferior.

Typical of the many small wooden timber droghers which ploughed the Atlantic during the last half of the nineteenth century, this barque is probably being kept afloat by her windmill pump and the timber in her. This vessel is of the kind built in Canada for the trade, but many old and strained ships were employed for the freight rates were low and the cargos sufficiently bouyant to float the ship home should the leaks become too bad. The adage was 'Pump her out and float her home.'

The deck cargo of deals is excessive and many ships were lost due to such overloading.

The British continued to build in British North America, but apart from mast timbers such as white pine, the export of lumber and, to a certain extent, of ships, stagnated until the end of the first decade of the nineteenth century. Factors inhibiting the trade were the lack of suitable return cargoes, prohibitive protectionist taxes, the cheap supply of softwoods from Scandinavia and the increasing use of teak in European shipbuilding. In 1807 the Treaty of Tilsit between Napoleon and Alexander of Russia effectively severed the northern European sources of supply. With the forests of England decimated, the timber trade from Canada began in earnest.

During the first half of the nineteenth century British North America lacked the population and development necessary to provide worthwhile westbound freight, thus ships, already limited to the ice-free months from April to December, were obliged to sail west in ballast or, if they were lucky, carried salt for the Newfoundland fisheries, or coal. Losses among the ships were enormous, particularly in the difficult navigation of the St Lawrence and during the later months of the season, when the North Atlantic begins to show her teeth. Lloyds imposed their heaviest premiums on ships sailing from Quebec during November.

The timber trade gathered momentum after the Napoleonic Wars. The problem of finding a westbound freight which at the same time augmented the settlement of British North America was, for the shipowner, neatly solved by the expansion of the emigrant trade, as described in my earlier chapter. With this incentive, the tonnage increased until, in 1845, 2000 vessels were employed. It was in the droghers that, in conditions which were often appallingly overcrowded and sometimes downright dangerous, the majority of desperate, famine-stricken Irish poor were transported to the New World.

The latter half of the nineteenth century saw the boom years of shipbuilding throughout the length of the American east coast. Many of the vessels launched around the shores of British North America were designed for the timber trade, among them the famous *Marco Polo*. However, lumber was also the ideal cargo for a tired old wooden ship. Ships which had for many years battled around Cape Horn with stressful cargoes such as coal and copper ore in the Chilean trade, racked and worn clippers and neglected hulks, were pierced with bow and stern ports and, to the peril of their crews, were then pumped outward and floated home until they fell apart in some Atlantic gale, or were written off.

During the first 2 decades of the century the vast timber resources of British North America began to be exploited, and around Quebec the coves and waterways became choked with huge quantities of timber, rafted from the hinterlands and awaiting shipment to Britain. In 1821, a preferential duty of 10s. a load was granted on Canadian timber, against 55s. on loads from the Baltic; this spurred merchants on both sides of the Atlantic to invest in the trade. Exports boomed, as did shipbuilding throughout the Maritimes. A vessel built in Canada was assured of her first cargo right on the doorstep, and the ship might sell for a good price in the Old Country. Many shipbuilding ventures were financed in Britain in the first place. In winter around the St Lawrence, while ice closed the navigation and farms were snowed under, the population cut timber and built ships. Every suitable cove sported its slipway, and shipbuilding tradesmen were at a premium. With a seemingly inexhaustible supply of timber, high returns and a favourable tariff, any scheme, if its aim was to transport more timber at less cost, was likely to be considered.

The trade

Around Quebec, timber was felled, to a large extent, during the winter months, when the logs could be sledded or hauled to the nearest frozen river. At the spring thaw the rivers brought the timber in rafts down to Quebec where a number of large sawmills ripped the logs into squared timber, deals, stavewood, boards and lathes suitable for shipping. Other squared timber was brought down from the lakes in rafts, and fleets of small craft delivered milled timber to the port.

The first ships would arrive from Europe at the end of April or the beginning of May, perhaps as many as 70 on a tide. On her way in, the Quebec boatmen could meet a vessel, board her on the run and make a deal with the master to provide facilities for the discharge of his salt or ballast and for subsequent loading.

The following account is from *Wooden Ships and Iron Men* by Frederick William Wallace, who wrote of the Quebec timber trade during the latter half of the century:

> The scene around the coves was one of tremendous animation. Ships, as far as the eye could see, were being loaded, towed in or out, or departing, sometimes under sail or with a tug-boat pulling them to a fair wind or open water. Ships of all rigs and nationalities, green-hulled, black-hulled, white-hulled, or with painted ports; sails stowed with a harbour furl or loose in the bunt-lines drying; clipper ships with sweeping lines and beautiful figure-heads and timber-droghing as a result of old age or a fill-in cargo between charters, with tall masts and sky-sail yards across; common timber-ships rounded up at the ends, 'built by the mile and cut off by the yard', homely but serviceable, and, alas! numbers of broken-down old packets – famous clippers, many of them, water-soaked and strained with hard driving – fit only for carrying a timber cargo, and the windmill pump working continuously and discharging a never-ending stream of water from the sodden holds. In the

latter years, the timber trade employed all the old worn-out crocks of square-rig, and Quebec presented a sad sight, with a fleet of 'has-beens' – Australian and California clippers and China tea ships, famous in nautical history, droghing deals and square-timber, pit-props and spool-wood, and with the Western Ocean sucking in and out of their started butts and warped planking.[1]

After discharging their salt, ballast or, if lucky, an inward cargo, the ships would be worked round to one of the many coves where timber, contained in booms, floated ready for loading.

Timber ships had bow and stern ports for taking long square timber into their holds. These would be knocked out, and booms and tackle rigged out over the bow and stern for the purpose of loading the timber. Engaged in this work were expert gangs of timber-stowers, mostly Irish, and rough, powerful men who could work like horses throughout the heat of a Canadian summer, and drink and fight with equal ability. These men were classed as timber swingers, hookers-on, holders, porters, and winchers. When the rafts of timber were floated alongside the ship, members of the stowing gangs took their stations on the squared logs in the water and deftly extricated the individual timbers from the mess and pike-poled them into position for loading. On the ship's fo'c's'le-head, other men superintended the manipulation of the tackles for raising the timber up into the open port and swinging it inside the ship. In the hold, other members of the gang sweated with cant-hooks and hand-spikes, stowing the wet and heavy cargo. The tackles used to be operated by muscle-power in the early days, with men tramping

Loading timber through bow ports

around the ship's capstan or turning a crab-winch, but later the portable donkey-boiler and steam winch were used . . .[2]

Once the ship was packed solid with timber, the question of a deck-load arose. The shippers would attempt to pile on every stick they could get aboard until she was overloaded, crank and unworkable. Most masters would grumble, but as in later years there were plenty of certificated men ashore seeking work under any circumstances, an outright refusal to load or sail put the protesting master out of work. The mates and men had no say and as for some owners, if the ship foundered, they lost nothing, for they were generally well insured.

Provided a vessel was not grossly overloaded and the deck-load was well secured, it was fairly safe during the summer months, but come fall and the winter gales, the losses rose appallingly. In 1872, in the month of December alone, 24 vessels were lost

out of a total of 57 for the whole year. Over 100 men perished, not to mention the suffering and privation of those who survived and the numerous near misses that must have occurred.

As far back as 1839 a British Government enquiry had pinned the main cause of losses in the trade on the carriage of excessive deck-loads, and the hardship the crews underwent stirred the British to pass an Act of Parliament. In this act it was forbidden to carry deck-cargoes on timber ships from 1 September to 1 May. In 1850 the navigation laws were repealed and no longer did the British have the sole right to trade. The British owners found they were handicapped by the law on deck-loads so, as usually happens when commerce finds itself thwarted by law, they found a way around it.

Large poops were built to house the cargo; some shippers carried this forward in the form of a spar-deck to the fo'c's'le and loaded the upper-deck below to the rail – thus effectively preventing the jettisoning any of the load if necessary. Spare spars were always carried on deck in sailing ships and the law allowed for this – in some ships the spares were sufficient to mast a fleet! Finally, the American side of the St Croix River provided a haven beyond the reach of British law. The law on deck-loads was later repealed after prosecutions persistently failed to bring the owners to account.

After the disastrous season of 1872, a Canadian shipowner, Henry Fry, denounced the lack of

The *Columbus* was one of the two great raft ships built in Quebec during the 1820s. Packed solid with timber, they were designed to only make a one-way passage and be broken up for the squared timber from which they were built. The *Columbus* safely delivered over 10,000 tons of timber to London, but, instead of taking her apart it was decided to sail her back for more. She broke up in the Atlantic. The second ship, *Baron of Renfrew*, was even larger but ran aground and broke up off Dover, scattering her 15,395 tons of ship and cargo, the equivalent loading of 45 ordinary ships, all along the French coast. At that time they were by far the largest wooden vessels ever built.

legislation on deck-loads, claiming that in his ships none were carried after 1 October. He drew a great deal of attention, resulting in a bill being passed to prohibit deck-loads after 1 October, but allowing for the carriage of deals not more than 3 ft high. This, of course, only applied to Canadian vessels. In 1874, when challenged by the British, Fry went to London and effectively proved his case to Lloyds and the authorities. A study showed that the carriage of deck-loads in the timber trade increased loss of property by 30 per cent and life by 40 per cent. The findings resulted in an act similar to that of the Canadians.

Two great raft ships

Among the multitude of ships built in British North America the most extraordinary must have been the *Columbus* and the *Baron of Renfrew.* Even today the

sheer size, simplicity and economy of their conception would be remarkable. In the 1820s it reflected the hard-nosed ingenuity and resourcefulness of the designers and engineers of the Industrial Revolution who were repeatedly presenting society, particularly in the maritime domain, with inventions and constructions with which it hardly knew how to cope. A grand scheme which might have revolutionised the bulk-timber trade across the Atlantic appears to have been doomed through misfortune, incompetence and greed, to become one of those colossal oddities of the nineteenth century.

Charles Wood was a true son of the Industrial Revolution. In 1811, after the death of their father, the brothers John and Charles Wood had taken charge of the family shipyard at Port Glasgow. On the stocks was Henry Bell's *Comet*, which became the first commercial steam vessel in Europe. Charles revolutionised steamship design by breaking away from the full-bodied sailing-ship hulls into which steam-engines had been installed. The *James Watt*, launched in 1820, incorporated the fine lines of oared craft with which Charles compared steam-powered vessels. Shortly afterwards, he left the shipyard, having found backers for his scheme to 'raft' timber

The famous *Marco Polo* was built at St John, New Brunswick to carry timber across the Atlantic. Reckoned as an ugly barn of a ship, after only two voyages she was purchased and fitted out by James Baines's Australian Blackball Line to carry emigrants to the antipodes. She made some remarkable passages under Captain 'Bully' Forbes, and sailed the Australian run for 15 years. The *Marco Polo* then continued in general trade until 1880, when, strained and sodden, she was condemned. For three more years she worked in the trade she was designed for, hauling timber across the Atlantic for a Norwegian firm, until, in 1883 she was deliberately run ashore on Prince Edward Island.

She is shown in the illustration at the height of her career, leaving Liverpool bound for Australia.

from Quebec, and was granted a 3-year contract to build two vessels, both considerably larger than anything the world had seen to that date.

His goal was to transport cheaply a very large quantity of timber across the Atlantic. By ignoring most of the accepted practices of shipbuilding and utilising the natural buoyancy of timber, it was possible to build huge vessels which would be virtually rafts. Apart from some basic hydrodynamic features such as stability and weatherliness, the hull would seem to need only the strength to contain its load and withstand the violence of the ocean. Even this quality could be pared, as Wood intended that the vessel should be dismantled for her timber at her destination, after being sold as a ship. This had some considerable financial advantage as the duty on timber imports could be thus avoided.

The *Columbus*

In 1823 the keel of the *Columbus* was laid in a large bay on the Isle of Orleans below Quebec, and as her colossal structure became apparent she began to attract the attention and comment of Quebecans and visitors. For almost her entire construction, squared timber was used. She was 301 ft overall, flat-bottomed, with a beam of 51 ft 4½ in. (15.66 m) and a depth of 29 ft 4½ in. (8.95 m). Her midship transverse sections were rectangular, with the deck beams protruding beyond her vertical sides. Surprisingly, some form was given her in the deck plan and the run of the chine towards the bow and stern, and if the simple elevations of her are representative of the actual shape, she may well indeed have been a good sailer as reported. To avoid damage to the timber, the seams were left uncaulked, the builders relying on the wet wood swelling to form a tight seam. One would have thought that, as the vessel was packed solid with timber, water-tightness would not have been essential, but it seems a vast amount of pumping was necessary and in the second ship, the *Baron of Renfrew*, a steam-engine was

installed to work the pumps and aid the loading and discharge of timber.

Many doubted the giant could be moved, but on 14 July 1823, with 4000 tons of timber already stowed through her bow and stern ports, and witnessed by thousands of spectators, the *Columbus* ponderously but surprisingly gently slid down the ways and entered the water. She was towed to anchor in the Orleans channel where her rig was set up and the remainder of her cargo of red and white pine was packed in. The vessel's registered tonnage was 3690 tons and her estimated capacity was 6300 tons. As the ship was to be dismantled for her timber at her destination, she was effectively transporting over 10,000 tons of timber. By comparison, most ships engaged in the trade at this period ranged between 300 and 400 tons, and a 500-ton ship would be considered large.

On 5 September 1824 the *Columbus* was towed downriver by Quebec's only steam tug, *Hercules*. On board was Charles Wood and a large crew of 80 commanded by Captain William McKellar. Prior to sailing, difficulties were encountered with some of the crew, who demanded higher wages. Further problems were found when it came to raising the anchors, and more tribulations were to come. Captain McKellar appeared distinctly nervous of the seagoing capability of the *Columbus*, and according to later statements of Charles Wood, had little knowledge of the St Lawrence and was not overly conscientious. Although warned by Wood to keep watch at night and to avoid the northern shore, McKellar did neither. After instructing the mate to maintain a course that would put her ashore, he turned in. That night the *Columbus* ran aground off Point de Betsiamites. By jettisoning part of her deck cargo of deals, and heaving off, the ship was refloated. One imagines that Wood was not very happy with his master, particularly as the latter, while directing the laying out of their one remaining anchor, wished to cut the cable, leaving the ship without any ground tackle. The order was

emphatically overruled by Charles Wood.

Once a good offing had been made, the tug was cast off and the *Columbus* made sail for the first time. Her size and low freeboard predictably made her a wet ship as soon as heavy weather was encountered. Conditions were miserable for the crew, who had no way of staying dry, but a watertight deckhouse at least kept the provisions safe. Three weeks out, the ship began to make water badly at the rate of over a foot an hour. Leaks had been expected and the pumps were so arranged that they could be manned by up to 60 men. In late October the Scilly Light was raised, to the relief of the crew, who had been continually pumping for weeks. In spite of their endeavours, which were encouraged by the promise of an extra guinea on their wages, the leak had gained 11 ft and by the time *Columbus* reached the Thames she was literally floating on her cargo, with 18 ft of water in the hold.

The pilot boarded the *Columbus* off Deal on 27 October and with the assistance of three tugs she was worked up the Thames to Blackwall, where, at the instigation of two of the partners, and contrary to Wood's instructions as to the berth, she was run aground on a site with a 15-ft curve, which broke the ship's back. Her arrival had been long heralded by the Press and crowds of sightseers turned out to see the ship, some of the crew quietly making a bit on the side allowing visitors on board at the charge of 2s. a head.

So far the whole undertaking had been a huge financial success, the ship and cargo together having safely delivered across the Atlantic timber valued at about £50,000. Finished with the delivery of the *Columbus*, Wood immediately returned to Quebec to supervise the building of the second and larger vessel, the *Baron of Renfrew*, the keel of which had been laid before his departure. Encouraged by the success of the venture and by assurances from Captain McKellar, who seemed to have had a remarkable change of heart, of the seaworthiness and sailing qualities of the *Columbus*, the team of backers made a fatal decision. This group, through their investment and contract with Wood, were the virtual owners of the vessels and had already ignored Charles Wood's advice and instructions, indicating a growing alienation between the builder and his backers. Inspired by what can only have been greed, and against Wood's intentions and orders, they prepared the *Columbus* for a return voyage, a voyage for which the ship was neither planned, nor in a fit condition to undertake.

In the spring of 1825, ballasted with chalk, the *Columbus* sailed for St John, New Brunswick. The inevitable happened. Under the stress of bad weather, she opened her seams. With 16 ft of water in the hold and choked pumps, three boats were prepared and she was abandoned. Fortunately a westward-bound vessel, the *Dolphin*, had been standing by and the crew were safely picked up with only the loss of one of their boats, that carrying the provisions. The *Dolphin* was a small ship of her time and the addition of about 80 to her complement resulted in considerable hardship and privation for all. The *Columbus* was 3 weeks out when abandoned, so the *Dolphin* had a fair way to go and adverse weather prolonged the voyage. She eventually made Cork, her stores expended and her crew and survivors exhausted. The *Columbus* broke up and scattered her 3690 tons of timber, over a third of the intended freight of the first voyage, all over the North Atlantic.

The second ship, *The Baron of Renfrew*, was launched in June 1825. Although only 3 ft longer than the *Columbus*, she was considerably larger, with a beam of 61 ft, depth of 34 ft and measured 5880 tons. She would deliver in one voyage her cargo of deals, logs, staves, masts and spars, ash oar rafters, lathwood and trenails, including the vessel herself, in total a staggering quantity of 15,395 tons, the equivalent of 45 conventional ships. Unfortunately, although she made the transatlantic voyage safely, mismanagement on the part of pilots and the owners got the *Baron* aground on Long Sand Head,

off Dover, where she broke up into three pieces which drove ashore on the French coast, to the delight of the local population.

Whatever the faults of the participators, it was an heroic scheme which, for ingenuity in construction and in the application of the natural resources of wind and water, deserved a better reward.

The *Marco Polo*

Of all the ships built in North America, perhaps the most renowned was the *Marco Polo*. Although she won her laurels in the Australian immigrant trade, she was built at St John, New Brunswick, as a large and simple timber drogher. Her keel was laid in the fall of 1850 at Marsh Creek, Courtenay Bay, St John – 'the most God forsaken hole possibly discovered'[3], according to a local. The huge tides of the Bay of Fundy leave the creek virtually bereft of water at the ebb and, as the *Marco Polo* was the largest ship ever built on the creek, it was planned to launch her on the spring tide. In April 1851, with her lower and topmasts already stepped and set up, she slid down the ways. A fresh breeze was blowing and as soon as she took the water the *Marco Polo* took charge and ran up the opposite side of the creek. Efforts to get her off failed, and as the tide ebbed she fell over and was nearly written off there and then by the dismayed builders and shareholders. Ultimately, by considerable excavation around the hull, she was floated off on the next spring tide 2 weeks later.

The local population considered the *Marco Polo* a very ordinary and ugly ship. Although she had hollow bows and sharper lines forward than other ships, she had a box-like midship section and the depth of a common carrier. When launched, she was flush-decked with a small house at each hatch, was fastened with black iron, and was uncoppered and entirely undecorated except for a full-length figure

of her namesake. To add to the apparent ugliness of this barn of a ship, her grounding had left a visible hog in the hull, a feature which some claimed accounted for her success as a fast passage-maker. The St John Shipping Register states simply:

> Ship 'Marco Polo', 1625 61/100 tons. Three decks and a half-poop. Length: 184.1 feet. Breadth admidships: 36.3 feet. Depth of hold amidships: 29.4 feet. Standing bowsprit. Square-sterned. No galleries. Owned by James Smith and James Thomas Smith.[4]

The *Marco Polo* only made two voyages in the Atlantic trade before she was sold to James Baines's Liverpool Blackball Line. Her first voyage was from St John to Liverpool with timber and then to Mobile, returning with cotton.

Under Captain James Nicol Forbes, or 'Bully' Forbes, the drogher made her reputation. Fitted out in the style of the Blackballers, with Cunningham's patent reefing aloft and plush accommodation below, refastened with copper and her stern decorated with an elephant, she made her first round voyage from Liverpool to Melbourne and back in the magnificent time of 5 months, 21 days. In Liverpool's Salthouse Dock, after this voyage, a banner between the fore and mainmast proudly proclaimed 'THE FASTEST SHIP IN THE WORLD'. Doubtless it was not just the qualities of the ship which enabled Captain Forbes to confound the sceptics when, before sailing, he claimed he would be back in the Mersey inside 6 months. Forbes had already built a reputation for making fast passages with ordinary ships. His nerve, seamanship and initiative were well known and his character is summed up in his boast after the *Marco Polo*'s first voyage: 'Ladies and gentlemen, last trip I astonished the world with the sailing of this ship. This trip I intend to astonish God Almighty!'[5]

The *Marco Polo* made no new record but did not discredit herself, getting home in 6 months. After this Forbes left to join the *Lightning* and, although she still made good fast passages, she was never to equal the time for her first voyage under Bully Forbes. For 15 years she encircled the earth on the Australian run, until, after 1867, she became so strained and sodden she was taken out of the trade and finally sold. In 1880 she was condemned in London but was bought by a Norwegian company and, complete with a windmill pump, spent her remaining years in the trade for which she had been built, timber droghing. She became so decrepit that, in July 1883 to prevent her foundering she was deliberately beached on Prince Edward Island. Her cargo of deals was salvaged but the *Marco Polo* became a total loss.

Built in 1866 as the iron steamer *Pereire,* this ship was converted to sail in 1888 and renamed *Lancing.* During her sailing years, she often worked the North Atlantic between longer voyages. She became renowned for her strength, imparted by her 2-inch (50.8 mm) plating, and her extraordinary speed. She beat a Danish mail steamer by one day on a passage from New York to Denmark, and was reputed to have sailed at 22 knots for 15 consecutive hours running her easting down to Melbourne. She was broken up in 1925.

The steel, 4914-ton, seven-masted *Thomas W. Lawson,* built by the Fore River Ship & Engine Co. at Bath, Maine in 1902. She was later converted to a bulk oil carrier and was wrecked on the Scilly Isles on the 13 December 1907. Of her nineteen crew, only three were rescued.

THE DEMISE OF COMMERCIAL SAIL

By the end of the nineteenth century, the steamers had usurped all the lucrative trades from the sailing ships. The larger and later sailers found employment on the long hauls around the Capes, leaving the North Atlantic to the schooners, fishermen and timber droghers. Occasionally, a windjammer might find brief employment in the Western Ocean, freighting cotton from the American south, or, as did the *Lancing,* running spoolwood from the St. Lawrence to Glasgow.

During the last decades of the nineteenth century attempts were made by American shipbuilders to build more economical sailing vessels by designing multi-masted schooners. These moderately-sized vessels encouraged the building of larger and larger schooners, culminating in 1900 in the first six-master, *George W. Wells,* and, in 1902, with the only seven-master ever built, the *Thomas W. Lawson.* Under-canvassed and clumsy, these very large schooners, which were intended to be easy to handle, were cursed by the seamen who worked to exhaustion on them, and by the officers who struggled to get them off every lee shore. Most were engaged in the coastal trade, but it was not unusual for them to cross the Atlantic, as did the *Thomas W. Lawson* on her final voyage.

When America entered World War I nearly every sailing vessel she possessed was employed for the war effort, including over a hundred of the large schooners. The war decimated the American fleet, and the fleets of every participating nation. After 1918, sailing ships fought a losing battle for existence as one by one they were wrecked, scrapped or laid

up. No new large ships were built to take their place and even the small schooners found it difficult to earn their keep and gradually they were taken out of service.

Here and there sail was still found to be worthwhile. The Portuguese Grand Bankers continued for another half century, and some citizens of the Massachusetts port of New Bedford found tasks for some of the smaller vessels.

The Cape Verde Packets

The links between New England and the Cape Verde Islands were forged in the eighteenth century when American whalers began to call at the islands to recruit the skilful seamen to be found among the mixed Portuguese and African population. These Cape Verdean whalemen began to settle in America, and like immigrants anywhere, sought to bring their families, a desire which was welcomed by New England cranberry bogs and textile mill owners who were always in search of labour. During the nineteenth century American ships calling at the islands to load salt and hides began to provide passages to New England for the Cape Verdeans who wished to emigrate and, before the end of the century, the American Cape Verdeans began to run their own vessels, taking general cargo to the islands and immigrants on the return voyage. This was the beginning of the Cape Verdean packet trade which was to end in 1970 when the last commercial sailing

Ernestina
Built for Grand Bank fishing as the *Effie M. Morrissey*, this schooner entered the Newfoundland and Labrador trade in 1914. She began a career in the Cape Verde-New England emigrant trade in 1948, making her final commercial transatlantic voyage in 1965. She was among the last of all sailing vessels operating in a trans-oceanic trade.

vessel to carry passengers left New Bedford, Massachusetts, bound for the Cape Verde Islands.

The description 'packet service' may be a little grand for the regular traders between New England and the Cape Verdes, for most of the vessels were schooners which had already passed their bloom of life engaged in fishing, whaling and piloting. The service was inaugurated in 1892 when Antonio Coelho purchased a 64-ton fishing schooner named the *Nellie May*. With an elderly ex-whaler as captain, 50 passengers who had each paid $15 for the voyage, and some general cargo, the *Nellie May* sailed from Providence bound for Brava. Early in the voyage the old skipper died, and the mate, knowing little of ocean navigation, missed the Cape Verdes and only discovered his mistake when they spoke to a passing steamer whose master told them they were 500 miles south of the islands. The very much relieved mate bought the *Nellie May* into the port of Furna on Brava Island after a passage of 45 days. Under a new skipper she made her return passage in 28 days, with 117 passengers in addition to her crew. Her next voyage out to the islands was protracted to 90 days, and when water and provisions ran out, the suffering drove two of the crew to throw themselves overboard.

The first voyages of the *Nellie May* were dramatic, and during the whole era of these packets, drama was never far away. Although the majority of passages were comparatively uneventful, incidents, damage and losses seemed to have been unacceptably high, a sad but understandable fact when nearly all the vessels were old and their voyage took them across the breadth of the ocean through storm and calm. Typical of the packets that vanished was the fate of the *Manta*, an old New Bedford whaler which sailed from Providence for the Cape Verdes on 8 November 1934 with 13 passengers, including 3 women and 6 children, 19 crew and a cow. She was never seen again. At about the same time another packet, the *Winnepesauke* out of New Bedford, also disappeared.

After World War II the Cape Verde sailing packets continued to operate. In 1945 the last commercial three-masted schooner, *Lucy Evelyn*, was bought by John Costa, an experienced packet captain. He had the passenger accommodation improved by the addition of a deckhouse and advertised the passage for $US150. Freight and passengers were slow to come forward, but finally there was sufficient to make the voyage worthwhile. The cargo manifest is interesting and would be typical for any small vessel supplying island communities. It included 13,000 ft of pine and 20 tons of cement for a new church, the piano and household goods of the pastor, 200 drums of kerosene, 3 cars, canned food, and clothing sent out to relatives. Teresa Neves, aged 60, was one of the two passengers; her sister had been lost in the *Manta*.

The *Lucy Evelyn* sailed on 9 May 1946, and although not one of her crew had ever had experience in a sailing ship and would not go aloft to set the topsails, she made an uneventful passage of 34 days. Her return voyage from Dakar in September and October was not so fortunate. In the first of a series of autumn gales she encountered, her mizzen boom was carried away and the rudder damaged. With a jury-rigged rudder, a second storm 280 miles off Block Island drove her back south-west to 250 miles off the North Carolina coast. Not able to steer, she was towed into Norfolk, Virginia, by the coastguard. Her subsequent coastal voyage home to New Bedford was also fraught with winter gales and blown-out sails, so that once more she had to be taken in tow and, with some difficulty, was got into New Bedford.

One of the old Cape packets still survives and has even taken on a new lease of life. She is the *Ernestina*, ex *Effie M. Morrissey*, which was given by the people of Cape Verde to the people of the United States of America and now sails out of New Bedford under the management of the Massachusetts Schooner Ernestina Commission.

The *Effie M. Morrissey* was built at Essex in 1894 as a Grand Banks fisherman. Her first skipper, William Morrissey, spared no expense in building her as strong and as fine as the shipwrights' art could make her. In the spirit of the era, she was designed for speed but, unlike some of the later, more extreme examples, she was a fine sea boat and carrier. She was sold out of the fishing industry in 1914 and sailed in the Newfoundland–Labrador trade under the ownership of Harold Bartlett until, in 1926, she was purchased by his nephew, the Arctic explorer Captain Robert Bartlett. Making numerous voyages to Arctic waters until the war years, and then sailing as a supply vessel for the US Navy, she continued under the ownership of Captain Bartlett until his death in 1946. She was bought by a group of ex-Navy men who intended to operate her as a South Pacific island trader, but she caught fire in New York and was deliberately sunk to save her, and the project was given up.

She was raised and, in 1948, was purchased by Louisa Mendes, the American daughter-in-law of an old Cape Verde packet skipper, Captain Henrique Mendes. From the first decade of the century Captain Mendes had owned and skippered a succession of Cape Verde packets (the *Effie M. Morrissey* was his thirtieth), all decrepit and several of which went down in the Atlantic leaving Mendes, his crew and passengers to be picked up by passing steamers. Captain Mendes renamed the schooner for his daughter Ernestina, and after removing her engine, repairing the damage caused by the fire and installing a galley on deck, she began a long career as a Cape Verde packet. In 1957, Captain Mendes, a veteran of 55 Atlantic crossings, made his last transatlantic voyage in the *Ernestina* before he retired to Fogo. In 1964, the *Ernestina* sailed back to Providence where she was enthusiastically welcomed by spectators and the Cape Verdean families. The schooner made one more voyage in 1965, but she could not compete with powered vessels and for the next 10 years sailed between the islands of the Cape Verde Archipelago.

Refitted by the Republic of Cape Verde to take part in Operation Sail 1976, the Bicentennial Parade of Ships in New York Harbour, she once more set out for America, but was dismasted in a gale not long after leaving the islands. The following year the *Ernestina* was given to the United States and, starting in 1982, she began a thorough 4-year refit in preparation for her present occupation as a school ship.

On 10 January 1970 the three-masted schooner *Tina Maria* sailed from New Bedford for Cape Verde. In heavy weather she foundered, ending the last voyage of the last Cape Verde packet. Barring chartered sailing vessels and small coastal craft, she was possibly also the last commercially-operated vessel in trade to attempt a transatlantic passage under sail.

End of a voyage.
A Bristol Channel pilot skiff puts her pilot aboard.

177

Glossary

aback: when the wind comes on to the fore side of a squaresail.

abaft: further aft or nearer the stern.

aft: behind or near the stern of a vessel.

aloft: up in the rigging.

backed: when the wind changes anti-clockwise.

ballast: any weight such as sand, stone, iron or water used to make a vessel more stable.

bare poles: when all sail has been taken in due to high winds.

beam: the breadth of a ship. Also a transverse structural member.

beat: making to windward.

bent: to made fast with a bend (as in hitched).

berthage: charges for a ship's berth alongside.

bilge: where the bottom of a vessel curves into the side. As sailing ships usually heel to some extent, this is where bilgewater collects.

bower anchor: one of the two anchors carried on the bows of a ship.

boxed: to drive a sailing vessel's head round by backing squaresails on the foremast.

bulwarks: the protective side of a ship rising above an exposed deck.

cable: the rope or chain attached to the anchor. From the standard lengths of a cable comes the distance measurement termed a *cable,* which is 200 yards, or approximately a tenth of a nautical mile.

careen: to beach or haul a ship over to one side by means of tackles from the masts to the shore to enable repairs and cleaning work to be done to the underwater part of the hull.

chains, chainplates: chains or metal straps which attach the shrouds to the hull.

channels: boards which spread the chains out from the vessel's side.

cleat: a wood or metal fitting with two arms to which lines can be attached. Also a wedge-shaped piece of wood nailed to a spar to prevent lines made fast to the spar from shifting.

clew: the aft, lower corner of a sail.

clinker (or clencher): boat or ship construction using overlapping planks. Also known as lapstrake.

close-hauled: general arrangement of a ship's sails when sailing as close as possible to the direction from which the wind is blowing.

come about: to tack, to alter course so as to turn into and through the wind to bring the wind on to the other side of the vessel.

companionway: originally the skylights of cabins below the quarterdeck, the term came to refer to the covering over an access to below and now is generally used for the ladder, or stairs.

crank: a ship which, due to her construction, or the stowage of her ballast or cargo, cannot sail without danger of capsizing.

cro'jack (crossjack): lower yard on the mizzen mast or the sail it supports.

crown: where the arms and shank of an anchor join.

deadeye: a round or heart-shaped block pierced with three holes used to secure standing rigging.

dead-reckoning: estimating position by course, speed, current and leeway alone.

draw (draught): measurement from deepest part of keel to the surface of the water.

embayed: the situation a vessel finds herself in when, through stress of weather, or poor windward performance, she is unable to beat out of a bay.

ensign: the flag of the nation to which a vessel belongs.

fathom: 6 feet or 1.83 m.

fetch (up and down): to be able to make some destination to windward close-hauled. To fetch up and down is to maintain a distance offshore or from an object by tacking back and forth. Also means the distance traversed by waves, generally the greater the fetch, the higher the seas.

floors: that part of a ship's framing which runs from the keel and keelson to the bilge.

flush-decked: having one continuous deck from forward to aft, generally understood as having no forecastle, quarterdeck or poop.

freeboard: distance from the water to the upper deck at its lowest point.

gaff: the spar which spreads the head of a four-cornered fore and aft sail.

gaff jaws: the forked end of a gaff which fits around the mast.

gammoning: powerful lashings which secured an earlier ship's bowsprit to the stem or beakhead.

gaskets: lines, sennit or strips of cloth used to secure the sails when furled.

groundswell: steep swells caused by the effect of the seabed on ocean swells in shallowing water.

gudgeons: the metal strap or fitting into which the pintle of a rudder fits. Gudgeons and pintles are the normal way of fitting any unbalanced rudder.

gybe: in a fore-and-aft rigged vessel, to turn away from the wind so as to bring the wind on to the other side, necessitating careful handling of the spars to prevent them slamming across.

hawse: where the anchor cable enters the ship.

heart (open heart): a heart-shaped block which serves a similar purpose of a deadeye except it has one large hole through which lanyards can be rove several times.

heave-to: to bring a vessel practically to a halt. In a sailing vessel this involves backing sails, normally on the main mast.

hog: a vessel is hogged when her keel is bent downwards towards the ends.

hounds: correctly the cheeks or shoulders which prevent the collars of the shrouds from slipping down a mast. Present usage applies the term to the point on a mast where the shrouds are attached.

hulk: originally a medieval vessel, the term hulk came to refer to any vessel no longer used as a seagoing craft but which served a purpose within the confines of a port. Hulks were often used as storeships, mast ships and, in the eighteenth and nineteenth centuries, as prisons.

in stays: a vessel is in stays when it is in the process of coming about on to another tack.

jackstay: any rope or wire stretched between two points to which something can be attached. On the forward upper quarter of the yard of a squaresail, jackstays are formed of metal rods; to these the sails are bent.

jettison: to throw overboard for the purpose of lightening and thereby easing a ship under stress of weather.

jib: a triangular sail set on its own stay and extended beyond the bowsprit by the jibboom. Nowadays, on small craft, the term is used for any of the smaller headsails.

jury-rigged: a temporary substitute made from materials to hand to replace a damaged rudder or rig.

kedge (anchor): a light anchor which can be laid out for warping.

to kedge: the process of using a kedge anchor to move the ship.

knot (speed): 1 nautical mile per hour.

landfall: the position at which a ship sights land after a passage.

leach: the aftermost edge of a sail.

league: about 3.18 nautical miles, approximately one-twentieth of a degree of latitude. The distance varies between countries, e.g., the old French league = approximately 2.3 nautical miles.

lee: the side away from the wind; or sheltered from the wind.

leeward: the direction downwind.

lie to: in heavy weather, to let the vessel lie to wind and sea with only sufficient sail to maintain her heading; usually about six points off the wind.

luff (of a sail): the leading edge of a sail.

mailletage: a method of protecting the underwater hull by nailing flat-headed iron nails into wooden sheathing with the heads so close together they form an almost continuous sheet. In a short time, rust closes any small gaps between the nailheads.

martingale: the stay which runs from the jibboom end to the dolphin striker and the guys which run from the striker up to the vessel's bow. The stay and guys serve to hold the jibboom down.

meridian: a line running from pole to pole, crossing all latitudes at right angles, also known as a line of longitude.

nautical mile: effectively one minute of latitude, or the accepted standard of 6,080 ft (1,852 m).

offing: the distance kept offshore to avoid dangers or made offshore on a tack before coming about.

orlop: the lowest deck, originally the deck laid on the lower beams and below the waterline.

overfalls: a tumbling, breaking sea caused by wind and tide rips, often over an irregular bottom.

parrel: a rope or iron collar which secures the centre of a yard or the jaws of a gaff to the mast.

pay-off: when the ship turns away from the wind, particularly after coming about.

points (of a compass): there are 32 compass points. Starting from N, they read N by E, NNE, NExN, NE, NExE, NNE, ExN, E . . . etc. Each point covers 11¼° of arc. A square-rigged sailing ship can be expected to be able to sail 6 points, or 67½° from the wind.

port: left hand side.

port tack: when a vessel is on a tack or reach, she is on the port tack when the wind blows from the left hand side.

pounding: when, in steep, rough seas, the bows of the ship fall violently into a trough, or the face of a wave.

pulling: rowing.

quarter: either side of the stern of a ship, or in that direction.

quarterdeck: the deck aft of the main mast or mizzen from which a sailing ship is commanded; usually the province of the officers.

race: tide race or rip. Where currents run very fast causing broken water.

rake: the distance from the vertical of stem, sternpost, or masts.

roach: the curve cut into the side or foot of a sail.

roundhouse: appears to have referred to the cabins formed by the poop on early ships. In the eighteenth and nineteenth centuries, deckhouses built on the quarterdeck or maindeck, often with the poop deck built over them. They are never round, but rectangular.

sag: when a keel is distorted so that the middle is lower than the ends.

St Elmo's fire: electrical discharges producing lights at the extremities of a vessel's spars, usually during thundery weather.

scantlings: any piece of timber of a particular standard square-section.

scurvy: physical disorder caused by a lack of vitamin C.

shank: the shaft of an anchor from the ring to the crown.

sheer: the longitudinal curve of the deck or gunwale.

shipped: to take aboard.

shoal: shallow water.

shrouds: the ropes or wires which support a mast transversely.

skysail: a squaresail set above a royal. From the deck up, some mid nineteenth-century ships could set a course, topsail(s), topgallant(s), royal, skysail and moonsail.

soundings: depths of water. A ship is within soundings when the bottom can be reached by a deep sea leadline. This is generally accepted to be within the 100 fathom line (183 m).

spar: any pole such as mast, boom, yard, etc.

staff (backstaff): an early instrument for measuring the angular height of a celestial body to ascertain latitude.

standing rigging: the rigging used to support masts; as opposed to running rigging by which the sails and spars are controlled.

starboard: right hand side.

staysail: a fore and aft sail hanked to a stay.

steerage: at first the accommodation space provided under the quarterdeck before the great cabin and used by those passengers who could not afford a cabin. During the emigrant years of the nineteenth century, whole 'tweendecks were used as steerage accommodation.

steeve: the angle of the bowsprit from the horizontal.

sternsheets: the seats in the stern of a boat.

stranding: driven aground by weather.

sweep: a large oar.

tack (of a sail): the forward, lower corner of a sail.

tack: a vessel going to windward is on a tack. A vessel tacking is making a series of legs to windward by zigzagging. Or a vessel coming about is tacking.

tack ship: come about.

taffrail: the curved wooden top of the stern of older sailing ships. Later the rail across, or round, the stern.

tiller: the arm by which a rudder is controlled.

tilt: the awning at the stern of a boat. Originally the decorated semi-permanent awning spread over curved supports in the extreme stern of a galley.

tom: to shore up with timber and wedges.

train oil: whale or seal oil.

trim: the way a ship floats in the water longitudinally. The trim can have a significant effect on the way a vessel sails

and usually requires a ship to sit a little deeper at the stern than the bow. The term is also used to describe the process of adjusting sails to the best effect.

tuck: used to describe the stern, generally below water.

'tweendeck/betweendeck: decks of vessels from the nineteenth century onwards which are below the upper deck.

variation: the difference between true north and magnetic north caused by variations in the Earth's magnetic field.

veered: wind change in a clockwise direction.

waist: the low midship part of a sailing ship.

warping: hauling a ship along by means of warps led to anchors or ashore.

watering: taking on fresh water, or going ashore to collect it.

wear: to bring a square-rigged vessel on to the other tack by turning away from the wind.

weather: in the direction from which the wind comes. Opposite of lee.

weatherly: able to sail well to windward.

weigh: to haul up an anchor.

yawl: a small ship's boat. Nowadays, a rig consisting of a main mast and small mast aft of the head of the rudder.

List of references

ALBION, R.G., *The Rise of New York Port (1815-1860)*. David and Charles, Newton Abbot, UK, 1970.

ALBION, R.G., BAKER, W.A., LABAREE, B.W., *New England and the Sea*. Mystic Seaport Museum, Mystic, 1972.

ANDERSON, R.C., *The Rigging of Ships in the Days of the Spritsail Topmast*. Conway, London, 1982.

ARMSTRONG, JOE C.W., *Champlain*. Macmillan, Toronto, 1987.

BARKHAM, M.M., ''Report on Sixteenth Century Spanish Basque Shipbuilding c.1550 to c.1600'' [manuscript]. Parks Canada, Ottawa.

BASS, G.E., *Ships and Shipwrecks of the Americas*. Thames and Hudson, London, 1988.

BATHE, B.W., G.B. RUBIN DE CERVIN, E. TAILLEMITE ET AL., *The Great Age of Sail*. Edited by Joseph Jobé, translated by Michael Kelly. Crescent Books, New York, 1977.

BATHE, B.W., G.B. RUBIN DE CERVIN, E. TAILLEMITE ET AL., *Seven Centuries of Sea Travel*. Leon Amiel, New York, 1973.

BIDDLECOMBE, CAPT. G., *The Art of Rigging*. First published 1848, reprinted by Edward W. Sweetman Company, New York, 1979.

BIGGAR, H.P., *The Voyages of Jacques Cartier*. Public Archives of Canada, 1924.

BINNS, ALAN, *Viking Voyagers*. William Heineman Ltd., London, 1980.

BOUQUET, M., *South Eastern Sail*. David and Charles, Newton Abbot, UK, 1972.

BOXER, C.R., *The Dutch Seabourne Empire 1600-1800*. Hutchinson & Co Ltd., London, 1965.

BRADFORD, W., with commentary by S.E. Morison, *Of Plymouth Plantation*. Alfred A. Knopf, New York, 1952.

BURWASH, D., *English Merchant Shipping 1460-1540*. University of Toronto Press, Toronto, 1947.

CARLETTI, F., *My Voyage Around the World: The Chronicles of a Sixteenth Century Florentine Merchant*. Translated by H. Weinstock, Pantheon Books, New York, 1964.

CARSE, R., *The Twilight of Sailing Ships*. Grosset & Dunlap, New York, 1965.

CHAPELLE, H.I., *American Small Sailing Craft*. Norton Inc., New York, 1951.

CHAPELLE, H.I., *The History of American Sailing Ships*. Bonanza Books, New York, 1935.

CHAPELLE, H.I., *The History of the American Sailing Navy*. Bonanza Books, New York, 1949.

CHAPMAN, F., *Architectura Navalis Mercatoria*. A. & C. Black (originally Adlard Books).

CHARLETON, W., *The Voyage of the* Mayflower II. Cassell and Company Ltd., London, 1957.

CHATTERTON, E.K., *The Merchantile Marine*. William Heinemann Ltd., London, 1923.

COHN, M. AND PLATZEN, M. K. H. *Black Men of the Sea*. Dodd, Mead & Co., New York, 1978.

COLEMAN, T., *Passage to America*. Hutchinson, London, 1972.

CONNEAU. CAPT. T., *A Slaver's Logbook or Twenty Year's Residence in Africa*. (From original manuscript.) Prentice-Hall, Inc., Englewood Cliffs, New Jersey, 1976.

CUTLER, C.C., *Greyhounds of the Sea*. Patrick Stephens, Wellingborough, UK, 1984.

DAWSON, S.E., *The St Lawrence Basin*. Lawrence and Bullen, London, 1905.

DODDS, J., AND MOORE, J. *Building the Wooden Fighting Ship*. Hutchinson, London, 1984.

DOW, G.F., *Whaleships and Whaling*. Argosy Antiquarian Ltd., New York, 1967.

EARLE, P., *The Wreck of the* Almiranta. Macmillan, London, 1979.

FUSON, H., ROBERT, *The log of Christopher Columbus*. International Marine, Maine, 1987.

GAGE, THOMAS, *New Survey of the West Indies [1651]*. Reprint, G. Routledge & Son, London, 1928.

GIFFARD, A., *Towards Quebec*. Her Majesty's Stationery Office, London, 1981.

GOSLING, W.G., *The Life of Sir Humphrey Gilbert*. Constable and Co., London, 1911.

GREENHILL, BASIL, *Archaeology of the Boat*. Wesleyan University Press, Connecticut, 1976.

GREENHILL, BASIL, *The Merchant Schooners, Vols I, II*. Percival Marshal, London, 1951.

GREENHILL, BASIL AND ANN GIFFORD, *The Merchant Sailing Ship*. David and Charles, Newton Abbot, UK, 1970.

HAKLUYT, R., *The Principal Navigations of the English Nation*. [8 volumes.] J.M. Dent & Sons, London, 1926.

HAKLUYT, R., *Voyages and Colonising Enterprises of Sir Humphrey Gilbert, Vols I, II*. Hakluyt Society, London, 1939.

HAKLUYT SOCIETY, *Spanish Documents concerning English Voyages to the Caribbean*. Second series No. LXII 1928. The British Library, London, 1928.

HAMILTON, E.J., *American Treasure and the Price Revolution in Spain*. Harvard University Press, London, 1934.

HARING, C.H., *Trade and Navigation between Spain and the Indies in the Time of the Hapsburgs*. Harvard University Press, London, 1918.

HARLAND, J., *Seamanship in the Age of Sail*. Conway Maritime Press, London, 1984.

HEPTON, P., *Captain William Wells and the Last Years of the Hull Whaling Fleet 1844-1869*. Malet Lambert Local History, Hull, 1984. [Originals, Malet Lambert High School, Hull.]

HEPTON, P., *William Wells, Master Mariner 1815-1880, Master of the "Truelove"*. Malet Lambert Local History, Hull, 1982. [Originals, Malet Lambert High School, Hull.]

HORNER, D., *The Treasure Galleons*. Dodd, Mead & Co., New York, 1971.

HOWARTH, D., *Dhows*. Quartet Books, London, 1977.

HURST, A.A., *Square-Riggers, the Final Epoch*. Teredo Books, Brighton, UK, 1972.

HUTCHINSON, W., *A Treatise on Practical Seamanship*. [1777.] Scholar Press, London, 1979.

HYDROGRAPHER OF THE NAVY, *Ocean Passages for the World*. Published by the Hydrographer of the Royal Navy, London, 1973.

INNES, H.A., *The Cod Fisheries: A History of an International Economy*. Yale University Press, London, 1940.

JENSEN, A.C., *The Cod: The Uncommon History of a Common Fish*. Thomas Y. Crowell Company, [?], 1944.

JONES G., *The Norse Atlantic Saga*. Oxford University Press, Oxford, 1964.

JONES, M.A., *Destination America*. Weidenfeld and Nicolson/ Thames Television, London, 1976.

KNIGHT, F., *The Golden Age of the Galleon*. Collins, London, 1976.

LANDSTROM, B., *Sailing Ships*. George Allen & Unwin, London, 1969.

LANDSTROM, B., *The Ship*. Allen & Unwin, London, 1961.

LEES, J., *The Masting and Rigging of English Ships of War, 1625-1860*. Conway Maritime Press, London, 1990.

LLOYD, C., *The British Seaman, 1200-1860*. Associated University Press, New Jersey, 1968.

LUBBOCK, BASIL, *The Arctic Whalers*. Brown, Son & Ferguson, Glasgow, 1955.

LUBBOCK, BASIL, *The Best of Sail*. Grosset and Dunlap, New York, 1975.

LUBBOCK, BASIL, *The Western Ocean Packets*. Brown, Son & Ferguson, Glasgow, 1977.

McGOWAN, A., *The Ship: Tiller and Whipstaff*. Her Majesty's Stationery Office, London, 1981.

MacGREGOR, DAVID R., *Merchant Sailing Ships, 1775-1815*. Argus Books, London, 1980.

MacGREGOR, DAVID R., *Merchant Sailing Ships 1815-1850*. Conway Maritime Press, London, 1984.

MacGREGOR, DAVID R., *Merchant Sailing Ships 1850-1875*. Conway Maritime Press, London, 1984.

McKAY, R., *Some Famous Sailing Ships and their Builder, Donald McKay*. 7 C's Press Inc., Connecticut, 1969.

MAGOUN, F.A., *The Frigate Constitution and other Historic Ships*. Dover, New York, 1987.

MARCIL, E.R., "Ship-rigged Rafts and the Export of Quebec Timber." *Neptune*, Spring, 1988.

MARCUS, G.J., *The Conquest of the North Atlantic*. Boydell Press, Woodbridge, UK, 1980.

MORRIS, R.D., *Pacific Sail*. David Bateman, Auckland, 1987.

MORRIS, R.D., *Sail Change*. David Bateman, Auckland, 1981.

MARTINEZ-HILDALGO, J.M., AND H.J. CHAPELLE, *Columbus's Ships*. Barre Publishers, Massachusetts, 1966.

MATTHEWS, F.C., *American Merchant Ships*. Series I and II. Dover, New York, 1987.

MORISON, S.E., *Admiral of the Ocean Sea*.

MORISON, S.E., *Christopher Columbus, Mariner*. Little, Brown and Co., Boston, 1955.

MORISON, S.E., *The Great Explorers*. Oxford University Press, New York, 1978.

NARES, LIEUT. G., *Seamanship*. [1862.] Gresham Books, Unwin Bros. Ltd., Old Woking, UK, 1979.

PARRY, J.H., *The Age of Reconnaissance*. Weidenfeld and Nicholson, London, 1963.

PARRY, J.H., *The Discovery of the Sea*. Weidenfeld and Nicholson, London, 1974.

PENALOSA, J. AND FERNANDEZ-GIMENEZ S., *Historia de la Navegacion*. Ediciones Urbion, Madrid, 1980.

PHILLIPS, CARLA RAHN, *Six Galleons for the King of Spain*. John Hopkins University Press, Baltimore, 1986.

QUINN, D.B., *England and the Discovery of America, 1481-1620*. George Allen & Unwin, London, 1974.

RITCHIE-NOAKES, N., *Liverpool's Historic Waterfront*. Her Majesty's Stationery Office, London, 1984.

SCNAUFFELEN, O., *Great Sailing Ships*. Adlard Coles, London, 1969.

THROCKMORTON, P., *The Sea Remembers*. Weidenfeld and Nicholson, New York, 1987.

THOMPSON, G.M., *Sir Francis Drake*. Book Club Assoc./Secker and Warburg Ltd, London, 1972.

UNDERHILL, H.A., *Masting and Rigging the Clipper Ship and Ocean Carrier*. Brown, Son & Ferguson Ltd, Glasgow, 1979.

VILLIERS, A., *The Quest of the Schooner* Argus. Hodder and Stoughton Ltd., London, 1951.

WALLACE, F.W., *In the Wake of the Windships.* Hodder and Stoughton Ltd., London, 1927.

WALLACE, F.W., *Wooden Ships and Iron Men.* Hodder and Stoughton Ltd., London, [1925-27?].

WARD, W.E.F., *The Royal Navy and the Slavers.* George Allen and Unwin, London, 1969.

WILLIAMSON, J.A., *A Short History of British Expansion.* Macmillan & Co Ltd., London, 1961.

WILLIAMSON, J.A., *The Cabot Voyages and Bristol Discovery Under Henry VII.* Hakluyt Society, Cambridge University Press, Glasgow, 1962.

WINCHESTER, C. (ed.) *Shipping Wonders of the World.* Vols I, II. Amalgamated Press, London, [1930s?].

WOODHAM-SMITH, C., *The Great Hunger.* Hamish Hamilton, London, 1962.

The Norse voyagers
1, 2 Marcus G.J. *Conquest of the North Atlantic.* Boydell Press. Woodbridge, Suffolk, 1980.

Christopher Columbus
1, 2, 3, 4, 5, 6, 7, 8, 9, 10 Fuson, R.H. *The Log of Christopher Columbus.* International Marine, 1987.

The Bristol merchants
1, 2, 3, 4, 5, 6, 7, 8, 9, 10, 11 Williamson J.A. *The Cabot Voyages and Bristol Discovery Under Henry VII.* For Hakluyt by Cambridge University Press. London, 1961.

Exploration of the North-American east coast
1, 2 Dawson, S.E. *The St Lawrence Basin.* Lawrence and Bullen. London, 1905.

3, 4, 5 Williamson J.A. *The Cabot Voyages and Bristol Discovery Under Henry VII.* For Hakluyt by Cambridge University Press. London, 1961.

6, 7 Morison S.E. *The Great Explorers.* Oxford University Press. New York, 1978.

8 Quinn. D.B. *England and the Discovery of America.* George Allen & Unwin. London, 1974.

9, 10 Hakluyt, Richard. *Principal Navigations Vol III.* Dent and Sons. London, 1926.

French voyages to North America
1, 2, 3, 4, 5, 6, 7 Hakluyt, Richard. *Cartier Narration.* Theatrum Orbis Terrarum Ltd. Amsterdam, 1967. Also: Biggar H.P. *The Voyages of Jacques Cartier.* Public Archives of Canada, 1924.

8, 9 Morison S.E. *The Great Explorers.* Oxford University Press. New York, 1978.

English trading voyages to the Caribbean
1 Spanish Documents concerning English Voyages to the Caribbean 1527-28. Hakluyt Society. Second Series No LXII 1928 Document No 21 [Diego Ruiz de Vallego to the crown New Segovia, April 21, 1568].

2, 3, 4, 5 and remainder of small quotes: Hakluyt, Richard. *Principal Navigations, The English Voyages Vol 7.* Dent and Sons Ltd. London, 1962.

English voyages of settlement
1, 2, 3, 18 Quinn, David Beers. *Voyages and Colonising Enterprises of Sir Humphrey Gilbert. Vol I and II.* Hakluyt Society. London, 1940.

4, 5, 6, 7, 8, 9, 10, 11, 13, 15, 16, 17 Hayes, Edward. "The Voyage of Sir Humphrey Gilbert to Newfoundland". From Richard Hakluyt. *Principal Navigations of the English Nation. Vol VI.* Dent and Sons. London, 1926.

12, 14, 19 "A Relation of Richard Clarke of Weymouth, master of the ship called the *Delight*". From Richard Hakluyt. *Principal Navigations of the English Nation. Vol VI.* Dent and Sons. London, 1926.

20 Strachey, William. *The Historie of Travell into Virginia Britania.* L.B. Wright and V. Freund (eds). Hakluyt Society. London, 1953.

Pilgrims
1, 2, 3, 4 Bradford, William, with commentary by S.E. Morison. *Of Plymouth Plantation.* Alfred A. Knopf. New York, 1952.

The Spanish treasure fleets
1, 6 Phillips, Carla Rahn. *Six Galleons for the King of Spain.* The John Hopkins University Press. Boston, 1986.

2 Vazquez de Espinosa, Compendium. From Earle, Peter. *The Wreck of the Almiranta.* MacMillan. London, 1979.

3 Gage, Thomas. *New Survey of the West Indies.* G. Routledge & Son. London, 1928.

4 Horner, David. *The Treasure Galleons.* Robert Hale and Co. London, 1971.

5 Dorell, John. 1670 account of the Islands to Lord Ashley. BL Egerton 2395 fos 472/6. From Earle, op. cit.

Dutch, Swedish and French voyages
1 A Translation from Armstrong, Joe. *C.W. Champlain.* Macmillan of Canada, 1987.

Eighteenth-century ships
1, 2 Hutchinson, W. A. *Treatise on Practical Seamanship.* Scholar Press. London, 1979.

The slave trade
1, 2, 3, 4, 5, 6, 7, 8, 9 Carletti, F. Translated by H. Weinstock. *My Voyage Around the World: The Chronicles of a 16th Century Florentine Merchant.* Pantheon Books. New York, 1964.

The Atlantic whaling industry
1, 3, 4 Lubbock, Basil. *The Arctic Whalers.* Brown, Son & Ferguson. Glasgow, 1955.

2 Dow, G.F. *Whaleships and Whaling.* Argosy Antiquarian Ltd. New York, 1967. Massachusetts Archives.

The Grand Banks
1 Villiers, Alan. *The Quest of the Schooner* Argus. Hodder and Stoughton. London, 1951.

The American transatlantic packets:
1 Coleman, Terry. *Passage to America.* Hutchinson. London, 1972.

2 Traditional. From the capstan shanty, *New York Gals* or *Can't you Dance the Polka.*

3 Traditional. Version from Hugil, Stan. *Shanties from the Seven Seas.* Routledge, Kegan and Paul. London, 1984.

The emigrant ships
1 Inscription on a monument commemorating an emigrant cemetery on Grosse Isle, Quebec.

2, 3, 6, 7 Woodham-Smith, Cecil. *The Great Hunger.* Hamish Hamilton. London, 1962.

4, 5 Extracts from the Diary of Robert Whyte 1847. From Woodham-Smith, op. cit.

8 Coleman, Terry. *Passage to America.* Hutchinson. London, 1972.

9 Letter from Vere Foster to Lord Hobart. 1851. Correspondence on the Treatment of Passengers on Board the Emigrant Ship *Washington*, H.C. 1851 Vol. 40. Also C/O Papers 384/88, item 351, Public Record Office. London.

The timber droghers
1, 2, 3, 5 Wallace, William. *Wooden Ships and Iron Men.* Hodder and Stoughton Ltd. London, [1920s?].

4 Wallace, William. *In the Wake of the Wind Ships.* Hodder and Stoughton Ltd. London, 1927.

Acknowledgements

All quotes have been acknowledged in the text, but I would like to offer thanks once more for the permissions to quote from the various sources. Although every effort has been made to establish copyright for the material published here, the author would like to apologize for any contravention which may have occured without his knowledge and invites holders of copyright in such cases to advise him or the publishers.

I would like to thank the staff of the following institutions for their generous assistance:

The Auckland War Memorial Museum Library; the Auckland Central Library; the National Maritime Museum, Greenwich; the Naval Museum, Madrid; the Department of Underwater Archaeology, Parks Canada, Ottawa; the Peabody Museum, Salem; the Museum of Plymouth Plantation, Plymouth, Mass.; Mystic Seaport Museum; Schooner Ernestina, New Bedford; Penobscot Marine Museum, Searsport; Bath Maritime Museum; Toronto Metropolitan Library; the Redpath Museum, Toronto; Institute of Maritime Archaeology, Roskilde; the Bristol Maritime Heritage Centre, Bristol; the Town Docks Museum, Hull; the Science Museum, London; Merseyside Maritime Museum, London.

For their personal assistance I would like to thank: Eileen and George Marcil of Quebec for their hospitality and help in that city; Lt.Cdr. John W. Beck R.N., Hon. Curator of the Falmouth Maritime Museum for providing information on the Post Office Packets; Eric Kentley, Bernard Bryant and John Graves of the National Maritime Museum, Greenwich for kindly allowing us to study the wealth of ship-models in storage; Dr. T. Wright, Director of the Science Museum, London for his warm assistance and advice; Robert Grenier, director, and Marcel Gringas, model-maker, both of the Department of Underwater Archaeology of Parks Canada, Ottawa; Carla Rahn Phillips for her helpful correspondence concerning the Spanish treasure fleets. Don Hamer, of Whangarei, New Zealand for collecting and supplying me with information I would otherwise have missed, and Timothy Morris for drafting the maps.

For their support and assistance while undertaking research I would like to thank the Ardizzi family of Toronto, the Quinn family of Grotton, Conn., Barbara and Len Cullen of Worthing, England, Patsy Cullen and John of Leeds, Paul O'Pecko of Mystic Seaport Museum and Captain Will Gates – Mayflower II Plymouth.

Finally, special thanks to Joy Browne, the editor; to Errol McLeary who had the complicated task of laying out the book; and to my wife Kathleen for her help and patience throughout the last few years.

Index